RADICAL BETRAYAL

How Liberals & Neoconservatives Are
Wrecking American Exceptionalism

ANDERS W. EDWARDSSON

Radical Betrayal: How Liberals & Neoconservatives are Wrecking American Exceptionalism

First Edition: 2023

Printed in the United States of America

10 9 8 7 6 5 4 3 2 1

ISBN-13: 978-1-959677-95-6 (Paperback)
ISBN-13: 978-1-959677-96-3 (Hardcover)
ISBN-13: 978-1-959677-94-9 (eBook)

Published by Defiance Press and Publishing, LLC

Bulk orders of this book may be obtained by contacting Defiance Press and Publishing, LLC. www.defiancepress.com.

Public Relations Dept. – Defiance Press & Publishing, LLC
281-581-9300
pr@defiancepress.com

Defiance Press & Publishing, LLC
281-581-9300
info@defiancepress.com

To Jen

Without you, life would have no meaning!

Table of Contents

Introduction...5

Chapter 1 | Once Upon a Time..12

Chapter 2 | A New Land 33

Chapter 3 | War and Peace 52

Chapter 4 | A Dual Revolution..75

Chapter 5 | A Defining Decade..107

Chapter 6 | Turning the Tide..139

Chapter 7 | An Exceptionalist Presidency 173

Chapter 8 | Bridge Presidents 199

Chapter 9 | From Hubris to Discord 230

Concluding Reflections 272

Appendix..288

Bibliography...290

"Our cause is noble; it is the cause of mankind."
George Washington | 1779

Introduction

On November 9, 2016, Americans woke up to President Trump. For many, it was a newsflash they had dreamt about but not dared to hope for. For others, it was a shock throwing them into a manic-depressive state of mind. Moreover, Trump's victory was first explained by talk about racism and a "whitewash" election which effects all upstanding citizens had an obligation to counter. However, after over half a decade of research—and increasing wisdom of hindsight—we can present a much more elaborate answer today. It is a complex tale about how Americans in 2016 felt that their country was failing because its leaders had surrendered to a globalist culture everyday folks didn't belong to—and encountered only through lost jobs, depraved TV shows, crime, and snarky comments about their political, religious, and traditional views delivered by "experts" in the news. Hence, Trump was no accidental president and his *Make America Great Again* slogan resonated because people felt the opposite—that America was not so great anymore. Still, this offers just a partial answer to why the highest office in the land was entrusted to Trump, because why didn't the job instead go to a career politician, like Ronald Reagan in 1980?

To answer this bigger question, it's necessary to take a step back and look at the big picture. Why have U.S. politics in recent decades become so bitter that the country seems to be falling apart? Whose fault is it? And what is the president's role in this process? Answers to queries like these are certainly also complex, especially since the problem has only gotten worse. As an example, a NYT/Siena College poll in 2022, showed that only 37 percent of Democrats agreed that "America is the greatest country in the world," and that a bewildering 53 percent of them stated they preferred socialism over capitalism. Hence, numerous Americans today no longer love their country—or at least loathe what it stands for. Which, in turn, means that many no longer believe in American Exceptionalism, or as it will here conveniently be called, Americanism. Which is key. Because this concept offers the main story of America, defines what the country is all about, and explains why people should be proud to live here. Thus, Americanism is a "glue" that unites people across economic, social, and other divides—and, as such, an indispensable force for keeping the country together. Moreover, given poll numbers like those above, America's problems today may seem to come mainly from the left. But, in addition to liberals, neoconservatives have been weakening people's belief in Americanism and implementing harmful policies for decades, so there's little room for a partisanship blame game here. The following study will explain how, when, and why the Founding Fathers' vision of America lost its sway among so many that Americans, in the end, turned to a New York businessman with no political experience to save the country.

Before beginning this study, some things need to be clarified. Most importantly, even if the meaning of "exceptional" (unusual, extraordinary) does not formally also include *better*, the term American Exceptionalism has implied superiority from its first known use by a London newspaper in the 1860s. Thus, both terms used in this book will mean that the U.S.

is different *and* better than other countries. Additionally, two opposites will be used to categorize exceptionalist views: *inclusive*, meaning that America can actively spread its political, social, and economic culture to other countries, and *exclusive*, denoting that America is so unique that other countries cannot successfully copy its model—at least not entirely. Also, *active* will mean the belief that spreading American qualities to others is a divine, moral, or another kind of duty, and *passive* the view that the U.S. should only function as a model for others to follow at will. Indeed, these classifications will, in many cases, be tentative. However, they are necessary and will make it possible to show how U.S. presidents' and others' exceptionalist beliefs have affected their worldviews and, therefore, their actions.

Furthermore, separating exceptionalist sentiments from common patriotic themes, slogans, arguments, and religious language is vital. For example, saying "America is great" is not an exceptionalist statement, just a patriotic hurrah. And: was President Harry S. Truman's habit of calling America "God's country" a sign of his exceptionalist views or religious beliefs—or both? Thus, to minimize the risk of over- and misinterpretations, the author has gone to great lengths to omit iffy examples of exceptionalist language in favor of such that fit the following definition: "A language referring to the U.S. as having a mission, leading the world, being a vital nation, having unique ideals, liberating other countries, and inspiring people [and] references to being on the right side of history and fighting for the right ideals."[1] On the other hand, since exceptionalist themes frequently blend into broader terms like "liberty," "democracy," and "capitalism," words such as Franklin D. Roosevelt calling America "the great arsenal of democracy" have been included.

---

1. John A. Dearborn, *Exceptionalist-in-Chief: Presidents, American Exceptionalism, and U.S. Foreign Policy Since 1897* (University of Connecticut: Honors Scholar Thesis, 2013), 23.

The word *meme* will be used to underline the fact that as ideas—and particularly entire worldviews and ideologies—are spreading through society from one person's mind to another's, they often behave as cultural equivalents to genes in that they replicate, mutate, and respond to selective pressures. Thus, they evolve. For example, "equality" is a meme central to Americanism and exceptionalist thinking that has changed meaning over time. In the U.S., this term was for a long time virtually unanimously understood as equality of opportunity; i.e., the absence of formal barriers—like demands for a noble heritage, a guild membership, or a specific ethnicity—for personal freedom and various forms of advancement. But, as demands for "leveling the playing field" and higher subsistence levels have increased, it has for many come to mean equality of outcome and is today used as an argument for egalitarian welfare systems like those in countries akin to France, Denmark, and Sweden.

Moreover, the feelings exceptionalist beliefs stir originate in Americans' *imaginations*. This term is widely used but commonly misunderstood. It's the human brain's ability to grasp abstract concepts like freedom, good, and evil. It shall not be confused with the intellect, which is people's ability to, e.g., willfully create and understand full-scale intellectual systems like Marxism and Americanism. However, since imagination precedes intellect, it frequently and often unconsciously affects people's political, philosophical, and other outlooks. For instance, someone who prefers equality of outcome over freedom is likelier to turn out a socialist than a free marketer. Also, if a person's imagination focuses more on what is realistic to achieve than what is desirable, his or her worldview tends to be restrained. Case in point, while nearly all the Founding Fathers were political moderates, the views of figures like philosopher Jean-Jacques Rousseau; the father of communism, Karl Marx; and libertarian stalwart Ayn Rand are often detached from practical restraints. Hence, political "daydreamers" tend to think that their visions are so right, grand, and tangible that their fulfillment justifies any means, making many ideologues good with harsh policies and even violence to reach their goals.

With a few thematical digressions, the analysis in this book has been organized chronologically. The first chapter offers a concise outline of the history of Western nationalism and the origin of Americanism. It explores the role of exceptionalist thinking in George Washington's foreign policy; Manifest Destiny; Andrew Jackson's reforming of U.S. political culture; and Abraham Lincoln's partial rewriting of the national ethos from freedom to equality. The second chapter describes the parallel growth of a modern U.S. left and an aggressive form of exceptionalist thinking in the context of late-nineteen- and early-twentieth-century ideological currents, including socialism and imperialism. A specific study of President William McKinley's exceptionalist defense of the Spanish-American War of 1898 is also offered. In Chapter 3, the analysis moves on to Woodrow Wilson, his worldview, and his attempt to create a New World Order after World War I. This chapter also shows how exceptionalism helped to restore America's original political and economic order after that war.

Chapter 4 presents more detailed portraits of individual presidents and analyses of their exceptionalist views and values. The first focuses on Franklin D. Roosevelt and the birth of modern liberalism through the New Deal, exploring how his form of exceptionalist thinking during World War II created the concept of human rights. It also probes Harry S. Truman's use of this "international exceptionalism" to engage the U.S. in the Cold War and how Dwight D. Eisenhower used Americanism to further a number of more conservative policies. Chapter 5 then examines the role of John F. Kennedy's exceptionalist oratory for the Democrats' liberal agenda and how Lyndon B. Johnson used similar language to bolster support for the Vietnam War and his Great Society program. In Chapter 6, the focus turns to the twin rise of American conservatism and the demise of post-World War II liberalism in favor of postmodern radicalism. Special attention is paid here to Richard Nixon's use of exceptionalist rhetoric, the Culture Wars, partisan polarization, and the emergence of neoconservatism. A study of Jimmy Carter's attempt to blame America's problems on its exceptionalist nature is also offered.

The last three chapters combine earlier findings into a critical analysis of liberals' and neoconservatives' abuse and consecutive weakening of Americanism in the post-Cold War era. Chapter 7 explores the paradigmatic role of Ronald Reagan's rhetoric. Specific attention is paid to his arguments regarding the Cold War and his Second American Revolution and how the latter accelerated the long-term split between Democrat and Republican worldviews. Chapter 8 then examines George Bush's attuning of exceptionalist views to the post-Cold War world, the Gulf War, the dissolution of the Soviet Union, and how Bill Clinton's globalist views became a bridge between an old and a new political paradigm. Finally, in Chapter 9, George W. Bush's use of nationalist rhetoric after 9/11, the features of Barack Obama's "critical exceptionalism," and Donald Trump's attempt to pull the U.S. back toward a less aggressive foreign policy are analyzed.

This book is an abridged version of the author's 2021 Ph.D. dissertation in Politics at the Catholic University of America in Washington, D.C. Changes are mainly editorial and linguistic, like cutting, compacting, and cleansing the text from academic gabble for better understanding. A handful of newfound examples, quotes, and reasonings have been added. Also, all footnotes except for direct quotes by historical actors and other scholars have been removed, but all sources used are still listed in the Bibliography. Moreover, I wish to thank Dr. Tech. Marcus Wallenberg Foundation for Education in International Industrial Entrepreneurship in Stockholm,

Sweden, for the full-time scholarship that in 2011 allowed me to start studying for a Ph.D. and begin a new life in America. I also want to thank the faculty and staff at The Catholic University of America in Washington, D.C., for their excellence and especially Professor Claes G. Ryn, who taught me to view U.S. politics in partly wholly new ways, and Professor John K. White for being chair of my Ph.D. committee. As well, thank you to Professor Josiah Baker at Methodist University in Fayetteville, North Carolina; Associate Professor Jan Kallberg at West Point, New York; Sven R. Larson, Ph.D., Montana; Policy Director John Hendrickson, Iowa; and Ken Hammet and Mike Oliver, my best friends in Florida, who have all read the manuscript and contributed with vital input and criticism. My deepest gratitude, however, as always goes to my wife, Jen. Without her patience, grace, and Shakespearean skills, neither my dissertation nor this book would ever have been finished. And, of course, despite all these people's best efforts, the responsibility for any remaining flaws, faults, and shortcomings rests squarely on the author alone.

> *"The eyes of all people are upon us."*
> John Winthrop | 1630

CHAPTER 1 |

Once Upon a Time

S ince the dawn of time, people have told stories about who they are, where they come from, and what sets them apart. Such tales give meaning to life and offer goals for our existence. Even in small tribes of hunter-gatherers, stories about forefathers' adventures are popular, and on the next step up in societal order—clans, which include hundreds or thousands of people dispersed over large areas—they become vital. Specifically, on the clan level, group narratives help people to decide if strangers they meet should be treated as friends or foes, explain the potentially devious nature of other clans, and more. And as diverse populations are merged into even larger collectives—states ruled by kings that most people will never meet or even see in person—even more elaborate (hi)stories are needed. These need to be powerful enough to bridge ethnic, social, economic, and other divides and explain complex circumstances like why different people live under one ruler, why men can be called out to fight faraway enemies, why everyone must pay taxes, and why people must accept the authority of royal minions like nobles, priests, and bureaucrats. Hence, by defining and discriminating between "us" and "them" and explaining conditions such as why a few are in charge and the rest must follow, nationalist narratives prop up political and bureaucratic structures and help hold larger bodies of people together. In the U.S., this political folklore is called Americanism, and it has until recently been one of the world's most powerful nationalist "glues."

Early Nationalism

Modern nationalism did not appear until the late eighteenth century, and America, followed by France, became one of the first countries to develop a full-scale modern national narrative. Yet, like many human phenomena, a primitive form of nationalism emerged when people in the Middle East some ten thousand years ago began forming agricultural societies. As hamlets grew into towns and cities with tens or even hundreds of thousands of inhabitants, the area became a political laboratory filled with competing city-states and small kingdoms. Sargon of Akkad became the first to merge numerous mini-states into an empire. Around 2300 BC, he united Mesopotamia with a mix of violence and bureaucrats, and to hold his realm together, he spun stories about himself as a guarantor of internal harmony and external peace. He also gave his reign a divine purpose by portraying himself as a favorite of the goddess Inanna, the patron of war, sex, justice, and political power. However, since the stories Sargon and his heirs told centered on themselves, not the people they ruled, a more profound feeling of national unity never developed. So, when facing internal problems and potent neighbors, the empire collapsed. And so did all early states except for Egypt, which was held together by its unique geography of a narrow river valley surrounded by deserts.

Hence, ancient people usually did not have time to form common identities. And with a Game of Thrones-like political-military drama storming around them, they continued to identify as members of smaller groups centered on shared ancestry and common gods. The prime example of this is the Jews. Their homeland never grew much larger than Massachusetts, but they developed such a strong identity that they have survived for over three millennia of hardship and harassment. Another example is the Greeks, who contributed to extending racial into a more ethnocultural form of nationalism. Briefly, they shared strong ethnic, linguistic, and religious bonds but were divided into city-states such as Athens and Sparta, which regularly fought each other. One event that did get them to cooperate was an invasion by the Persian Empire in the 490s BC, but as soon as that threat vanished, they started scuffling again. Then, the Peloponnesian War 431-404 BC became so exhausting that the Macedonians, a rough bunch of cousins to the Greeks from the north, could subdue the whole area around 350 BC. Their King Philip II forced them to join a confederacy under his rule by arguing that they should be united since they all spoke the same language and prayed to the same gods.

Building upon his deeds, Philip's son Alexander the Great became the first European to create a full-scale empire. In the 330s BC, he conquered most of the known world from Greece to India. And to hold this enormous realm together, he had to offer something more than just a royal house and threats of violence. By fostering economic and intellectual interchange by erasing borders and forcing people from different areas to work together, he formed Hellenism; a mix of local customs, Greek language, religion, philosophy, and architecture that came to dominate the eastern Mediterranean basin. And even if this only became an elite culture, it became a crust strong enough to hold larger states together. Indeed, when Alexander died in 323 BC, his empire split, but only between his leading generals who became rulers over a handful of mid-sized kingdoms held together by—and further developing—Hellenism.

With this, the idea of using culture to forge large states was in the air, and it was picked up by the Romans, who improved its use. While empires from Sargon's Akkad to Alexander's Greeks had often been created in haste and fallen as soon as weak leaders came around, the Romans took centuries to turn their city-state into an empire. This slow process allowed conquered people to assimilate and made Latin the *lingua franca* of the Western Mediterranean. Moreover, because Rome was a republic, the Romans saw their state as rooted in the people and themselves as citizens, not simple subjects to power. Also, as their dominion grew, they gradually extended citizenship to conquered peoples. And since this came with certain rights, like voting in local assemblies and going to court, millions of outsiders, in time, got a vested interest in a state that, at its height, stretched from the British Isles to the Persian Gulf. Moreover, after Rome in 27 BC turned into a monarchy, its emperors became worldly sovereigns and *pontifex maximums*, the highest spiritual leaders in the land. Thus, they got a significant influence not only over people's bodies but also over their minds.

The emperor's spiritual role in the fourth century AD grew further when Christianity was made the state religion. However, by then, the Roman Empire had been split in two. This division was first meant for administrative purposes only. Still, since the Greek-Hellenistic half was more prosperous, its history took its own route and survived for another thousand years as the Byzantine Empire. By contrast, in the West, after Germanic barbarians sacked Rome in AD 476, no new emperors were named, and during the following Dark Ages, the area broke up into a mosaic of warrior states whose people started to grow their own national identities. For example, the Franks, a tribe living west of the Lower Rhine who had picked up Latin culture and language, became forefathers to the French, while Teutonic tribes further east—that the Romans had never formally conquered and therefore spoke Germanic languages—became ancestors of today's Germans.

Still, memories of Rome meaning peace and prosperity survived, e.g., in art, literature, and the Catholic Church, and from the eighth century, European history became a line of efforts to reunite the continent. First, in AD 800, the Pope crowned the Frankish king Charlemagne emperor of a "Holy Roman Empire" extending from the Baltic Sea to northern Italy. But, after his death, the empire soon split, and Europe through the Middle Ages remained a cluster of mostly small-to-midsized kingdoms, principalities, duchies, prince-bishoprics, free cities, and other semi-independent areas. Then, from around 1500, the Austrian royal house of Habsburgs gained prominence before in order Spain, Sweden, France, Germany, and Russia/Soviet Union also tried to establish their European empires. Moreover, after the fall of communism in 1989, all Western and Central European countries except Iceland, Norway, Switzerland, and a few Balkan nations have joined the European Union; an entity whose leaders, like their monarchical and dictatorial forerunners, define themselves as natural wardens of European peace, wealth, and splendor.

Significantly, the only country (so far) to leave the E.U. is the U.K. After centuries of Roman rule, Britain first looked much like the rest of Europe. However, its history soon began to differ so much that it essentially became a non-European country. In short, the British Isles were, in turn, invaded by Picts, Scots, Angles, Saxons, Jutes, Friesians, Danes, and Norwegians before William the Conqueror finally triumphed in the Battle of Hastings in 1066. His victory allowed for the political scene to settle and for the idea of England as one state to take root. Moreover, in 1215, King John was forced to sign the Magna Carta; a kind of constitutional document, e.g., dividing political power between the king, parliament, and courts and giving rights to people as individuals rather than as members of groups like the aristocracy. As a result, England began to develop a society marked by widespread political influence, power-sharing, and an early form of modern individualism. Also, after losing the Hundred-Year War against France in 1453, England began to redraw from continental affairs to build an island empire including Wales, Ireland, and Scotland.

Roots of Americanism

The English started flexing their muscles after blocking Spain's bid for European supremacy by sinking its Armada in 1588. But as a nation of seafarers, they looked beyond Europe and started founding colonies across the Atlantic. What's more, for a long time, the settlers living along North America's eastern seashore continued to see England as their home country and themselves as full-worthy Englishmen. However, because of the distance, the colonies weren't politically incorporated with England, and their inhabitants never gained access to the Parliament. So, when royal governors began to squeeze the colonists' rights in the 1700s, they could only complain. The 1776 Declaration of Independence thus became a catalog of complaints about the king and Parliament's un-English behavior and the American Revolution a forced act aimed to protect the colonist's rights as "free Englishmen." Given this, it would not have been strange if the Founding Fathers had created a European-like country with a king, nobility, and state church. However, instead, they created an entirely new political system they hoped would be a model for freedom-seeking people worldwide.

Three things are vital to grasp the impact of this episode. First, the colonies' culture had been transformed for over a century by, among other things, access to free land, local self-rule, and the free-spiritedness coming from living far away from kings, dukes, and other nobles. Thus, Americans had become more individualistic, more free market, and more wary about the abuse of political power than the people back home. In a word, they were distilled Englishmen. Second, the Pilgrims had brought themes and ideas that swayed them to view North America as a new Promised Land and themselves as "new Israelites" living in a land blessed by God and meant for higher purposes; stories in turn going back to a mix of Biblical themes, a twelfth-century tale about Roman Britain as the place where Joseph of Arimathea hid the Holy Grail, and Tudor Era rhetoric about England being God's "elect nation." Third, the Founders mixed ancient Greek and Roman wisdom with Christian beliefs, English practices, and Enlightenment thinking. For instance, the Declaration's elevating of certain rights to self-evident truth reflects Enlightenment idealism; the Constitution's limits upon the power of government echo the English political tradition, and the ethics deemed necessary for a well-functioning republic were Christian.

Furthermore, persuading people at home and abroad that the U.S. had the right to revolt against the English required a strong supporting narrative. Consequently, Americans became the first people to develop a full-scale *civil religion*. This term means the set of beliefs buttressing a modern state where people no longer primarily believe in religious reasons for their political regime (as Medieval Europeans had believed kings to rule by divine right). Instead, a civil religion gives citizens historical, philosophical, ideological, and other worldly reasons to love their country. For example, in more contemporary times, Soviets were told they lived in the world's first classless society and had to abide by the party guiding them toward a communist Utopia; Germans that their fate was to dominate Europe; and Swedes that they should work hard and pay high taxes because their country is looked upon as an avantgarde welfare state. And in America, the story became that the nation had to play a role in History as a model of freedom.

However, since the U.S. lacked a history and people were intensely religious, American civil religion became a halfway house between secular and traditional beliefs. In fact, nearly all nationalist themes have Christian models. Among other things, they include tales about an Exodus (people leaving for a promised land); a Genesis (the American Revolution); a Moses-like founder (George Washington); prophets (Thomas Paine); a Jesus figure (Abraham Lincoln); apostles (John Adams, Benjamin Franklin); martyrs (John F. Kennedy, Martin Luther King Jr.); a Devil (Benedict Arnold); sacred spaces (Gettysburg, Arlington Cemetery); places for pilgrimage (Mount Vernon, Mount Rushmore); sanctified holidays (July 4, Memorial Day); holy scriptures (the Declaration of Independence, the U.S. Constitution, both displayed on altar-like displays in the National Archives); and sacred hymns (Star-Spangled Band, America the Beautiful). Washington, D.C., can also be seen as a Jerusalem with "political temples" such as the Capitol, the White House, and the Supreme Court, plus minor shrines for national heroes like Jefferson and Lincoln.

Still, secular ideas also strongly contributed to American culture. For example, the U.S. inherited institutions and principles like the Common Law system, political power-sharing, and the view that elites should have few legal privileges directly from England. Central to the exceptionalist matrix also naturally became the English "freedom tradition" at large. To get a correct perspective on this last issue, we should recall that the English Civil War of 1642–1651 took place parallel with the formative years of the early English colonies in North America. It taught the colonists things like standing up against recognized governments and the pros and cons of the republican government of Oliver Cromwell. In addition, when the Parliament a few decades later limited the king's power through the Glorious Revolution, the 1689 English Bill of Rights not only revived the spirit of the Magna Carta. By drawing attention to whether political authority originates from above, Heaven, or from below, the People, it also stirred democratic debate in England and the colonies.

To boot, philosopher John Locke enhanced many themes of the Glorious Revolution. His rebuke of the old, medieval order of divine authority, absolute monarchy, and a pyramid-like socioeconomic organization would later fascinate, amongst others, Thomas Jefferson. He merged Locke's ideas about a modern society with economist Adam Smith's free market thinking into a vision of the U.S. as a group of semi-independent agrarian states. As we will see, this vision would have enormous consequences and helped make *freedom* and *equality* the founding principles of the Union. However, it should be noted that Locke can be read in different ways. Above all, his views of liberty, private property, citizenship, and the ties between them can be seen as arguments for small governments, low taxes, and few regulations *or* for government reallocating resources between people. In turn, these readings lead to two views of equality: *equality of opportunity*, which accepts the differences in wealth and other fallouts freedom produces, and *equality of outcomes*, which demands taxation, entitlements, and regulations to confiscate and reallocate private resources. Both readings have also existed parallel throughout U.S. history, but the first, minimalistic government-equality of opportunity view continued to dominate political and other discourses well into the twentieth century. However, from the end of the 1800s, the second view did start to become ever more important. But we are not there yet.

Furthermore, since the American Revolution took place in the eighteenth century, Enlightenment thinking had at least three impacts on U.S. civil religion. First, the view that logic and science can be used to "decode" Reality and make everything possible merged with the Puritan striving for *perfection* and the idea that America, its people, and society must be flawless before the Second Coming of Christ can happen. This created a belief that the Declaration and the Constitution are both ideal documents ordering a perfect society; a sureness so rigid that already Jefferson, who believed that laws and political institutions must evolve with human progress, grumbled, "Some men look at constitutions with sanctimonious reverence and deem them, like the ark of the covenant, too sacred to be touched."[2] Perfectionism has since also marked American's Christian beliefs as well as political movements from Abolitionism, Prohibition, and Progressivism to the Great Society, the Reagan Revolution, and the War on Terrorism, whose ambitions all have known—or at least respected— few boundaries. Also, the perfectionist meme renders everything un-American as potentially faulty or even devious by nature. Because as one historian writes about Americans: "If moral fervor stirs our better angels, moral fever spurs our demons."[3]

Second, the individualistic spirit of the Enlightenment changed the meaning of "freedom." Europeans, including Early Americans, had for millennia held a traditional Christian view of this notion in the sense that a man should be free to "willingly surrender to the will of the Lord." Hence, freedom had been seen as the right to join a church or other community and live up to its ideals (think the freedom to join an Amish society and agreeing to give up modern comforts to live according to its rules). The Enlightenment nurtured a more modern, individualistic view of freedom: the right to live according to your will if it does not interfere with others. However, because of Americans' deep religious and strong communitarian (valuing the good of the community over individualism in politics and society) bents, this development became so slow that it is still partially incomplete. Nevertheless, this shift makes U.S. history a tale of how Americans first turned from a traditional to an individual to an atomistic view of freedom, of which the latter has become so extreme

---

2. Thomas Jefferson, "Thomas Jefferson to Samuel Kercheval" (July 12, 1816) on *Library of Congress*, accessed May 15, 2018, https://www.loc.gov/resource/mtj1.049_0255_0262/.

3. James A. Morone, *Hellfire Nation: The Politics of Sin in American History* (New Haven: Yale University Press, 2003), 3.

that it today threatens the unity of U.S. society by making people igno-rant or even hostile to cultural, religious, and other communal duties and sentiments.

Third, Enlightenment thinking permeated the term "We the People." It is Roman in that the legitimacy of political power in the U.S. derives from its citizens. But, even if the Founders talked about the people as "the homogeneous bedrock of America," the majority of them still wanted the best, brightest, and most virtuous to rule. Jefferson penned to John Adams: "The natural aristocracy I consider as the most precious gift of nature for the instruction, the trusts, and government of society."[4] And in Federalist No. 10, James Madison wrote: "Democracies have ever been spectacles of turbulence and contention; have ever been found incompat-ible with personal security or the rights of property; and have in general been as short in their lives as they have been violent in their deaths." Hence, the Founders were elitists, not democrats. Unsurprisingly, there-fore, many would over time come to disagree with this view. In fact, Americans instantly developed a fear that the country's new elites risked betraying them and the republic just as the old British one had done. Two significant upshots of this became an inclination for conspiracy thinking and that the people, in the end, turned away from the Founders' view of the president as an apolitical, first-among-equals figure above politics toward him being a "man of the people" and a guardian against elites.

What is more, the Founders' flexible worldview and the unprecedented move to declare independence allowed them to conduct two grand politi-cal experiments. The first was to create a government without an execu-tive. It was carried out in the 1781 Articles of Confederation. However, this experiment failed and led to the creation of the presidency in the

---

4. Thomas Jefferson, "Natural Aristocracy" in *The Imaginable Conservative* (May 1, 2018), https://the imaginativeconservative.org/2018/05/natural-aristocracy-thomas-jefferson.html.

1789 U.S. Constitution. The practical reason for this was the need for one man to lead and defend the nation. Another more esoteric but still important motive was that Americans also wanted a leader above party politics. This urge is best explained by placing it in a sociological context. It's an impulse, like the one compelling Russians to call their Tzar "little father" and Swedes to see their king as a public ally against aristocrats, tax collectors, and other *herrar*. And if we allow ourselves to theorize, this identical tendency amongst politically, socially, religiously, and culturally diverse scores of peoples point to the fact that the urge has a genetic root in humans' attraction to strong father figures. Anyhow, the U.S. president was made both head of state and commander-in-chief *and* given a role much like an (elected) monarch. Already Washington introduced royal ways like taking a "coronation tour" across the country, forming a cabinet, delivering a yearly state of the nation address, giving dinners for dignitaries, tea parties for commoners, and more.

This "monarchical presidency" got another boost from the Founder's second experiment, which was to create a nation without a state church or even an officially declared religion. It not only inflated the U.S. civil religion to fill the same political-psychological role state churches and religions played in Europe. It also gave the president a dual role as the nation's political and spiritual leader. Hence, his function became similar to the Roman emperor's position as *pontifex maximus*. And because presidents, unlike European monarchs, do not have an archbishop, a pope, or any other force constricting their (civil) religious views, their influence upon Americans' imagination regarding their country's nature, historical goal, and international role became technically unbound. In addition, they have come to serve as raw models for what should be considered good public behavior and private morality. Unsurprisingly, therefore, Americans would for long tend—again like Europeans their monarchs—to see the president almost as a demigod figure. And needless to say, this is a political power tool few presidents have been able not to (ab)use and the main reason why they still today have such paradigmatic roles.

As a working example, George Washington had just been sworn in when he was forced to answer the question about how America's mission to change the world could be fulfilled. Or, more precisely, should the U.S. actively spread its system and ideals, or should it only function as a model? The specific reason for this was that when the French, in June 1789, staged their revolution, many Americans felt a moral and ideological duty to support them. But Washington said no. One motive was that he judged a total upending of the French's over thousand-year-old societal order destined to fail, another was that he felt that the U.S., still lacking natural borders and a standing army, couldn't afford foreign adventures. And his decision set a vital precedent. Later, in his 1796 Farewell Address, Washington laid down a "great rule of conduct," meaning that America should strive for solid economic relations but have "as little political connection as possible"[5] with other countries. And Jefferson—who initially supported the French Revolution but changed his mind in due course— made this policy bipartisan by including it in his 1801 Inaugural Address.

Washington's and later John Adams's economic policy became a similar yardstick. And just as with foreign policy, grim realities more than grand principles came to decide the details. Principally, all Founders ascribed to what we today call a free market economy. However, since national independence relied on economic self-sufficiency, Washington's political isolationism was complemented by his Secretary of the Treasury Alexander Hamilton's economic mercantilist view that the U.S. should be one market but that domestic production—at least for the foreseeable

---

5. George Washington, "Farewell Address" (September 19, 1796), *The American Presidency Project* (henceforth *APP*), accessed May 9, 2017, https://www.presidency.ucsb.edu/node/200675.

future—needed to be protected from foreign competition. And as the U.S. grew into a continental-scaled economy where states and regions specialized and competed, trade barriers worked in most Americans' favor for a long time. Hence, with isolationism keeping the country out of world (military) affairs and protectionism shielding its economy, the so-called *American System* formed that, with some deviations, was to be kept in place until World War II.

Another "founder effect" that must be noted is that North America's vastness and natural riches combined with early American Christian traditions, English heritage, and Enlightenment thinking created an optimistic, vigilant, and vibrant culture focused on exploration, experimentation, and risk-taking. This not only preserved and rejuvenated old Puritan traits like a high work ethic and an outstanding level of industriousness but long conserved a strong focus on marriage, family, honesty, and community—including things such as taking care of most things locally, giving generously to charities, and socializing sin (because society is supposed to be defamed by individuals' mistakes). A corresponding effect was that public and private discourses became marked by—and to this day retain—a bombastic tone. For example, politics, business, sports, and everyday talk are in America characterized by an unusually colorful language jammed with highbrow and emotional code words like "glorious," "huge," "awesome," and "amazing."

Because of all this and more, American society and culture from the start became (or was at least viewed as) genuinely exceptional. Its large-scale thinking, unbound optimism, and ethos about hard work, diligence, and good spirit are also indeed unique and have for nearly three centuries made possible unprecedented individual successes as well as both private and public massive projects such as the Eire Canal, transcontinental railroads, and the Moon Programs. Because, as President Theodore Roosevelt would say, "We Americans love big things!"[6] Already when traveling the land in the 1830s to compare the U.S. with Europe, French scholar Alexis de Tocqueville concluded:

> The position of the Americans is therefore entirely excep-
> tional and it is quite possible that no democratic people will
> ever be similarly placed. Their strictly Puritanical origin,
> their exclusively commercial habits, even the country they
> inhabit, which appears to divert their minds from the study
> of science, literature, and the arts, the nearness of Europe
> which allows them to neglect such pursuits without relaps-
> ing into barbarism, a thousand such reasons, of which I
> have only been able to signal only the main ones, must have
> focused [sic!] the American mind, in this unusual manner,
> upon purely practical objects. Everything—his passions,
> needs, education, circumstances—seems to unite in inclin-
> ing the native of the United States earthward. Only religion
> persuades him to raise an occasional and absent-minded
> glance to heaven.[7]

Please note that this quote does not—as some have tried to imply—offer an early identification of Americanism and American Exceptionalism per se. Instead, it is a harsh judgment of intellectual affairs in the U.S. Yet, Tocqueville's words prove how different America was viewed already back then. In addition, his mentioning of religion as Americans' only "higher" interest is of specific interest since the religious side of U.S. nationalism clearly showed when Americanism—or, more specifically, some of its exceptionalist features—fused with a European philosophy at that time.

---

6. David Frum, *How We Got Here: The 70s: The Decade That Brought You Modern Life (For Better or Worse)* (New York: Basic Books, 2000), 22.

7. Alexis de Tocqueville, *Democracy in America and Two Essays on America* (London: Penguin Books, 2003), 525f.

MANIFEST DESTINY

A vital source of the American think-big mentality is that the sluggish farm-by-farm westward expansion of the East Coast colonies since the 1600s after independence turned into a geopolitical process marked by quantum leaps like the Louisiana Purchase (1803). This for almost a century left the U.S. with a surplus of land that had profound intellectual and ideological effects. First and foremost, the abundance of land convinced Jefferson—and what later became the Democratic Party—that geographic expansion was *the* way to build and sustain long-term what he called an "Empire of Liberty." This idea was consistent with the market-oriented but still agriculture-focused thinking of the French so-called physiocrats and was as simple as it was elegant. Concisely, continued expansion would keep America a loose union of semi-independent agrarian republics free from modern perils such as big cities, "commerce," and industrialization. Hence, Jefferson's vision of America's future was not what we today call capitalist but a small-scale *bourgeoisie* society; an image that to this day lives on—not just through movies and TV shows but also right-wing political rhetoric—in many people's romantic view of rural and small-town America.

However, since territorial conquest was traditionally associated with European monarchy and militarism, expanding the country demanded good-sounding justifications. On this issue, some turned to John Locke, who had argued that since American Indians did not mix soil with labor as farmers, the land was free for the taking. However, the spirit of the times offered a more simple and gracious case than this theoretical argument. When the French Enlightenment around 1800 combined with German Romanticism and transformed medieval feudal state ideology into civil religions/modern nationalism, a joint spiritual and worldly assertion for Europe's ongoing colonization of Asia and Africa was born. Exactly, since the West, through rows of geographical, historical, religious, and other circumstances, had soared far ahead in technological, military, and other aspects, seizing control over underdeveloped areas was portrayed not as conquest but as a moral duty meant for "civilizing" less advanced people for their own good. And this argument sounded so good that Americans picked it up to defend their redeeming of "the Wild West."

In 1845, journalist John L. O'Sullivan dubbed the western expansion of the U.S. *Manifest Destiny.* However, the sentiment dated back to the early 1800s, the Louisiana Purchase, and the Lewis and Clark expedition when Jefferson wrote that the U.S. one day would "cover the whole northern, if not the southern continent, with a people speaking the same language, governed in similar forms, and by similar laws."[8] Such "continentalism" was later also preached by John Adams' son and future president himself John Quincy Adams: "North America appears to be destined by Divine Providence to be peopled by one nation, speaking one language, professing one general system of religious and political principles, and accustomed to one general tenor of social usages and customs."[9] But, Quincy Adams' vision, stemming from a more moderate mind than Jefferson's frivolous imagination, was limited to North America. In 1821, he gave a July Fourth oration approving of George Washington's isolationist line, saying that the U.S. "goes not abroad in search of monsters to destroy." He also warned about the effects of an aggressive foreign policy:

> [America] well knows that by once enlisting under other
> banners than her own, were they even the banners of foreign
> independence, she would involve herself, beyond the power
> of extrication, in all the wars of interest and intrigue, of

8. Walter LaFeber, *The American Age: United States Foreign Policy at Home and Abroad since 1750* (New York: W.W. Norton & Company, 1989), 51.

9. Walter A. McDougall, *Promised Land, Crusader State: The American Encounter with the World Since 1776* (New York: Houghton Mifflin, 1997), 78.

individual avarice, envy, and ambition, which assume the
colors and usurp the standard of freedom. The fundamental
maxims of her policy would insensibly change from liberty
to force. The frontlet upon her brows would no longer beam
with the ineffable splendor of freedom and independence;
but in its stead would soon be substituted an imperial
diadem, flashing in false and tarnished lustre the murky
radiance of dominion and power. She might become the
dictatress of the world: she would be no longer the ruler of
her own spirit.[10]

Ironically, it was Quincy Adams who two years later, as Secretary of State, wrote the Monroe Doctrine. This policy declared that since Latin America had gained independence from Spain and Portugal, European intervention in the New World would now be seen as potentially hostile acts against the U.S. And even if this claiming of a big brother role in the Western hemisphere was first a show of support for other people's independence, it did open the door for U.S. meddling in the Caribbean that later would spell the end of George Washington's foreign policy.

President Andrew Jackson continued to use continentalism in the next decade. He was a passionate expansionist, and the effects of his presidency, in many ways, became massive. Four things need to be mentioned. First, through populist rhetoric, Jackson made Jefferson's yeoman farmer of the interior, rather than the "natural aristocracy" along the East Coast, the political backbone of the country. That he happened to be in office when many states changed their voting regulations to include all white men, at the same time as the right to vote was still dependent on owning land (or other property), also pinned a democratic badge on expansion to new areas where Americans could acquire such property. In addition, the need

10. John Quincy Adams, "Celebrating the Declaration of Independence," (July 4, 1821) *Teaching American History*, accessed September 22, 2018, http://teachingamericanhistory.org/library/document/speech-on-independence-day/.

to open space for white settlers allowed Jackson, with his Indian Removal Act of 1830, to start expelling American Indians from their homes east of the Mississippi (and prepared the land for the latter half of the Indian Wars, whose effects would be felt into the first quarter of the twentieth century). Thus, the "Trail of Tears" of some sixty thousand natives between 1830 and 1850 out West was conducted in the name of democracy, making them early victims of an active form of exceptionalist thinking.

Second, mass democracy replaced the intricacies of republicanism with straightforward "democratism" as an American quality ready for export. Indeed, the widening of U.S. democracy triggered a movement led by the English Reform Act of 1832, which, by citing the expansion of suffrage in America, commenced a century-long extension of voting rights across Europe (which in turn boosted a more activist view of America's global mission at home). Beforementioned John L. O'Sullivan, for instance, called the geographic expansion of the U.S. a step in "America's inevitable upward march to first-rate status."[11] He also fused democratism with Christianity by arguing that since "democratic principles [are] the animating force of Christianity," it must be the end goal of History. Like contemporary European thinkers such as Auguste Comte and Karl Marx, he too furthered this destiny-bound view by dividing human history into phases stretching from barbarism, through theocracy, statism, and aristocracy, to democracy—a grand progress no one could be allowed to stand in the way of.

Third, being the first president to define himself as an anti-elitist, Jackson once and for all began to alter Americans' view of the president from the Founders' august "first among equals" figure into a "man of the people" who should act as an agent for the average citizens' needs and wishes.

---

11. John D. Wilsey, *American Exceptionalism and Civil Religion: Reassessing the History of an Idea* (Downers Grove, IL: IVP Academic, 2015), 81.

Indeed, this change would take a good century or more. Nevertheless, the vision of America as a "folksy" country—rather than a politically and philosophically sophisticated Enlightenment experiment—with this became a political, cultural force and opened a vertical battlefield between elitists and populists that, in time, became a central feature of U.S. politics. As we will see, from around 1900, the number of self-proclaimed plebeian candidates for—and victors of—the U.S. presidency has also increased dramatically.

Fourth, because the West, during the 1800s, experienced the rise of "scientific" racism, Jacksonianism and Manifest Destiny came to suggest Anglo-Saxon superiority. However, on this issue, exceptionalist thinking cut both ways. On the one hand, racist views regarding American Indians were, besides defending their mistreatment at home, used as an alibi for the Mexican-American War of 1846–1848. Because, while Mexicans earlier had been seen and treated as at least semi-Europeans, racist reasoning now made their "brownness" an obstacle to successfully governing themselves—and adding the Southwest to the U.S. a caring deed. On the other hand, the exceptionalist view of America as a land of freedom embedded in Manifest Destiny did contribute to ending slavery.

This is because Abraham Lincoln was convinced that exceptional qualities defined America, and as a politician, military leader, and theorist of U.S. nationalism, he profoundly changed people's views of America during the Civil War. Specifically, describing the U.S. as humanity's "last best hope of earth,"[12] his most critical deed was to declare that the Declaration's words "all men are created equal" included all, not just white, men. By doing so, he initiated a long-term shift of political focus from freedom to equality that would have massive consequences far beyond the slavery

---

12. Abraham Lincoln, "Second Annual Message," (December 1, 1862) *APP*, accessed February 5, 2018, https://www.presidency.ucsb.edu/node/202180.

issue. By stressing salaried work—"free labor"—over slavery, Lincoln also revitalized the Protestant work ethic, outlined the modern concept of the American Dream, and prepared the U.S. for large-scale capitalism. In addition, he reformed several religious-based exceptionalist views and norms. Most importantly, he challenged the idea that America could do no wrong because Providence guided its actions. E.g., by refusing to argue that God was on the North's side in the Civil War and instead saying he hoped the North was on God's side, he modernized the use of religious-based civic arguments by making it harder to use them as scapegoats for bad political decisions. Finally, a small but powerful change impelled by Lincoln was to stop referring to *these* United States and use the singular instead. Thus, he expedited the already changing view of the U.S. from a group of semi-independent states to that of one nation, which was—among many other things—a long-term requirement for a stronger federal government. A big political turn in that direction would also follow this small linguistic twist.

"We need Hawaii just as much and a good deal more than we did California. It is Manifest Destiny."

William McKinley | 1898

CHAPTER 2 |

A New Land

The 1890s represent a watershed in American history. The decade started with the end of the Indian Wars with the Wounded Knee Massacre and the Frontier's closing in 1890. And after that, important events took place virtually every year. For example, in 1893, the burst of an economic bubble led to a recession and a wave of violent strikes; in 1895, America passed the U.K. as the world leader in industrial output; the 1896 election of William McKinley marked the beginning of the Progressive Era; and in 1898, America stepped forward as a great power through the Spanish-American War. Moreover, historian Frederick Jackson Turner predicted that since "Going West!" so far had been the essence of American culture, the vanishing of the Frontiers would change the nation by redirecting the "energies" of the people. And it did. Due to industrial development, massive immigration, and rapid urbanization following its path, the country changed so profoundly that some began to argue for creating a federal welfare state. At the same time, U.S. foreign policy changed so drastically that the country experienced an outburst of traditional imperialist behavior, including the acquisition of overseas outposts. Consequently, parallel with America beginning to take the first

33

steps toward expanding the federal government, it abandoned George Washington's foreign policy entirely. When entering World War I in 1917, Thomas Jefferson's vision of a Union of semi-independent republics was thus on its way out, and America's original socioeconomic order to survive intact only for another decade and a half.

THE TECHNOCRATIC TURN

In the nineteenth century, the West moved from agricultural to industrial societies. In America, the shift became a painful mental as well as a material process that led to a "frontier anxiety" that lasted into the 1930s. For example, in 1921, President Warren G. Harding would say that "the base of the pyramid of civilization which rests upon the soil is shrinking through the drift of population from farm to city."[13] However, as big changes tend to do, industrialization offered marvelous opportunities next to upsetting blows. As Americans left the often meager but stable security of villages and small towns for cities equally ridden with gloom and opportunity, their minds opened to new social, cultural, and political views that, among other things, affected the national narrative. Until then, the national storyline had been that Americans left to themselves (with God's help) had turned a continent of wilderness into a thriving civilization stretching from sea to shining sea. But now, despite a general optimism fostered by technological, medical, and other advances, some milieus changed in ways that *lessened* people's view of the U.S.

The roots of this illogical development were that in America, critiques of social, economic, and other circumstances had not ended in 1776. On the contrary, religion, republicanism, and communitarianism offered healthy counterweights to the country's worldly culture, and criticisms

---

13. Warren G. Harding, "First Annual Message," (December 6, 1921), *APP*, accessed May 5, 2017, https://www.presidency.ucsb.edu/node/206691.

of things like capitalism, slavery, and excessive individualism had fumed from the start. In the second half of the 1800s, the Civil War and a series of economic panics also upset people's confidence in the U.S. model and tilled the soil for the radical reading of John Locke. The ideas of European thinkers such as John Stuart Mill, the founder of social liberalism; August Comte, the father of positivism (the belief that everything can be understood through logic and reason); and Karl Marx, the guru of communism, also gained some traction. As a result, at the same time as Americans became the wealthiest people in history, complaints about, e.g., poor working conditions, inadequate housing, and bad sanitation grew together with calls for female suffrage, unemployment insurance, and old-age pensions. And naturally, as scholars, media personalities, and others turned their focus from triumphs to troubles, demands on politicians to "do something" rose.

The program of the Populist Party, launched in 1891, reflected this partly new political atmosphere. It painted a dull picture of life in America:

> We meet in the midst of a nation brought to the verge of
> moral, political, and material ruin. Corruption dominates
> the ballot-box, the Legislatures, the Congress, and touches
> even the ermine of the bench. The people are demoralized;
> most of the States have been compelled to isolate the voters
> at the polling places to prevent universal intimidation and
> bribery. The newspapers are largely subsidized or muzzled,
> public opinion silenced, business prostrated, homes covered
> with mortgages, labor impoverished, and the land concen-
> trating in the hands of capitalists. The urban workmen are
> denied the right to organize for self-protection, imported
> pauperized labor beats down their wages, a hireling standing
> army, unrecognized by our laws, is established to shoot them

down, and they are rapidly degenerating into European conditions.[14]

Indeed, this image did not reflect the popular picture of America. But, as populist movements tend to do, it offers a snapshot of spreading attitudes at the time. Still, the Populist Movement was only a political precursor and a general romantic and backward-looking force. A much more elitist, aggressive, and futuristic faction, with the grander ambition to speed up History by removing the Founders' political and economic systems, was already in the making.

The background is that the blast of technological and scientific break-throughs in the second half of the nineteenth century had two critical political consequences. First, a worldly Utopia, resting upon belief in human perfectibility, finally seemed within reach. This was particularly true in America, the birthplace of modern marvels like the assembly line, skyscrapers, telephones, and cars. The only thing seemingly missing was to remove the shackles and let bureaucrats, architects, engineers, and other do-gooders get to work. Hence, twirls of red strings were drawn between political action and scientific progress on the societal detective board, forming a view about rule by experts." Second, one specific outcome of this hype was Social Darwinism. We will return to this pseudoscience, but we can note here that just like climate change today, everyone who wanted to be thought "serious" supported it. The only query was if society could be perfected simply by changing people's behavior from the outside, through reforms, or if improvements demand internal changes also? And not so surprisingly, experts of various forms recommended a mix of politi-cal reforms and selected breeding through birth control, abortions, and euthanasia.

---

14. Donald B. Johnson & Kirk H. Porter. *National Party Platforms 1840-1972* (Chicago: University of Illinois, 1973), 89ff.

Furthermore, the political philosophy giving voice to this new world-view was progressivism, which compared with European ideologies such as communism, socialism, and Christian democracy seems weak and elusive. The reason for this is that Americans, by and large, have always remained distrustful of political power and that *pragmatism*—a character-istic American school of thought asserting that theories should be mea-sured by their practical usefulness, not dogmas or ideology—was said to be scientists' only loadstar. And to some extent, existing American mores and cultural traits did dampen the influence of extreme political and other ideas. Case in point, in the U.S., a country with over 120 million people in 1930, approximately 60,000 "idiots" and other "unproductive" people were to be forcibly sterilized in accordance with eugenics laws, while in Sweden, with only six million, the number became around 65,000. Nevertheless, Progressivism is a radical—and essentially anti-American—philosophy defined by an "aspiration to turn the university into the fourth branch of the of government,"[15] whose core idea is a kind of secular mil-lenarianism: that humanity had finally progressed enough to become fully aware of itself and its potential.

Moreover, modern science's claim that everything is relative—a notion seemingly proven by Albert Einstein in 1915—and the belief that every-thing old, formal, and traditional was deformed and/or inefficient got a special ring to it in "the world's first modern country." Because of this, Newton was out and Darwin in and change became a goal in itself. Among many things, this meant that the Founding Fathers' classic view of human nature was dismissed, and their ensuing take on politics (as a dirty and deranged business that forever needs to be restrained) thought to be wrong. Instead, progressives, through reason and logic, wanted to

---

15. Charles R. Kesler, *I Am the Change: Barack Obama and the Crisis of Liberalism* (New York: Broadside Books, 2012), 54.

turn government into a productive force and, through education, adapt the populace for whatever they, the elite, found fit. This also brought into the political crosshair the oldest and most formal thing in America—the Constitution. Like the Founders, it was deemed outdated and too rigid for the modern era. And so was the politically minimalistic, economically *laissez-faire*, and sociocultural traditional order it had been written to create, uphold, and protect. Hence, the progressive project became to "modernize" America by federalizing and democratizing all essential aspects of private life and public affairs—and for this to happen the Constitution had to go, or at least be shoved aside.

Given this, the Progressive Movement was destined to mature into a left-wing spectacle. As academics akin to philosopher John Dewey, economist Thorstein Veblen, and future President Woodrow Wilson became central to its development, they created a political platform for social or "modern" liberalism in America that, behind a veneer of pragmatism, became revolutionary in nature. Sometimes, this also showed early. For example, in 1909, philosopher and to-be co-founder of American radicalisms dreadnaught *The New Republic* Herbert Croly argued that the U.S. could only be saved by a government spreading wealth more evenly. In 1914, journalist Walter Lippmann, soon to be one of American liberalism's leading voices, declared modern society so complicated that it demanded "scientific government."[16] Similarly, while the American Economic Association's ambition was to make the U.S. Government "an educational and ethical agency whose positive aid is an indispensable condition of human progress,"[17] voices within the Jesus Movement, under the motto "What would Jesus do,"[18] wanted political action to right social

16. Walter Lippmann, *Drift and Mastery* (published 1914; reprint Madison, WI: The University of Wisconsin Press, 1985).

17. Leonard Liggio, "Intolerance and Intervention," (August 1983) *Reason Magazine*, accessed August 14, 2020, https://reason.com/1983/08/01/intolerance-and-intervention/.

18. Eric Foner, *The Story of American Freedom* (New York: W. W. Norton & Company, 1998), 130.

wrongs. For example, a Baptist minister wrote, "we now have such scientific knowledge of social laws and forces [that] we have reached the point where we can make history make us."[19] Because of this, one historian writes:

> During the early twentieth century, it was not uncommon
> to hear leading Americans from a wide range of political and
> religious backgrounds articulate intuitive visions proclaiming human natural goodness and the ability of politics to
> transform society and even the world. Interpretations of
> social and political disorder as products of the inefficient
> management of institutions or of the incomplete realization
> of progress, equality, or democracy became more frequent
> in the United States. Increasingly, the person perceived as
> deserving of society's attention and praise was the one who
> had great plans to serve and save mankind.[20]

Nonetheless, this left-wing radicalism was to take over half a century to be publicly more fully revealed. And outside politics, progressivism would spread even slower. One reason for this was Americans' devotion to individualism and freedom, another was that radicals disagreed about what needed to be done and how to do it. Consequently, the Progressive Era, in the end, only produced a handful of laws and regulations intended to battle corruption, wily business practices, and immoral conduct. Indeed, these were based on the belief that political and bureaucratic means could direct human behavior, but they were only pebbles compared to the Mount Utopia radicals dreamt of. Informatively, the only large-scale national social engineering project before the 1930s became Prohibition; a reform based more on religious beliefs than ideological convictions—

19. Bradley C. S. Watson, *Progressivism: The Strange History of a Radical Idea* (Notre Dame, IN: University of Notre Dame Press, 2020), 54.
20. Justin Garrison, *An Empire of Ideals: The Chimeric Imagination of Ronald Reagan* (New York: Routledge, 2013), 42.

and a fiasco so complete that the U.S. still today deals with the crime and the Mafia it created.

Even so, the Progressive message had two looming effects. First, it moved the focus from traditional sources of progress, such as individual work, saving, and enterprise, toward political, bureaucratic action. To wit, it shifted people's hope of a better life from the marketplace to the political meeting (and medical operating) room. Second, the Puritan tendency to socialize sin by holding society responsible for sinners' mistakes was rejuvenated. This view had largely been lost during the nineteenth century through the spread of modern individualism, but now a twisted mirror image of it made entre: that it was society's obligation to fix "sins" like individual poverty, illness, and unemployment through federal welfare systems. Indeed, rank-and-file Americans were not yet ready for this since states, counties, and people still took care of most issues. However, since what happened in Washington, D.C., and within academic ivory towers for most remained of marginal-to-no interest, radicals could bid their time and slowly but steadily push political, academic, and bureaucratic discourse in their direction. In steadily widening circles, therefore, the American inclination for perfection merged with the modern belief in infinite progress and nurtured the image of the U.S. as a defective creation that could be fixed through logic, reason, and political top-down strokes.

In other words, in the 1890s, the U.S. saw the rise of a modern political left that, like its European counterpart, focused on leveling social, economic, and other differences by political means more than cultivating opportunities for people themselves to improve their situation. And for this to happen, as one scholar writes, "the eighteenth-century Constitution based on the eighteenth-century notion of a fixed human nature with static rights, had in turn to be transcended by a modern or living constitution based on the evolutionary view."[21] In order, an ideological reshuffling within and between the parties also commenced. Until then, the Democrats had been America's right-wing party in many ways. Following Jefferson and Jackson, it had stood, e.g., for small government, low tariffs, *laissez-faire*, and individual freedom. However, after the Civil War, by stressing states' rights and becoming the home of segregationists and the Ku Klux Klan, the party had parked itself in the middle of a political desert. These latter circumstances namely confined it to the Old South, and after Lincoln's VP, Andrew Johnson, left the White House in 1869, for almost half a century, only one Democrat, Grover Cleveland, was elected president.

Therefore, after taking a beating in the 1894 midterms and William McKinley's landslide two years later, William Jennings Bryan, a firebrand orator, took the lead. As the Democrat's presidential candidate in 1896, he, among other things, picked up on a long-time populist cry for "free silver." In doing so, he blamed Eastern bankers for the sad state of the economy and demanded unlimited coinage of silver. Indeed, this policy would have meant rampant inflation, and economists harshly condemned it. However, Bryan spoke passionately about how humanity should not be crucified "upon a cross of gold" and alluded to Jackson's stand against "the encroachments of aggregated wealth" in ways that moved millions. And even if he didn't win in 1896, or when he ran again in 1900 or 1908, this was only the beginning. In the following decades, the Democrats—caught up in a self-propelling double helix of need to win votes and attracting radicals—would continue to move left by substituting its traditional plank of support for, e.g., limited government, a free economy, free trade, and states' rights for a message of higher taxes, federal regulation of marketplaces, redistribution of wealth, and protectionism.

Contrariwise, as heir to the more government-friendly and mercan-

---

21. Kesler, *I Am the Change*, xvi.

tilist-isolationist Federalist legacy of George Washington, John Adams, and Alexander Hamilton, the Republican Party, since its inception in 1854, was more of a centrist alliance. It was firmly capitalist for sure, but among its pillars was sturdy support for tariffs, industrialization, public education, social harmony, and Yankee Protestantism; a religious variety emphasizing things like the Puritan work ethic and giving in to the itch to fight evils like gambling and alcohol by laws and regulations. After the Civil War, the GOP had consequently become a natural home for a broad spectrum of capitalists, farmers, skilled workers, and people mainly appreciating the established order of things. However, from the 1890s, the party seemed to be moving right. This was at first mainly a relative shift caused by the Democrats' leftward drift. However, the impression was reinforced in 1898 when a group of Republicans suddenly decided to abandon George Washington's foreign policy.

THE SPANISH-AMERICAN WAR

A most ironic effect of progressive's talk of the U.S. as an imperfect society is that it made a foreign policy aiming to spread the American system *more* likely. The logic behind this is that as Americans began to admit problems at home and launch reforms to correct them, they still so strongly believed that God and/or History had made the U.S. unique that they thought they also knew what was best for others. Thus, progressives in both parties every so often became reformers at home and imperialists abroad. However, the U.S. didn't change foreign policy simply because of progressives' urge to improve the world, or any other "prime mover" for that matter. What happened depended on a mix of material needs for some individuals and companies, the U.S. becoming rich enough to act as a great power, political ideas, idealistic urges, some Americans being tantalized by Europeans' "scramble for Africa," and that America seemingly (with Canada in British hands, Mexico filled with non-whites, and the Frontier closed) was running out of space. Combined, these memes started a debate about America's future and international role in which most voices pointed in the same direction—that the only areas left to expand into were the Caribbean and the Pacific and that the country, by not doing so, was flouting its mission to remake the world.

Therefore, in 1895, President Cleveland began to break the seal of George Washington's foreign policy. He did so by extending the Monroe Doctrine to declare all matters within the Western hemisphere a potential U.S. interest and prevent Europeans from forcefully collecting debts owed by Latin American countries. Earlier that year, a fire had also been lit that was to lead the U.S. to step forward as a full-fledged great power. Specifically, Cuba had always tantalized Americans. Already Jefferson toyed with the idea of adding the island to the Union and, especially after attaining Florida in 1822, the prospect of admitting the resource-rich tropical paradise as a state persisted. However, alien in language and culture, plus racially non-white, throughout the nineteenth century, it remained in Spanish hands.

Nevertheless, Americans reacted strongly when the local population revolted against their Spanish overlords. Also, the press took the uprising and ran with it. And the support went far beyond the East Coast "yellow press" contest between William R. Hearst's *New York Journal* and Joseph Pulitzer's *New York World,* typically blamed for whipping the people into a war frenzy. Even in the Midwest, the heartland of American isolationism, a common editorial theme became that "Spain violated American interests in the Caribbean and that her presence in that area was inimical to the consummation of America's 'manifest destiny.' "[22]

---

22. George W. Auxier, "Middle Western Newspapers and the Spanish American War, 1895-1898," *The Mississippi Valley Historical Review,* Vol. 26, No. 4 (Mars, 1940), 524.

Now, the "splendid little war" that followed and was to change U.S. foreign policy forever indeed got nearly all markers of a traditional colonial war. However, the argument for it from the start was that the U.S. had a moral responsibility to free and an obligation to "civilize" the Cubans so that they could enjoy the same level of wealth and success as Americans. I.e., the same arguments Europeans used to defend their colonization of Africa and parts of Asia. The popularity of this opinion also led to similar calls in Congress. For instance, on March 17, 1898, Republican Senator Redfield Proctor from Vermont would declare: "Not until peace comes and the [Cubans] can go back to their country, rebuild their homes, reclaim their tillage plots, which quickly run up to brush in that wonderful soil and clime, and until they can be free from danger of molestation in so doing. Until then the American people must, in the meantime, care for them."[23]

However, since foreign policy is a presidential prerogative and President Cleveland belonged to the old school that rejected the idea of the U.S. intervening abroad for ideological reasons, the progress toward war became slow. In 1896, after public support for intervention jumped further when the Spanish opened a network of concentration camps across Cuba, Cleveland still ensured that the U.S. would not interfere. And in his 1897 Inaugural Address, his successor William McKinley promised to continue "the policy of non-interference with affairs of foreign governments wisely inaugurated by Washington."[24] Even so, the latter was forced to increase his pressure on the Spanish by the following year until war became impossible to avoid. Still, even in his final request for congressional approval to invade Cuba in April 1898, he emphasized a general humanitarian reason

23. Redfield Proctor, "Cuban Reconcentration Policy and its Effects," (March 17, 1898), *Latin American Studies*, accessed February 1, 2017, www.latinamericanstudies.org/1895/reconcentration-camps.htm. Emphasis added.

24. William McKinley, "Inaugural Address," (March 4, 1897), *APP*, accessed June 4, 2018, https://www.presidency.ucsb.edu/node/205278.

more than any exceptionalist duty for the intervention: "In the name of humanity, in the name of civilization, in behalf of endangered American interests which give us the right and the duty to speak and to act, the war in Cuba must stop."[25]

Nonetheless, since Americans did go to war not to protect or expand their homeland but to liberate and carry out change on behalf of others, a balanced account must be that the Spanish-American War happened primarily because of a new, activist form of Americanism's missionary notion. Thus, the invasion marked a fundamental shift in U.S. foreign policy, and citizens and pundits alike viewed it as America was finally living up to its destined role. At this time, Americans also started using *exemptionalist* claims that America could ignore international rules because of her special status. For example, after the war, naval officer and historian Alfred T. Mahan would say that if the U.S. had violated international law to help Cuba, so what? This violation was no worse than when people before the Civil War had illegally aided fugitive slaves.

Certainly, there was opposition to the war. But most of its critics were worried less about Cuba than the war leading to further conquest. And they were to be proven right. Two events on June 15, 1898, show these points. With the U.S. invasion now rolling, the American Anti-Imperialist League, which included members as different as steel magnate Andrew Carnegie, author Mark Twain, and labor leader Samuel Gompers, gathered in Faneuil Hall, Boston, where Samuel Adams once had argued for independence from the U.K. There, speakers protested that the U.S., next to Cuba, would take Puerto Rico and the Philippines from Spain. One thundered, "We are not here to oppose war [but] to insist that a war begun

---

25. William McKinley, "Message to Congress Requesting a Declaration of War With Spain," (April 11, 1898) *APP*, accessed June 4, 2018, https://www.presidency.ucsb.edu/node/304972.

in the name of humanity shall not be turned into a war for empire."[26] And another clarified that the war risked "sacrifice the principles on which the Republic was founded" and that America, by perusing it, added itself "to the list of oppressors of mankind."[27] Hence, the Anti-Imperialists did not question America's right to invade a foreign country to liberate it but worried that the war would derail into something incompatible with the Declaration and the Constitution.

That same day, in Washington, D.C., Congress met to discuss whether the U.S. should annex Hawaii, which, against an opposition led by its ex-Queen Liliuokalani, had long been ruled by American settlers. And emotions ran high here, too. While Republican House Speaker Thomas Reed saw the seizure of another country as absurd as "annex[ing] the moon" and refused to preside over the session, other opponents quoted George Washington and Abraham Lincoln. But others reasoned like the House member who argued that opposing seizing Hawaii was "antediluvian and thorough stupidity."[28] And while some did express themselves more crassly—"a Great manufacturing nation [like the U.S.] must find new markets for our energy and enterprise"—most agreed with the member who matched these views: "We need not, nor do I believe we will, enter into a conquest of force but, to the contrary, our higher civilization will be carried across the Pacific by the white and peaceful wings of our rapidly increasing commerce."[29] Thus, the annexationists carried the day and a few weeks later, on July 4, a resolution passed that turned Hawaii into a U.S. colony.

The same cocky attitude later marked the U.S. Government's dealings

---

26. Stephen Kinzer, *The True Flag: Theodore Roosevelt, Mark Twain, and the Birth of American Empire* (New York: Henry Holt and Company, 2017), 6.
27. Ibid.
28. Ibid, 8.
29. Ibid.

with the areas conquered from Spain. And the political language was now quickly becoming utterly entangled with the moral overtones. In February 1899, McKinley said that America, by accepting the Paris Peace Treaty," which formally ended the war and transferred what was left of Spain's empire to the U.S., was "obeying a higher moral obligation which rested upon us."[30] This obligation, he also said, was to help the former subjects to the Spanish crown to gain freedom and prosperity. However, the local population's wishes were not given much consideration. Guam, in the Western Pacific, had by then already been placed under the U.S. Navy's control by Executive Order; Puerto Rico was, through the 1900 Foraker Act, to be organized into an unincorporated territory with only a limited degree of popular government; and Cuba, which could formally not be annexed because of a prewar decision, was given independence in 1901, but only after the Platt Amendment guaranteed that the island remained within the U.S. fold.

In the end, therefore, only the Philippines created a headache. Located halfway around the world, much larger, densely populated, and culturally different even compared to Spain's Caribbean outposts, many Americans initially felt reluctant to deal with it. McKinley, for example, started by floating the idea to keep only a sliver of the archipelago as a coal station for American ships, while others wanted to grant the islands instant independence. However, after the Filipinos revolted against their new rulers, even previous war opponents changed their minds. For instance, William Jennings Bryan crowed: "Behold a republic gradually but surely becomes the supreme moral factor in the world's progress and the accepted arbiter of the world's disputes—a republic whose history, like the path of the just, 'is as the shining light that shineth more and more unto the perfect

---

30. Richard V. Pierard & Robert D Linder, *Civil Religion & the Presidency* (Grand Rapids, MI: Academie Books, 1988), 133.

day.' "[31] And eventually, McKinley also had a change of heart. After coming out for annexation of Hawaii—"It is Manifest destiny"[32]—he made up his mind also about the Philippines.

During a tour of his political home turf in the isolationist Midwest, McKinley first, in nearly sixty speeches, tested the ground for colonial expansion and exceptionalist arguments, e.g., by saying that the war with Spain had been fought "in a holy cause."[33] Clearly, a president measuring the opinions of "normal folks" on such an important question would never have occurred to the Founders. In fact, it had probably been impossible only a few years earlier. But times were changing, and after getting the answers he wanted from his voters, he returned to Washington, D.C., and continued to emphasize the idealistic side of what was happening. For instance, he told a group of visiting clergymen that he had had an epiphany one night while walking the White House's corridors about that it was now America's duty to "educate the Filipinos, and uplift them and civilize them and Christianize them, and by God's grace to do the very best we could by them, as our fellow-man for whom Christ also died."[34]

In these examples, the power of exceptionalist thinking is made clear. Or, more specifically, the power of activist exceptionalist thinking. Because, even if annexation of conquered territories violated maybe not the words of the Constitution but definitively the spirit of the Declaration, most people's worries (President McKinley included) were subdued by the belief in a mission to "civilize" conquered lands before, maybe, granting them independence. And people now took this task very seriously. Even usually

---

31. Robert Endicott Osgood, *Ideals and Self-Interest in American Foreign Policy: The Great Transformation of the Twentieth Century* (Chicago: The University of Chicago Press, 1953), 87.

32. Ernest R. May, *Imperial Democracy: The Emergence of America as a Great Power* (Chicago: Imprint Publications, 1991), 244.

33. Stephen Kinzer, *The True Flag: Theodore Roosevelt, Mark Twain, and the Birth of American Empire* (New York: Henry Holt and Company, 2017), 82f.

34. May, *Imperial Democracy*, 253.

well-mannered Republican mandarins could lose their temper over it. As when Republican Senator George F. Hoar from Massachusetts said that America, by accepting the Treaty of Paris, risked looking like "a cheap-jack country raking after the cart for the leavings of European tyranny," and his Connecticut colleague Orville Platt exploded: "The literal application of the Senator's doctrine would have turned back the Mayflower from our coast and would have prevented our expansion westward to the Pacific Ocean."[35] And since Platt's attitude became dominant, Cuba became only the first in a long row of U.S. interventions in the Caribbean known as the "Banana Wars" that would last until 1934.

Moreover, the views used to defend these post-1898 interventions not seldom mingled with racial biases. Republican Senator Albert J. Beveridge from Indiana said: "God has not been preparing the English-speaking and Teutonic peoples for a thousand years for nothing [and] made us the master organizers of the world to establish a system where chaos reigns."[36] And Massachusetts Republican Senator Henry Cabot Lodge passionately agreed:

> [To abort America's] mighty movement westward [to]
> the shores of Asia, to the very edge of the cradle of the
> Arians [. . .] would be a wrong to humanity, a dereliction
> to duty, a base betrayal of the Filipinos who have supported
> us [. . .] and in the highest degree contrary to sound morals
> [since America] has a great mission in the world—a mission
> of good, a mission of freedom.[37]

Clearly, what ripped through America from around 1900 was thus a

---

35. Kinzer, *True Flag*, 105.

36. Albert Jeremiah Beveridge, "If this be imperialism . . ." in Bob Blaisdell (ed.), *Infamous Speeches: From Robespierre to Osama bin Laden* (Mineola, NY: Dover Publications, Inc., 2011), 62f.

37. Michael J. Hostetler, "Henry Cabot Lodge and the Rhetorical Trajectory," in Jason A. Edwards & David Weiss, *The Rhetoric of American Exceptionalism: Critical Essays* (Jefferson, NC: McFarland & Company, Inc., Publishers, 2011), 125.

wave of both popular and political support for traditional imperialism reinforced by exceptionalist claims and racist arguments. Still, most Americans denied behaving like Europeans. For example, President McKinley, in his second 1901 Inaugural Address, assured that the U.S.' actions were poles apart from European colonialism because Americans were inherently different:

> The American people, entrenched in freedom at home, take
> their love for it with them wherever they go, and they reject
> as mistaken and unworthy the doctrine that we lose our own
> liberties by securing the enduring foundations of liberty to
> others. Our institutions will not deteriorate by extension,
> and our sense of justice will not abate under tropic suns in
> distant seas.[38]

And after an anarchist later that year shot McKinley dead, defending foreign policy ventures with exceptionalist arguments became standard. In a "corollary" to the Monroe Doctrine, his successor Theodore Roosevelt assured that Americans from now on would intervene on Europe's behalf in any conflict with Latin America. Hence, he aggressively confirmed the U.S.'s role as a great power and a hegemon throughout the Western hemisphere. Roosevelt too repeatedly underscored that America had the right and a sacred obligation to go abroad. Like when he, in 1905, spoke in front of the Alamo in Texas, a prime symbol of U.S. might:

> We can not decide whether we will be great or not. The only
> thing we can decide is whether, being great, we will do well
> or do ill. We have got our duty in the world. We must do
> our duty to others, and we must do our duty to our selves.

---

38. William McKinley, "Inaugural Address," (March 4, 1901) *APP*, accessed September 12, 2019, https://www.presidency.ucsb.edu/node/205282.

[. . .] We have duties in connection with the great position we have taken. We can not shirk these duties. We can do them well or do them ill, but do them we must.[39]

To finish, Roosevelt's successor William H. Taft lacked Roosevelt's animated persona and theatrical genius. But he didn't differ on America's new role and mission. In his 1909 Inaugural Address, he noted that "The governments of our dependencies in Porto Rico and the Philippines are progressing as favorably as could be desired" and that the U.S. "in each dependency is upholding the traditions of civil liberty and increasing popular control which might be expected under American auspices."[40] Undeniably, comments like these from Roosevelt and Taft could be disregarded as mere cynical remarks, concealing economic and other traditional great power motives for interfering in other countries' affairs. Yet, as indicated by the pattern of ambitious nation-building projects from Cuba to the Philippines, the spike in international involvement after 1898 was at least partly driven by a sincere belief in the rightfulness to spread American values overseas. Taft's successor would also take giant new steps both to reform America and remake the world—plus use plenty of exceptionalist rhetoric to defend these actions.

39. Theodore Roosevelt, "In front of the Alamo," (April 7, 1905) *Theodore Roosevelt*, accessed February 15, 2017, http://www.theodore-roosevelt.com/images/research/txtspeeches/132.txt.
40. William Howard Taft, "Inaugural Address, (March 4, 1909), *APP*, accessed June 4, 2018, https://www.presidency.ucsb.edu/node/207216.

"The world is not looking for servants, there are plenty of these, but for masters, men who form their purposes and then carry them out, let the consequences be what they may."

Woodrow Wilson | 1907

CHAPTER 3 |
War and Peace

After acquiring outposts in the Caribbean and the Pacific Ocean, President William McKinley and his successors continued to flex America's new role as a great power. Before entering World War I, the U.S. was to send troops five times to Nicaragua; four times to Cuba and Honduras; three times to Panama and the Dominican Republic; twice to Mexico; and once each to China, Korea, Samoa, and Haiti. The reason behind these actions varied, but arguments for them regularly reflected the new, aggressive form of Americanism gaining ground after the Spanish-American War. For instance, President Theodore Roosevelt defended continued involvement in Cuba by stating, "I know of no action by any other government in relation to a weaker power which showed such disinterested efficiency in rendering service." At this time, presidents also began to claim that their duties were global. For example, in 1906, Roosevelt stepped in and negotiated a peace treaty between Russia and Japan, and his successor William H. Taft openly expressed support for a coup in Nicaragua ousting the country's leader José Zelaya. Hence, patterns were set and habits created that continue to this day. Still, Roosevelt's and Taft's words and actions were only bleak forerunners to what was to come. After winning the White House, Woodrow Wilson became the formulator of modern U.S. foreign policy and the founder of a rhetorical tradition that still today buttresses its goals. In a word, the time for America to go abroad in search of monsters to kill had begun.

DAYS OF WILSON

With a few exceptions, nineteenth-century presidents "stayed in place and on the script," meaning that they accepted the limited domestic role given to them by the Founding Fathers. Apart from Andrew Jackson, they also did not use the presidency for demagogy to whip up the passions of crowds or turn the people against the country's elites. However, as the U.S. became a great power and pressure for reforms grew, this order was destined to fall; if not before when Theodore Roosevelt became president. He was a time-typical *machismo* leader, an energic persona, a flamboyant nationalist, and a progressive, which most notable deed is that he concluded Andrew Jackson's alteration of the U.S. from a Congress-led republic into a mass democracy with the president as a tribune-like agent of the people. The time to do this was also now ripe. All Roosevelt needed to do was to say that "all powers not delegated are reserved," meaning that he, as president, could do anything that the Constitution did not expressly forbid him to do. Indeed, this was the very opposite of what the Founders had intended. Still, because of the *Zeitgeist* (the spirit of the era), he got away with it and turned the presidency into a full-blown partisan office.

Furthermore, though Roosevelt often alluded to U.S. history and national grandeur, he seldom used overt exceptionalist rhetoric. One reason is that the presidency's rhetorical traditions held back even a political juggernaut like him, another is that he quickly seemed to realize what other progressives would struggle with throughout the twentieth century: that exceptionalist rhetoric does not lend itself well to arguing for radical reforms. Or put differently, because Americanism is a statement concept—"the U.S. is the greatest country in the world"—using exceptionalist themes and arguments for change is tricky since it suggests something is wrong with America. Yet, after 1900, two forms of exceptionalist rhetoric developed—one conservative, focusing on the need to stick with the Founding Fathers' principles of small government, low taxes, state rights, etc., and one radical, based on arguments that the U.S. must change, possibly even contrary to the Founders' ideas, to stay great. And the latter after 1900 became so demanding that President Taft, himself sort of a progressive, in 1910 felt obliged to pledge to "'stand with the Constitution' in the face of the progressives' attack on the Supreme Court and the rule of law, and their advocacy of direct government, overregulation of businesses, and the widespread expansion of federal power."[41]

Roosevelt's oratory before and after leaving the White House further exemplifies this split and the political importance of the two rhetorical forms of Americanism. As president, he mostly used the first conservative form but felt free to utilize the second radical variant more afterward. As in 1910, when he, in a speech in Osawatomie, Kansas, presented his full-blown progressive post-presidential "New Nationalism" agenda. It was centered on the claim that the U.S. system placed more importance on property rights than human welfare, and he thus demanded that the federal government should create a new socioeconomic regime "under which each man shall be guaranteed the opportunity to show the best that there is in him."[42] This was to happen through reforms such as national insurance for the elderly, disabled, and unemployed, an eight-hour workday, farm relief, and a federal income tax. And all this needed to be done both to catch up with Europe and because America was

41. Watson, *Progressivism*, 117.
42. Theodore Roosevelt, "The New Nationalism," (August 31, 1910) *Theodore Roosevelt*, accessed February 15, 2017, http://www.theodore-roosevelt.com/images/research/speeches/trnationalismspeech.pdf.

. . . the central feature of the history of the world; for the
world has set its face hopefully toward our democracy; and,
O my fellow citizens, each one of you carries on your shoul-
ders not only the burden of doing well for the sake of your
own country, but the burden of doing well and of seeing
that this nation does well for the sake of mankind. [43]

Thus, as ex-President, Roosevelt used the notion of America as a model
as an argument for reforms pointing *away* from the country's original
socioeconomic system. And by doing so while running for the GOP's 1912
presidential nomination and—after losing that battle against President
Taft—as a third-party candidate for his Progressive Party, he set a crucial
example for progressives. Because, since demands for active alterations (as
opposed to change aimed to restore something that has been lost) must
often be explained—and as a future president would say, "When you're
explaining, you're losing"—this strategy turned out less than optimal.

Nevertheless, in 1912, all three presidential candidates claimed the
progressive mantle. And since Roosevelt's run split the Republican vote,
it was, in the end, the Democratic candidate Woodrow Wilson who got
the chance to implement his program, arguably because he was the best to
bury his radicalism in fuzzy exceptionalist talk. On the campaign trail, he
said things like, "I believe that God presided in the inception of this nation
[. . .] to show the way to the nations of the world how they shall walk in
the paths of liberty."[44] And in office, he continued to "speak American."
In his 1913 Inaugural Address, he picked up where Roosevelt had left
off by using exceptionalist arguments for his domestic agenda. Referring
to the Puritan theme of the U.S. as a nation born free and virtuous but
constantly threatened by forces of decay, plus teasing Americans bent for

43. Theodore Roosevelt, "The New Nationalism," (August 31, 1910) *Theodore Roosevelt*, accessed February
15, 2017, http://www.theodore-roosevelt.com/images/research/speeches/trnationalismspeech.pdf.
44. Dearborn, *Exceptionalist-In-Chief*, 60.

perfectionist thinking, he said: "Our duty is to cleanse, to reconsider, to restore, to correct the evil without impairing the good."[45] That year, in his presidential July Fourth address, he also mobilized fallen Union soldiers from the Battle of Gettysburg for his policies. Speaking *in situ* in Pennsylvania, he asked people to view them as actors in the drama of U.S. history:

> These venerable men crowding here to this famous field have set us a great example of devotion and utter sacrifice. They were willing to die [so] that the people might live. But their task is done. Their day is turned into evening. They look to us to perfect what they established. Their work is handed on to us, to be done in another way, but not in another spirit. Our day is not over; it is upon us in full tide.[46]

However, Wilson had change, not restoration, in mind. In his Inaugural Address, he said: "The Nation now seeks to use the Democratic Party [. . .] to interpret a change in its own plans and point of view [because] some old things [. . .] have dropped their disguises and shown themselves alien and sinister."[47] As an ideologue, he also held radically different views than average Americans. During his earlier academic career, he had rebuked the U.S. political system by arguing that many of its particulars were outdated. Above all, he detested the Founders' mechanisms of checks and balances and separation of powers since they slowed down the political process and forced the three branches of government to deliberate. Because, even if this may have been a good and necessary thing back in 1789, since nearly all essential matters (according to Wilson) had since been settled

---

45. Woodrow Wilson, "Inaugural Address," (March 4, 1913) *APP*, accessed June 4, 2018, https://www.presidency.ucsb.edu/node/207576.

46. Woodrow Wilson, "Address at Gettysburg," (July 4, 1913) *APP*, accessed February 21, 2017, https://www.presidency.ucsb.edu/node/206406.

47. Wilson, "Inaugural Address," (March 4, 1913) *APP*, accessed June 4, 2018, https://www.presidency.ucsb.edu/node/207576.

with logic and scientific accuracy, there was no longer any need for this. More specifically, he had also declared that the Constitution's focus on negative freedoms was "increasingly felt to be oppressive"[48] and that the document made it hard to steer society in the right direction—which, for him, meant forsaking federalism and turning the U.S. into a European-like top-down nation-state.

Nonetheless, Wilson planned to talk his way around Americans' political hearts into their brain with logical arguments. Hence, he trusted Americans to be rational enough to accept his ideas, disregarding the established orders age, success, and popularity. And to fathom how Wilson could believe this, we need to compare his view of human nature and statecraft with the Founders.' Based on ancient philosophy and Biblical perceptions, the latter saw humans as imperfect beings with a fixed (or, in modern parlor, genetic) mix of virtues like temperance, wisdom, and love and vices such as pride, greed, and envy. They also realized that politics—because of human irrationality and the fact that historical circumstances are never identical—is a delicate art, not a precise science. In contrast, Wilson had a positive view of human nature, which led him to believe that if enlightened leaders skillfully explained what needed to be done, people would understand and follow. And since no one, according to Wilson, was more enlightened or skillful than Wilson, he was the man for the job to drag America out of History and into the future. However, he did realize that traditional political language would not work well for this operation, so he often avoided it. For instance, when he in 1913 chose to be the first president since John Adams to deliver his State of the Union in person, he left it empty of exceptionalist themes on domestic issues. And it worked. In his first term, he pushed through several long-standing

48. Larry P. Arnn, *The Founders' Key: The Divine and Natural Connection Between the Declaration and the Constitution and What We Risk by Losing It* (Nashville: Thomas Nelson, 2012), 9.

progressive requests, including lower tariffs, popular election of senators, and a federal income tax.

On the other hand, while Americanism is a culturally conservative force nationally, exceptionalist language about the U.S. being a beacon of freedom, etc., is easily jerked into calls for action abroad. Wilson thus used plenty of such rhetoric for such ends. And despite grievances about America's present home state, he believed so strongly in the country's mission that he could not separate his love of the country from its international role. In addition, being a religious man, he saw spreading its virtues as a political *and* holy duty. He once said that the U.S. was "born to exemplify that devotion to the elements of righteousness which are derived from the revelations of Holy Scripture."[49] This language also reflects a critical element of Wilson's self-image, which was that God had picked him to "restore America" as a model for democracy. When handed a crisis for the established world order in the form of World War I, he, therefore, didn't hesitate to be the first to entirely abandon the Founders' view of America as a model, not an implementor, of freedom. And even before taking the U.S. to war, he turned his focus from domestic reforms toward creating a New World Order.

Concisely, Wilson's world vision resembled German philosopher Immanuel Kant's idea about a future where eternal peace was warranted through cooperation and economic interdependence between democratic republics. This view had been aired in America before, e.g., by President Ulysses S. Grant, who said, "I believe that our Great Maker is preparing the world, in His own good time, to become one nation, speaking one language, and when armies and navies will be no longer required."[50]

---

49. John Kenneth White, *Barack Obama's America: How New Conceptions of Race, Family, and Religion Ended the Reagan Era* (Ann Arbor: The University of Michigan Press, 2009), 159.

50. Ulysses S. Grant, "Inaugural Address," (March 4, 1873) *APP*, accessed June 4, 2018, https://www.presidency.ucsb.edu/node/203658.

Besides, what was to be Wilson's trademark idea, a League of Nations, had been presented by Theodore Roosevelt after winning the Nobel Peace Prize for brokering a Russian-Japanese peace treaty in 1906. However, Kant's and Roosevelt's concepts had previously been disregarded as naive non-starters. However, after Europe plunged into war in 1914, they would soon seem like great ideas. Thus, Wilson declared the U.S. (in the form of himself) the world's "chief interpreter" of democracy and began sketching on a new international order. In this way, he became the formulator of modern U.S. foreign policy. And it hit a chord since his plans fitted most Americans' aversion to war, their "think-big" tradition, and the techno-cratic-positivistic spirit of the day. Blinded by exceptionalist pride, many also expected other people to be equally persuaded and simply follow their president's suggestion. However, European leaders frequently disregarded his plans, cementing Americans' resistance to join the war themselves in the process.

But, like ideologues often do when faced with scorn and resistance, Wilson's determination only hardened. His public transformation into a political fanatic can be tracked by quotes. When he interfered in Mexico in 1914, he said that he only wanted "to teach the South American repub-lics to elect good men"[51] but also to turn the whole region into a realm with U.S.-like governments and economies. Then, in 1915, he stated that America's "only reason for existence as a government, [is] to show men the paths of liberty."[52] When renominated for the presidency in 1916, he said: "We are to play a leading part in the world drama whether we wish it or not" and "We shall lend, not borrow; act for ourselves, not imitate

51. Don Wolfensberger, "Congress and Woodrow Wilson's Military Forays Into Mexico: An Introductory Essay," *Wilson Center*, accessed December 28, 2017, https://www.wilsoncenter.org/sites/default/files/ACF18F1.pdf.
52. Richard Gamble, "Savior Nation: Woodrow Wilson and the Gospel of Service," Paper presented to *The Philadelphia Society*, April 21, 2001, accessed February 27, 2017, https://phillysoc.org/gamble-savior-nation-woodrow-wilson-and-the-gospel-of-service/.

or follow; organize and initiate, not peep about merely to see where we may get in."[53] And in 1918, when faced with the prospect of a German victory after Russia's surrender at Brest-Litovsk, he pledged America to a perhaps endless war: "Force, force to the utmost, force without stint or limit, the righteous and triumphant force which shall make right the law of the world and cast every selfish dominion down in the dust."[54] Hence, Wilson not only turned John Quincy Adams on his head and, like the Greek daemon Hercules, set out into the world to find monsters to destroy. He also revealed an ever-since more noticeable authoritarian vein of American "liberalism" that runs up to today's "cancel culture." We will hence return to this.

THE GREAT WAR

World War I amplified the tug-of-war between foreign policy isolationists and activists the Spanish-American War started. Still, tradition and division between electorally influential groups—especially German-Americans and Irish-Americans, of which the former resented support for the Entente and the latter despised the British—carried the day when Wilson declared U.S. neutrality on August 4, 1914. However, this decision also fit his personal agenda. As a critic of the global balance of power system, which had produced general peace since the Napoleonic Wars, he hoped to broker "a just peace" and create a new political world order. But, all of Wilson's diplomatic attempts failed. The main reason for this was that what he saw as the autocratic nature of the Kaiser regime clashed with his exceptionalist views. However, before the war, Germany had been

---

53. Woodrow Wilson, "Address at Sea Girt, New Jersey Accepting the Democratic Nomination for President," (September 2, 1916) *APP*, accessed March 14, 2017, https://www.presidency.ucsb.edu/node/206580.

54. Woodrow Wilson, "Speech at the Opening of the Third Liberty Loan Campaign, delivered in the Fifth Regiment Armory, Baltimore: 'Force to the Utmost,' " (April 6, 1918) *APP*, accessed December 10, 2018, https://www.presidency.ucsb.edu/node/206655.

almost as democratic as the U.K. and France, but Wilson simply ignored this fact. And since this swayed him to demand a democratized Germany, which required an Allied victory, his call for "a peace without victory" sounded dishonest. It was also Wilson's hostility to Berlin, together with German blunders like the Zimmerman Telegram (wherein Germany promised Mexico to regain Arizona, New Mexico, and Texas if joining their side) that drew America's slide into the conflict.

The events dotting the timeline leading to war tell the story. Growing frantic over that his "peace work" didn't work out, Wilson, on January 22, 1917, made Roosevelt's idea of a "League for Peace" his own. He said it would make the Monroe Doctrine the "doctrine of the world" and added: "These are American principles, American policies. We could stand for no others. And they are also the principles and policies of forward-looking men and women everywhere, of every modern nation, of every enlightened community. They are the principles of mankind and must prevail."[55] Convinced that this meant that the U.S. would join the war, Germany declared unrestricted submarine warfare in the Atlantic a week later. And after several American ships had been torpedoed, the U.S. finally joined the fray. In his war message to Congress on April 2, 1917, Wilson publicly transmuted from peace dove into war hawk and brusquely presented the conflict as a crusade for freedom that the U.S. was destined to join:

> The world must be made safe for democracy. Its peace must
> be planted upon the tested foundations of political liberty.
> We have no selfish ends to serve. We desire no conquest, no
> dominion. We seek no indemnities for ourselves, no material
> compensation for the sacrifices we shall freely make. We are
> but one of the champions of the rights of mankind. We shall

---

55. Woodrow Wilson, "Address to the Senate of the United States: 'A World League for Peace'," (January 22, 1917) *APP*, accessed March 17, 2017, https://www.presidency.ucsb.edu/node/206603.

be satisfied when those rights have been made as secure as
the faith and the freedom of nations can make them.[56]

Thus, Wilson used exceptionalist language to motivate America's entry into the war. By entering the war as an "associate, not an ally" of the U.K. and France, he also not only defined the U.S.' aims as different from the Allies.' He also turned his plan for a new world order into a war goal.

Furthermore, since Wilson for years had described the warring sides' objectives as "virtually the same," the decision to join one of them as a crusade for freedom demanded some serious marketing. This job fell on the Committee on Public Information (CPI). It at first appeared to be a traditional wartime propaganda agency. However, besides producing "normal" war propaganda, the CPI got the role of "educating" the American people about Wilson's new world order and making his policies "known to every village crossroads in this country and in remote corners of foreign lands."[57] In other words, the president's persona and ideas were elevated beyond the nation and its ideals.

To do this, the CPI mobilized all available mediums like newspapers, posters, radio, and movies. It even invented some new propaganda techniques, including about 75,000 "Four Minute Men" that were hired to give over seven million stump speeches, mainly in movie theaters, to sell war bonds and arouse enthusiasm for the war. A typical speech sounded like the following:

> Now, then, do you want to take the slightest chance of
> meeting Prussianism here in America? If not, then you'll
> have to help in summoning all the resources of this country

---

56. Woodrow Wilson, "Address to a Joint Session of Congress Requesting a Declaration of War Against Germany," (April 2, 1917) *APP*, accessed March 17, 2017, https://www.presidency.ucsb.edu/documents/address-joint-session-congress-requesting-declaration-war-against-germany.

57. Alan Axelrod, *Selling the Great War: The Making of American Propaganda* (New York: Palgrave MacMillan, 2009), 81.

for the giant struggle. For resources will win the war. Here's the way you can help save our resources. Instead of throwing money away on unnecessary things, buy Thrift Stamps, 25 cents, and War-Savings Stamps, $4.12, worth $5 in five years, 4 per cent compound interest. They're good as government money; like a mortgage on the U.S.A. Here's one of the War-Savings Certificates, and here's a Thrift Card. Ask at any post office, any bank, or store wherever you see a W.S.S. sign. It is up to us. We, the people, must win the war.[58]

The CPI's activities would become a huge success. And it was not the only organization that threw itself into a frenzy to awaken patriotism. For instance, idealistic belligerency showed itself among the clergy. Plenty of preachers had supported the Spanish-American War two decades earlier, and now many also supported Wilson's war. And well-read in Americanism's Christian scope and habitually seeing things in black and white, good and evil, "their enthusiasm for the war [became] an acknowledged extension of their theological progressivism."[59] Likewise, Congress organized a contest asking people to compose an "American Creed" declaration, and the winner was later presented by the House of Representatives as a resolution:

> I believe in the United States of America as a government of the people, by the people, for the people; whose just powers are derived from the consent of the governed, a democracy in a republic, a sovereign Nation of many sovereign States; a perfect union, one and inseparable; established upon those principles of freedom, equality, justice, and humanity for which American patriots sacrificed their lives and fortunes.
> I therefore believe it is my duty to my country to love it, to

---

58. "Four Minute Speech 1918," *Mr. Richman's Blog*, accessed December 29, 2017, https://rickmanhchs.files. wordpress.com/2016/02/four-minute-speech-article.pdf.

59. Richard M. Gamble, *The War for Righteousness: Progressive Christianity, the Great War, and the Rise of the Messianic Nation* (Wilmington, DE: ISI Books, 2003), 3.

support its Constitution, to obey its laws, to respect its flag, and to defend it against all enemies.[60]

In the summer of 1917, Wilson also established *The Inquiry*, a group of over a hundred experts directed to analyze the world and present strategies for the peace process. Indeed, its work was supposed to be neutral, but since its members knew of Wilson's new world order scheme and many were technocrats, they took their task as a bureaucratic marching order. Consequently, they treated historical and cultural problems, including border disputes around the world with roots often stretching back hundreds or even thousands of years, as meek, practical issues that could be resolved by the stroke of a pen and, perhaps, simple majority referendums. Thus, many of their findings and recommendations became dubious but were nonetheless used as a base for Wilson's final peace plan, the Fourteen Points. He presented it on January 8, 1918, in a speech that, because of its international theme, lacked patriotic clichés but contained an avid plea for a League of Nations. And after the war, he didn't even bother to hold back. In his 1918 State of the Union, delivered in December of that year, just weeks after the canons in Europe had gone silent, he said that the U.S. was now "to give order and organization to this peace not only for ourselves but for the other peoples of the world as well, so far as they will suffer us to serve them."[61] However, winning the war had been the easy part, and Wilson was to meet his Waterloo after it.

THE BATTLE OF THE LEAGUE

Since war propaganda always overflows with pompous rhetoric, it would be easy to dismiss Wilson's portrayal of World War I as a war for freedom

---

60. William Tyler Page, "The American Creed," *USHistory.com*, accessed May 20, 2019, http://www.ushistory.org/documents/creed.htm.

61. Woodrow Wilson, "Sixth Annual Message," (December 2, 1918) *APP*, accessed March 16, 2017, https://www.presidency.ucsb.edu/node/207603.

and democracy as hyperbole. However, as in the case of the Spanish-American War, this is wrong. The sentiment among Americans—and not least the opinion of most elites—was that the country's traditional isolationism had become outmoded. Also, the idealistic-aggressive form of Americanism used to promote Wilson's ideas convinced many that the war, at its core, was a unique ideological and not traditional geopolitical conflict. At the war's end, therefore, millions had been persuaded to see Germany as evil and the time as ready for a new world order making similar bloodbaths in the future impossible. Wilson, therefore, sailed off for the 1919 Paris Peace Conference with a smile and the ambition to give the world a "scientific" peace treaty, saying that he hoped to return "with the happy assurance that it has been possible to translate into action the great ideals for which America has striven."[62]

However, like an overtly impressive but poorly planned building, the scale and scope of Wilson's plan doomed it. A debate about the League started already in March when Massachusetts Republican Senator Henry Cabot Lodge, a supporter of Theodore Roosevelt's original "peace league" idea but soon-to-be leading skeptic of Wilson's plan, debated President of Harvard University (and fellow Republican) Lawrence Lowell on the first draft of the Versailles Treaty. The exceptionalist language in this discussion became limited to a few comments by Lodge about the U.S. being "a great moral asset of Christian civilization" and that world peace was best favored by keeping "America as she is [. . .] in her ideals and in her principles."[63] Still, these remarks are some of the first modern examples of a leading opponent's use of exceptionalist arguments rather than a proponent of a vital new policy. And as soon as the debate after Wilson submitted the Versailles Treaty's final version started in earnest, they became legion. For

---

62. Ibid.

63. *The Lodge-Lowell Debate of the Proposed League of Nations* (Boston: Old Trust Company, 1919), 52.

example, the president told the Senate:

> It is thus that a new role and a new responsibility have come to this great nation that we honor and which we would all wish to lift to yet higher levels of service and achievement. The stage is set, the destiny disclosed. It has come about by no plan of our conceiving, but by the hand of God who led us into this way. We cannot turn back. We can only go forward, with lifted eyes and freshened spirit, to follow the vision. It was of this that we dreamed at our birth. America shall in truth show the way. The light streams upon the path ahead, and nowhere else.[64]

Thus, by asking Congress to make the U.S. the warden of his new world order by becoming a League member, Wilson suggested scrapping George Washington's "great rule of conduct" and throwing away a century of successful U.S. foreign policy. Approval of joining the League of Nations should also only have been a formality. To the left, Democrats were lured by the siren song of "international liberalism," the plan's rejection of power politics, and support for international organizations. And since the League idea originally came from Theodore Roosevelt, many on the right, including influentials like ex-President Taft, also supported the plan.

However, Wilson had gone so far in Paris that joining the League would mean surrendering national independence and destroying "the traditional American role in world affairs that had been built over generations."[65] Thus, the question of membership turned into the most brutal political debate since the issue of slavery. And even if the use of exceptionalist arguments in this brawl with modern standards seems low, Internationalists, who wanted America to join the League without reservation, Reservationists,

---

64. Woodrow Wilson, "Address to the Senate on the Versailles Peace Treaty," (July 10, 1919) *APP*, accessed November 4, 2018, https://www.presidency.ucsb.edu/node/310230.

65. Jason A. Edwards, "The Fight Over the League of Nations: Rhetorical Tension within America's Exceptionalist Narratives," *Ohio Communication Journal* 47 (October 2009), 278.

who wanted to join with exemptions, and Irreconcilables, who did not wish to join, all used them.

Overall, however, League supporters most ferociously employed Americanism and especially Wilson advocated for the U.S. to join with messianic devotion. He argued that the Senate should ratify the treaty because it would allow America to "fulfill [its] sacred promise to mankind" and that the League offered "the leadership we said we wanted, and now the world offers it to us. It is inconceivable that we should reject it."[66] In this speech, given during a nationwide tour to get senators to approve his plan, he also stated that it was not only the right but the duty of the U.S. to spread its societal model—and that American's exceptional qualities made it possible for them to do so without corrupting themselves. It is arguably the best example of an active use of Americanism to win a political debate before World War II. And even in defeat he refused to give up. In 1920, after forcing the Senate to vote no to membership in the League by refusing to compromise with the Reservationists, Wilson, in his last State of the Union, still argued that leading the world toward democracy was "the manifest destiny of the United States."[67]

Two more things should be mentioned. First, during World War I, the "Wilsonian spirit," thanks to the CPI, sank so deeply into the collective mind that Americans' worldview afterward, despite some backlash, partly changed forever. This spirit also convinced the U.S. foreign policy establishment so completely that spreading American virtues became a political given and a political, bureaucratic driving force largely independent of electoral results. Second, the war affected Europeans and Americans in very different ways. In 1914, the former had greeted it as a politically,

66. Woodrow Wilson, "Address at the Mormon Tabernacle in Salt Lake City, Utah," (September 23, 1919) *APP*, accessed March 20, 2017, https://www.presidency.ucsb.edu/node/318159.

67. Woodrow Wilson, "8th Annual Message," (December 7, 1920) *APP*, accessed on April 3, 2017, https://www.presidency.ucsb.edu/node/207615.

socially, and culturally tonic event that would resolve multiple political disputes and—in line with the Social Darwinist attitude—cleanse the participating nations from weak human elements. However, four years of grievous casualties turned most Europeans into pacifists hellbent on avoiding another war at all costs. But for Americans, who did not have liability for the war and whose intervention had brought it to a quick end, war remained a certainly undesirable but still viable alternative. Hence, two still-defining features of modern Western politics took form.

RETURN TO NORMALCY

The victory in World War I created national pride, confirmed the U.S.'s standing as a great power, and gave the country new roles, e.g., as the world's top creditor nation. Also, the Wilsonian legacy of spreading American ideals made it impossible to withdraw from world affairs again fully. On the other hand, lingering isolationism, the decision not to join the League of Nations, and the deaths of activist firebrands Theodore Roosevelt and Woodrow Wilson confined future activities. What's more, in the 1920s, a wave of revisionist interpretations of World War I and the moral rightfulness of America to join it partly wrecked the image of the conflict as a war for democracy. As a result, general fatigue concerning foreign policy set in. Running for the presidency in 1920, Republican Senator Warren G. Harding from Ohio summoned up the public mood by saying:

> America's present need is not heroics, but healing; not nostrums, but normalcy; not revolution, but restoration; not agitation, but adjustment; not surgery, but serenity; not the dramatic, but the dispassionate; not experiment, but equipoise; not submergence in internationality, but sustainment in triumphant nationality.[68]

68. John W. Dean, *Warren G. Harding* (Times Book, 2004), 57.

Specifically, as an alternative to Wilson's progressive-internationalist line, Republicans adopted an updated but still passive variant of traditional U.S. foreign policy under the banner America First. This term had been used during the war to indicate patriotic unity, but it was now given the meaning of a return to the original principles that made the U.S. exceptional in the first place. And the people approved. After winning a landslide victory with over 60 percent of the popular vote, Harding could pepper his Inaugural Address with noncommitting phrases such as "our representative government is the highest expression and surest guaranty of both" and "surely there must have been God's intent in the making of this new-world Republic." He also stated that the U.S. would not again try to direct "the destinies of the Old World" and that "a world super-government is contrary to everything we cherish and can have no sanction by our Republic."[69] Thus, he reintroduced a foreign policy according to which the U.S. would function only as an example.

Nonetheless, Harding, along with his VP and to-be successor, Calvin Coolidge, pursued a more "open" form of U.S. foreign policy than before the war. It, e.g., focused on expanding international trade, embraced Roosevelt's original idea about an obligation-free "association of nations," and promoted deals like the 1921–1922 Washington Disarmament Conference, limiting great powers' navies' tonnage; the 1928 Kellogg-Briand Peace Pact, wherein the U.S. and fourteen other countries officially outlawed war; and the 1932 Stimson Doctrine, declaring that the U.S. refused to recognize border changes achieved by force. Harding and Coolidge also initiated what would later become known as a "Good Neighbor Policy" that maintained but softened the U.S. involvement in Latin America. And when the two used exceptionalist language to sell these policies, they did it to defend the America First principle. For exam-

69. Warren G. Harding, "Inaugural Address," (March 4, 1921) *APP*, accessed June 4, 2018, https://www.presidency.ucsb.edu/node/206688.

ple, after Harding's death in August 1923, Coolidge, in his first State of the Union, said:

> Our country has one cardinal principle to maintain in its foreign policy. It is an American principle. It must be an American policy. We attend to our own affairs, conserve our own strength, and protect the interests of our own citizens; but we recognize thoroughly our obligation to help others, reserving to the decision of our own Judgment the time, the place, and the method.[70]

Furthermore, while war damage fostered a gloomy mood in Europe, in the U.S., an economic boom created a period of (over) optimism as surplus production, not scarcity, for the first time in human history, was the biggest problem. This created an easy-minded culture. According to literary critic Irving Babbitt, post-war America became worldlier, more individualistic, and often confused material and moral progress. It was also in the 1920s that the "American Dream" took on its modern, materialistic connotation. Contributing to the ballyhoo was too that the booming economy turned the U.S. into a counter-proof to claims (mainly coming from Europe) that socialism was the wave of the future. Thus, foreshadowing the Cold War, a "soft power" contest between the U.S. and Soviet Russia began as American culture went global, e.g., through movies, music, and consumer goods. These "tastes of America" not least affected Europe's lower and middle classes, seeking an alternative to the continent's old monarchical order, and pulled segments of that continent's industry into the mass-producing era. Accordingly, at the end of the decade, a *NY Times* reporter in Europe declared that "Isolation is a myth [. . .] The United States is ever present."[71]

70. Calvin Coolidge, "First Annual Message, (December 06, 1923) *APP*, accessed January 8, 2019, https://www.presidency.ucsb.edu/node/206712.

71. Frank Costigliola, *Awkward Dominion: American Political, Economic and Cultural Relations with Europe, 1919-1933* (Ithaca: Cornell University Press, 1984), 263.

Despite this, except for "standard" patriotic rhetoric and occasional exceptionalist hurrahs regarding foreign policy, Americanism at this time seems only to have been employed in domestic politics. In fact, compared to before the war, when progressives had primarily used such language, conservatives seem mostly to have used it to argue for a rollback of Wilson's "war socialism" system of government-sat production goals, quotas, and regulations. Still, even in such circumstances it was scarce. Numerous reasons can be imagined for this. One is that the still weak presidency and strong local and regional focus of U.S. politics and media did not favor peacetime nationalistic rhetoric. Another is that the American model did partly fade compared to Soviet Russia and Fascist Italy as they started drowning the world in propaganda about fostering rapid modernization through their top-down, government-run economies. And whatever the cause, as the Wilsonian vision of a new democratic, capitalistic world order evaporated, Americans turned inward, enjoying illegal drinks and jazz at speakeasies, watching Charlie Chaplin movies, and following Babe Ruth's baseball career instead of worrying about Europe and other distant problems.

Still, the dismantling of Wilson's "war socialism" put focus on the inherent conflict between European ideologies and the American system. And even if, as one scholar writes, "the liberalism of the 1920s would lose the evangelical, moral fervor of earlier progressivism,"[72] for the first time in U.S. history, ideological differences became noticeable—or at least permanent. Presidents Harding and Coolidge's Secretary of Commerce Herbert Hoover, therefore, after gains for radical candidates in the 1922 midterms, ventured into the porticos of political philosophy to develop a modern variant of Americanism that would update and make the GOP's political profile clearer. As a classic self-made millionaire from Iowa who had made a fortune as a mining engineer, e.g., in Australia and earned

---

72. Watson, *Progressivism*, 115.

a world reputation as an aid worker in Europe at the end of World War I, he seemed like a good candidate for the job. However, as a progressive Republican and technocrat by both nature and training, his attempt became over-ambitious, too weak, and highly complex.

In *American Individualism* (1922), Hoover explained how his years abroad had convinced him that America's democracy stemmed foremost from the country's strong form of individualism and that he wanted to protect it from threats from both the left and the right. As a Progressive, he was also no friend of the "rogue individualism" and freewheeling economy of the nineteenth century, which he described as "every man for himself and the devil take the hindmost."[73] His ambition was thus to draw a middle ground between capitalism and socialism. But, as with all such undertakings, the alternative became blurry. For instance, while Hoover desired to preserve capitalism, keep taxes low, and balance the budget, he also wanted to help people fulfill their American dreams by "leveling the playing field" with political and bureaucratic means. He also wished to cultivate an attitude of "cooperative individualism" through public service and far-reaching government/business cooperation without letting society slide into socialism, which he—based on his European experiences and the "ghastly failure of Russia"—loathed most of all.

Despite his dim message, Hoover was in 1928 elected president and made his Inaugural Address true both to the GOP's America First foreign policy and his domestic progressivism. In the first area, he said he wanted to strive for "a distinction based upon confidence in our sense of justice as well as our accomplishments within our own borders and in our own lives." And in the second, he promised, among many other things, to eradicate poverty and introduce universal healthcare. However, within a

---

73. Herbert Hoover, *American Individualism* (New York: Doubleday, Page & Co., 1922; reprint with an Introduction of George H. Nash, Stanford: Hoover Institution Press, 2016), 43.

year, the worst economic crisis in U.S. history took precedence over all his plans, and he instead had to come up with a crisis program. At first, Hoover tried to fight the Great Depression through a balanced budget and an uneasy mixture of free-market and interventionist policies. When this didn't work, his technocratic view that the U.S. Government "ought to plan more, as if in a war"[74] then exerted itself, leading him to introduce political measures not too far behind Wilson's "war socialism." And lastly, most damaging of all, by signing the 1930 Hawley-Smoot Act that increased nine hundred import duties, he helped ignite a global trade war.

Still, because Hoover's balanced budget policy and tariffs resembled the "American System," the public first supported them. But this didn't last long. Just as the good times of the 1920s had boosted support for America's original socioeconomic system, the Great Depression quickly became perceived as a result of its flaws, and both public and political faith in free markets, non-intervention, and balanced budgets began to collapse. This downfall was advanced by extremist left- and right-wing propaganda spilling over from Europe, the spread of new economic theories like Keynesianism, and increased support for statist alternatives such as social democracy, modern liberalism, communism, and fascism. Moreover, Hoover undermined America's international standing by matching his "cooperative individualism" at home with "independent internationalism" abroad. This policy was based on his view that the world needed far-reaching Americanization but that "it was futile to try to impose American ideals upon other peoples by arms or treaties."[75] Consequently, he tried to spread American virtues by securing voluntary cooperation between countries, but because the Great Depression hit, this turned into a political *cul-de-sac*.

---

74. Amity Shlaes, *The Forgotten Man: A New History of the Great Depression* (New York Harper Perennial, 2008), 31.

75. Joan Hoff Wilson, *Herbert Hoover: Forgotten Progressive* (Long Grove, IL: Waveland Press, Inc.), 55.

It should finally be noted that Hoover did not use much exceptionalist or typical patriotic rhetoric to defend himself or his policies. The reasons for this are blurred, but one was that nationalistic jargon did not come naturally to him. Instead, like many of his European political contemporaries, he preferred a for people still familiar war-like rhetoric centered on terms like "defense," "front," and "attack." However, such words did not help him battle the Great Depression's army of fear, despair, and need. On the contrary, it probably only served to deepen people's anxieties. Still, Hoover did end his presidency with an exceptionalist appeal to his successor to preserve the American order:

> We have builded [sic] a system of individualism peculiarly
> our own which must not be forgotten in any governmental
> acts, for from it have grown greater accomplishments than
> those of any other nation. On the social and economic sides,
> the background of our American system and the motivation
> of progress is essentially that we should allow free play of
> social and economic forces as far as will not limit equality
> of opportunity and as will at the same time stimulate the
> initiative and enterprise of our people. In the maintenance
> of this balance the Federal Government can permit of no
> privilege to any person or group. It should act as a regula-
> tory agent and not as a participant in economic and social
> life. The moment the Government participates, it becomes a
> competitor with the people.[76]

Clearly, after losing in a landslide, Hoover realized that Americans' views had been twisted by the hardship of the Great Depression in ways that did not go well with the country's philosophical heritage. And like Wilson twenty years earlier, his successor would not let a good crisis go to waste.

---

76. Herbert Hoover, "Annual Message to the Congress on the State of the Union" (December 6, 1932), *APP*, https://www.presidency.ucsb.edu/node/207748, accessed May 17, 2017.

*"The democratic aspiration is no mere recent phase
in human history. It is human history."*

Franklin D. Roosevelt | 1941

CHAPTER 4 |

A Dual Revolution

What triggered the Great Depression, why it became so severe, and why it came to last for so long are still contested questions today. But whatever the answers are, in November 1932, the crisis carried Franklin D. Roosevelt to the White House in a landslide victory that changed America forever. Because even if his New Deal did not fix the economy, parts of it amassed into a rudimentary federal welfare state that—as people got used to turning to "D.C." for help and services—pushed the country over a mental tipping point into uncharted political territory. Indeed, most Americans were not ready for a more radical left-wing turn, so he was forced to hold back. And after winning reelection in 1936, political, economic, and other objections, including many from within FDR's own party, killed his political momentum. Still, the New Deal permanently changed the domestic U.S. political discourse by finally shifting the political focus from what the federal government shouldn't do to what it could do. In the same way, as events in Europe and East Asia began sliding toward a new world war, Americans' view of their country's role in the world was set to change. This became a slow process unfolding over several years, driven by FDR's active view of the U.S.'s role and a steady increase in his use of exceptionalist themes and arguments to convince Americans that it was their duty to combat fascism. Thus, thanks to the Great Depression and World War II, FDR finished what his cousin Theodore and Woodrow Wilson had begun—breaking up the Founding Fathers' socioeconomic system and abandoning George Washington's foreign policy.

A BREAK WITH HISTORY

To what degree Herbert Hoover deviated from American dogma to fight the Great Depression is debatable. For nearly a century, he has been scorned for doing too little, too late. Yet, in 1974, a former federal administrator said that "the whole New Deal was extrapolated from programs that Hoover started."[77] And today, quite a few economists argue that his meddling prolonged the depression. So, a balanced judgment must be that Hoover did believe in Americanism enough not to contest the country's sociopolitical heritage head-on but did things going well beyond what the Founding Fathers would have deemed acceptable. Moreover, it was definitively his successor Franklin D. Roosevelt who ultimately broke with the country's socioeconomic regime. An archetypal upper-class New Englander, he did believe in Americanism, but he had an even stronger belief in his own abilities and historical role. FDR was also a skillful political strategist, a shrewd power player, and a born orator, without whose inspiring voice U.S. history would have unfolded differently. And much more statist and internationalist than his cousin Theodore, he put the U.S. on a dual track to become a welfare state and an ideological superpower.

However, FDR didn't run as a reformer. In 1932, he offered much talk but no plan to fight the Great Depression. And the reason for this was simply that he didn't have one. Lacking deeper ideological convictions,

---

77. Paul Johnson, *A History of the American People* (New York: HarperCollins Publishers, 1997), 741.

he chatted with Americans about politics in familiar terms, like the virtue of low taxes and a balanced budget. Also, knowing that most voters still believed in America First, he traded his internationalism for a muted form of isolationism. Subsequently, FDR often attacked Hoover from the right, saying things like the president engaging in "reckless and extravagant" spending and wanting to "center control of everything in Washington." At one point, his vice-presidential candidate John Garner even accused the sitting president of "leading the country down the path of socialism."[78] Only on a few occasions did FDR touch upon how to fight the depression—and his long-term political goal. And when he did so, he did it in such ambiguous terms that listeners lacking philosophical schooling possibly didn't realize what he was saying.

Two speeches stand out here. The first was given at Oglethorpe University in Atlanta, Georgia, on May 22, 1932. It focused on alleged failures of the U.S. economic system, and FDR began by contrasting present needs with what he defined as the illusionary wealth of the 1920s. He mocked those who had believed in the established economic system to have thought they could "sit back and read in comfort the hieroglyphics called stock quotations, which proclaimed that their wealth was mounting miraculously without any work or effort on their part." He also said that this "dazzling chimera were lent not only the voices of some of our public men in high office, but their influence and the material aid of the very instruments of Government which they controlled." In other words, he likened capitalism to a Ponzi scheme. Moreover, after identifying the origin of the depression to be "not an insufficiency of capital [but] an insufficient distribution of buying power coupled with an over-sufficient speculation in production," he accused those who resisted change to be

---

78. Otto Friedrich, "FDR's Disputed Legacy" (February 1, 1982), *Time*, accessed July 1, 2019, http://content.time.com/time/subscriber/article/0,33009,954983,00.html.

"sitting tightly on the roof-tops in the flood." Still, besides empty nods to "planning" and demands for "bold, persistent experimentation,"[79] he offered no solutions.

In the second speech, given four months later at the Commonwealth Club in San Francisco, FDR first went deeper into what he thought had triggered the Great Depression. In short, he blamed it on the victory of Thomas Jefferson's minimalist view of governmental tasks over Alexander Hamilton's more statist line around 1800. After glossing over that this had created such a vibrant economy that America soon became the world's most prosperous country, FDR continued by suggesting that the current "Machine Era" rendered so many economic and other truths obsolete that a paradigm shift was necessary. In support of this, he echoed Turner's "Frontier Thesis" by arguing that since there was no longer a "safety valve in the form of a Western prairie to which [people] can go for a new start," the U.S. had reached its "last frontier." Moreover, his fix for this was "a re-appraisal of values" and to rewrite America's social contract from equality of opportunity to equality of outcome. Because the "task now is *not* discovery or exploitation of natural resources, or necessarily producing more goods" but . . .

> . . . the soberer, less dramatic business of administering
> resources and plants already in hand, of seeking to reestab-
> lish foreign markets for our surplus production, of meeting
> the problem of under consumption, of adjusting production
> to consumption, of *distributing wealth and products more
> equitably*, of adapting existing economic organizations to the

---

79. Franklin D. Roosevelt, "Address at Oglethorpe University in Atlanta, Georgia" (May 22, 1932) *APP*, https://www.presidency.ucsb.edu/documents/address-oglethorpe-university-atlanta-georgia, accessed May 12, 2023.

service of the people. The day of enlightened administration has come.[80]

Hence, FDR argued that the time of personal freedom to succeed and prosper was over. He also called for "economic planning [. . .] for a long time to come." And to obscure this break with American tradition, he finished with an aimless but exceptionalist-sounding appeal: "Faith in America, faith in our tradition of personal responsibility, faith in our institutions, faith in ourselves demands we reorganize the new terms of the old social contract. We shall fulfill them, as we fulfilled the obligations of the apparent Utopia which Jefferson imagined for us in 1776 . . ."[81]

This speech makes 1932 as pivotal in U.S. history as 1776, 1789, and 1861. Because what FDR did was not only elevate the technocratic turn into a ruling philosophy and open a door for a European-like welfare system supported by an "administrative state" that instantly began to morph into an uncontrollable fourth branch of government. By "extending progressive thought to its logical political conclusion," he also cast off a seven-hundred-year-old principle of Magna Carta by insisting that "rights must be understood as collective rather than individual."[82] This advanced the divorce of the Declaration from the Constitution initiated by Theodore Roosevelt and Woodrow Wilson. Specifically, since the two documents complement each other—the former by expressing the spirit of U.S. independence and the latter by keeping the U.S. Government small—the two must be disconnected to allow a radical agenda. And since the Constitution is popular and hard to change, the only way to do this is to misrepresent its intent by reinterpreting its language. To that end, FDR, in his first Inaugural Address, would state that the U.S. was "the

---

80. Franklin Delano Roosevelt, *Great Speeches* (Mineola, New York: Dover Publications, Inc.), 21ff. Emphasis added.

81. Ibid, 26f.

82. Watson, *Progressivism*, 30.

most superbly enduring political mechanism the modern world has produced" since the Constitution (in his view) allowed an expansion of the U.S. Government. He would later also say that it should be seen only as "an instrument designed to fulfill the ends, commitments, or promises of the Declaration."[83]

Still, aware that his ideas stood opposite Americans' basic political instincts, FDR, after the election, continued to assure that all he wanted to do was to preserve America's uniqueness. For instance, he once defended the New Deal as a "war against those conditions which make revolutions—against the inequalities and resentments which breed them."[84] By the same token, he often invoked patriotic code words like "the Pioneer." However, FDR typically used such metaphors to support deviations from traditional policies. Like when he, accepting renomination in 1936, said that "Philadelphia [the site of the convention] is fitting ground on which to reaffirm the faith of our fathers," only to directly recycle his argument from his Commonwealth Address: "The age of machinery, of railroads; of steam and electricity; the telegraph and the radio; mass production, mass distribution—all of these combined to bring forward a new civilization and with it a new problem for those who sought to remain free."[85] Similarly, when he used specific exceptionalist notions, he usually used them in radical senses, like talking about *equality* in the meaning of outcome, not opportunity. Hence, in several ways, he used Americanism against itself.

In the same way, even if a broader secularization of American politics

---

83. Willmoore Kendall & George W. Carey, *The Basic Symbols of the American Political Tradition* (Washington, D.C.: The Catholic University of America Press, 1970; reprint 1995), xxii.

84. Franklin D. Roosevelt, "Address at the Democratic State Convention, Syracuse, N.Y.," (September 29, 1936) *APP*, accessed June 11, 2020, https://www.presidency.ucsb.edu/documents/address-the-democratic-state-convention-syracuse-ny.

85. Franklin D. Roosevelt, "Acceptance Speech for the Renomination for the Presidency, Philadelphia, Pa." (June 27, 1936) *APP*, accessed December 6, 2017, https://www.presidency.ucsb.edu/node/208917.

was underway, FDR, as a low-key but earnest Christian, praised God more than America's virtues and leaned towards a liberal form of Christianity. For example, he frequently stroked the historical relationship between the Progressive Movement and parts of the religious community by assigning radical policies touches of Christian rightfulness. And in his 1933 Inaugural Address, when he blamed the Great Depression squarely on Wall Street, he alluded directly to the Bible's tale about Jesus in the temple overthrowing the tables of the money changers as a contemporary policy model: "The money changers have fled from their high seats in the temple of our civilization."[86] Another example of FDR supporting his ideological goals with religious language is when he told a group of Protestant ministers: "We call what we have been doing 'human security' and 'social justice.' In the last analysis, all of these terms can be described by one word, and that is Christianity."[87]

Furthermore, even if the day-to-day effects of FDR's ideological shift would not become evident for a few decades, some contemporary friends and foes noted their novelty. John Dewey, for instance, observed that "an inner split" had taken place in American liberalism and that FDR's new form saw "the business of the state" as the advancement of "all modes of human association in which the moral claims of the members of a society are embodied."[88] Because of this, FDR occasionally had to admit that a historic shift was taking place. But, he always did so by wrapping the news in good-sounding language, like when he said that "government in a modern civilization" must create a "democracy of opportunity."[89] Throughout the 1930s, the statist boldness of the New Deal also revealed itself in

---

86. Franklin D. Roosevelt, "Inaugural Address," (March 4, 1933) *APP*, accessed January 12, 2018, https://www.presidency.ucsb.edu/node/208712.

87. Mary E. Stuckey, *Defining Americans: The Presidency and National Identity* (Lawrence, KA: University Press of Kansas, 2004), 236.

88. Michael Novak, *Choosing Our King* (New York: MacMillan Publishing Co., Inc., 1974), 156.

89. Roosevelt, "Acceptance Speech . . ." (June 27, 1936).

support of "structuralist" and other radical theories. However, since some of these partly resonated with traditional streaks of American culture, they often slipped into discourses unnoticed. For example, the Puritan habit of socializing individual sins reappeared as arguments for governmental unemployment benefits and poverty programs. In fact, the whole welfare state concept can be seen as a perverted variant of this attitude.

It was also the New Deal's alienness that broke it. After winning reelection in 1936, FDR almost immediately began to lose his political momentum. There are three reasons for this. One, that the Great Depression, despite the New Deal, continued. Two, that Americans, on balance, were not ready to yield control over their lives to either politicians or "experts." And three, that FDR, to get through radical legislation, in early 1937, tried to "pack" the Supreme Court with extra liberal justices. This last power grab infuriated the nation and shattered "the magic" surrounding his presidency. As a result, even Democrats, like the party's 1928 presidential candidate Al Smith, began accusing FDR of abandoning the "fresh air of free America [for] the foul air of communist Russia."[90] Naturally, though, most critiques came from the right. For example, when the economy took a new nosedive in 1937, the National Association of Manufacturers (NAM) blamed the slump on New Deal regulations, bureaucratization, and tax increases. One of their pamphlets declared: "Give freedom to the brains and energy of men. Do not paralyze them with dictatorship, do not cause them to atrophy under regimentation, do not render them impotent with initiative killed. Turn them loose—inspire them . . . reward them in good old American free enterprise fashion."[91]

---

90. Robert Dallek, *Franklin D. Roosevelt: A Political Life* (New York: Viking, 2017), 247.

91. Burton St. John, III, "Re-Contextualizing Americanism: The National Association of Manufacturers' Jeremiad for Free Enterprise During the Roosevelt Era," Edwards & Weiss (ed.), *Rhetoric of American Exceptionalism*, 73.

STORM CLOUDS

By 1939, the New Deal was effectively over, and public opinion had shifted toward more traditional and business-friendly stances. However, this news drowned in the war drums echoing across Europe and Asia, and FDR was focused instead on formulating a new internationalist form of Americanism. And on this issue, his main point was identical to Wilson's—that world peace could be saved only by making more countries democratic. To convince the American people of this, FDR had begun a campaign in October 1937 through his so-called Quarantine Address. Symbolically held in the capital of American isolationism, Chicago, it suggested isolating totalitarian regimes that violated international treaties marking "the process of civilization toward a condition of law and order." It also painted Americans' hopes of escaping world developments as naïve because "there is a solidarity and interdependence about the modern world, both technically and morally, which makes it impossible for any nation completely to isolate itself from economic and political upheavals in the rest of the world."[92] However, FDR did not suggest any more specific actions, and isolationism ran so deep that his talk did not change public opinion, which was reflected in the *America First* movement; a group of activists including Walt Disney, Charles Lindberg, and Gore Vidal.

Consequently, at the outbreak of World War II on September 3, 1939, FDR could only declare U.S. neutrality. In sum, he claimed that since neutrality would protect America's societal system, it would serve the world and that the U.S. would stop "war from coming to the Americas. For that, we have historic precedent that goes back to [. . .] George Washington."[93] However, FDR's specific arguments differed from Wilson's a quarter cen-

92. Franklin D. Roosevelt, "Address at Chicago," (October 5, 1937) *APP*, accessed July 20, 2017, https://www.presidency.ucsb.edu/node/208843.

93. Franklin D. Roosevelt, "Fireside Chat," (September 3, 1939) *APP*, accessed July 20, 2017, https://www.presidency.ucsb.edu/node/209990.

tury earlier. A most profound difference is that he urged Americans to actively discriminate between the warring sides because "even a neutral has a right to take account of facts."[94] A few weeks later, he also said: "Destiny first made us, with our sister nations in this hemisphere, joint heirs of European culture. Fate seems now to compel us to assume the task of helping to maintain in the Western World a citadel wherein that civilization may be kept alive."[95] Hence, FDR, for practical purposes, did declare America a political, moral, and cultural ally to France and the U.K. And this time, from the start, both elites and over 80 percent of Americans openly favored an Allied victory. Yet, not even Germany's *Blitzkrieg* occupation of Western Europe from Nordkapp, Norway, to Burgundy, France, in 1940 affected Americans' opposition to themselves entering the war.

Even so, after securing an unprecedented third term in November 1940, FDR increased his effort to compel Americans to fight fascism. Within three weeks, he gave three speeches comprising all but a direct call for the U.S. to enter the war. In a New Year's address on December 29, FDR began with a warning that not "since Jamestown and Plymouth Rock has our American civilization been in such danger as now" and concluded that the future of freedom hung upon turning the U.S. into "the great arsenal of democracy."[96] A week later, he pushed the analysis further in his 1941 State of the Union. It coincided with introducing a Lend-Lease Bill, making military aid to the U.K. possible, and, in a progressive fashion, ascribed the world's problems to socioeconomic evils. Precisely, FDR linked the survival of democracy to "four essential human freedoms."

---

94. Ibid.

95. Andrew Glass, "FDR assails neutrality laws, Sept. 21, 1939," (September 21, 108), *Politico*, accessed December 28, 2021), https://www.politico.com/story/2018/09/21/fdr-assails-neutrality-laws-1939-826061.

96. Franklin D. Roosevelt, "Fireside Chat," (December 1940) *APP*, accessed July 20, 2017, https://www.presidency.ucsb.edu/node/209416.

The first is freedom of speech and expression—everywhere in the world. The second is freedom of every person to worship God in his own way—everywhere in the world. The third is freedom from want—which, translated into world terms, means economic understandings which will secure to every nation a healthy peacetime life for its inhabitants—everywhere in the world. The fourth is freedom from fear—which, translated into world terms, means a world-wide reduction of armaments to such a point and in such a thorough fashion that no nation will be in a position to commit an act of physical aggression against any neighbor—anywhere in the world.[97]

We will return to these points. First, FDR two weeks later rounded off his "war drive" in his third Inaugural Address. In a most uncommonly exceptionalist speech, he depicted U.S. history as a progression from George Washington's creation of a nation, through Abraham Lincoln's preservation of the Union, to the present day when it was now his turn to save the country from external threats. He, therefore, called upon Americans "to recall what our place in history has been, and to rediscover what we are and what we may be" and offered them the set answer that democracy would triumph, but only if America acted against fascism as it had acted against the Great Depression, meaning "quickly, boldly, decisively [. . .] within the three-way framework of the Constitution of the United States."[98] FDR also declared democracy "the most humane, the most advanced, and in the end the most unconquerable of all forms of human society" and praised it as *the* propelling force of history: "The democratic aspiration is no mere recent phase in human history. It is human

---

97. Franklin D. Roosevelt, "Annual Message to Congress on the State of the Union," (January 6, 1941) *APP*, accessed July 20, 2017, https://www.presidency.ucsb.edu/node/209473.

98. Franklin D. Roosevelt, "Third Inaugural Address," (January 23, 1941) *APP*, accessed July 17, 2017, https://www.presidency.ucsb.edu/node/210116.

history. It permeated the ancient life of early peoples. It blazed anew in the middle ages. It was written in Magna Carta."[99] In years to come, he would also repeatedly return to this theme. In 1943, for instance, he said that the Axis Power's blocking of free people's "forward movement across history" must fail since "those who put their faith in the people"[100] will always prevail.

Returning to FDR's four freedom themes, the importance of his linking of political democracy to specific societal and economic conditions, plus his view that America should lead this process, is critical to understand many of his actions during World War II. A few things about them thus need to be noted. Superficially, the four freedoms may seem like standard Americanisms. However, while the first two equate the traditional "negative" freedoms of speech and religion, the latter two, freedom from fear and want, are "positive" freedoms, or *rights*, which cannot simply be granted but must be politically provided for. Thus, to make his freedoms come true, FDR needed both a continued upending of domestic U.S. politics and a new foreign policy. Or more specifically, to eradicate want and fear at home, America needed a welfare state more extensive than the New Deal and the world an aggressive U.S. foreign policy focused on—or at least not being negative to—regime change and nation-building.

Consequently, to prepare Americans for a more full-scale welfare state after the war, FDR drew on the legacy of the New Deal and, by degrees, extended the meaning of his four freedoms until they combined became indistinguishable from social democracy. This happened in his 1943 State of the Union when he declared it the duty of the U.S. government to protect citizens from "all major economic hazards [. . .] from the cradle

---

99. Ibid.

100. Franklin D. Roosevelt, "State of the Union Address," (January 7, 1943) *APP*, accessed July 23, 2017, https://www.presidency.ucsb.edu/node/209971.

to the grave."[101] However, FDR's variant of this European ideology got two distinct features rooted in exceptionalist thinking. First, the U.S. cannot ask other countries to follow its example if its society and democracy aren't sound according to progressive standards. Thus, perpetual reforms of domestic systems and institutions aimed at perfecting America are a requirement, not a choice. Too, to keep America number one, reforms cannot be formulated only from the wishes of the American people but must always aim to match and preferably exceed foreign realities. Second, because the U.S. is *the* modern country, other nations should not only accept global U.S. leadership but conduct political, economic, and sociocultural reforms leading to the (progressive-like) Americanization of their societies. I.e., to American liberalism's autocratic bent, FDR added an imperialist ethos similar in form but totally different in kind to Americanism's missionary precept.

Specifically, besides laying the foundation for a federal welfare state at home, FDR made *democratism*—people's right everywhere to participate equally in politics—and *human rights*—an international variant of the Bill of Rights—goals of U.S. foreign policy. Already before his Four Freedoms Speech he had declared, "Of course, the peoples of other nations have the right to choose their own form of Government. But we in this nation still believe that such choice should be predicated on certain freedoms which we think are essential everywhere."[102] Hence, there was no room for substantial variation in political, economic, and social systems in an Americanized world. In August 1941, FDR made this overt by including his four freedoms in the Atlantic Charter. This document, in which he and Winston Churchill (whose country at the time was in such dire need of U.S. support that he had to agree to anything and everything

---

101. Ibid.

102. Franklin D. Roosevelt, "Annual Message to the Congress," January 3, 1940, *APP*, accessed July 25, 2017, https://www.presidency.ucsb.edu/node/210437.

FDR demanded) presented their vision of the post-war world, was nothing but a "bold attempt [. . .] to internationalize the New Deal."[103] And since this Charter a few years later would frame the declaration of the United Nations (see below), its implications became immense, making human rights the base for countless post-war both domestic policies and international declarations. Hence, a progressive variant of international Americanism and structures for its implementation was forming.

After Japan attacked Pearl Harbor on December 7, 1941, FDR's work began to pay off. He began to drum up support for war efforts and post-war plans by arguing that it was time for Americans "to cleanse the world of ancient evils, ancient ills."[104] And even if Americanism and exceptionalist themes continued to play only a supportive role in most of his speeches, his optimism about America's errands and obligations in the world seemed as endless as Wilson's. For example, in 1943, FDR equated the U.S. government's responsibility of caring for homecoming American soldiers with the duty "to restore [Axis-occupied] peoples to the dignity of human beings, masters of their own fate, entitled to freedom of speech, freedom of religion, freedom from want and freedom from fear."[105] As with World War I, his acts and language were also supported by nationalist and exceptionalist jargon flourishing everywhere. For example, many so-called *Liberty* ships built for the military were named after signers of the Declaration.

As a result, FDR's four freedoms sank deep into the American psyche. And before formally entering World War II, many Americans began to express support for the idea of global American hegemony. In February

---

103. Elizabeth Borgwardt, *A New Deal for the World: America's Vision for Human Rights* (Cambridge, MA: Belknap Harvard, 2005), 3.

104. Franklin D. Roosevelt, "State of the Union Address," January 6, 1942, *APP*, accessed August 7, 2017, https://www.presidency.ucsb.edu/node/210559.

105. Franklin D. Roosevelt, "Fireside Chat» (July 28, 1943) *APP*, accessed August 14, 2017, https://www.presidency.ucsb.edu/node/210292.

1941, news magnate Henry R. Luce wrote in *Life Magazine* that it was now America's "time to be the powerhouse from which the ideals spread throughout the world" because "unlike the prestige of Rome or Genghis Khan or 19th Century England, American prestige throughout the world is faith in the good intentions as well as in the ultimate intelligence and ultimate strength of the whole American people."[106] Moreover, by inspiring painters like Norman Rockwell and novelists such as John Crowley, FDR's vision came to dominate popular culture in ways that are still notable. For instance, after the war, the Four Freedoms Plaza became the headquarters for Marvel Comics superheroes *The Fantastic Four*, who fight for American-like justice and freedom on a global scale. Thus, the four freedoms at long last loosened the iron grip of George Washington's foreign policy over the American mind.

Truman & The Cold War

On April 12, 1945, Vice President Harry S. Truman was tossed into the Oval Office by the sudden death of FDR. And for the first time since George Washington's passing, or at least Abraham Lincoln's murder, Americans became as chocked as Europeans are after the death of a bellowed monarch. Moreover, Truman was forced to spend his first year fathoming many issues that FDR had not informed him about (including the Manhattan Project), and dealing with that the war's end created a hard-to-navigate mix of budding optimism, fears about a post-war recession, and risks of an isolationist backlash among leaders and citizens alike. Hence, his presidency got a rocky start. However, his upbringing in an archetypal Middle-American backwater in Missouri gave him a hardworking, honest, and blunt personality that survived this test. It also made him sincerely religious and a more steadfast believer in Americanism than his

---

106. Henry R. Luce, "The American Century," *Life Magazine* (February 17, 1941), 64.

cosmopolitan predecessor. For example, he often called America "God's country."[107] And, what his folksy rhetoric lacked in grace, he offset with candor. In his first message to Congress, he said: "Our forefathers came to our rugged shores in search of religious tolerance, political freedom, and economic opportunity. For those fundamental rights, they risked their lives. We well know today that such rights can be preserved only by constant vigilance, the eternal price of liberty!"[108]

This speech is politically enlightening, too. As noted, Americans' social, economic, and other views so far had forced progressives to depict reforms as harmless steps in line with—or at least not contrary to—American tradition. Even FDR in his heydays had claimed to do nothing but to protect the exceptional nature of the U.S. However, thanks to the collectivist sentiments nurtured by the New Deal, the four freedoms, and World War II, Truman could, to some degree, move beyond this mental roadblock. In a word, he no longer felt forced always to assert that his policies aligned with tradition. Hence, he felt confident in shifting the burden of political proof toward conservatives, demanding them to explain why reforms allegedly benefitting the weak, the needy, and the general public should *not* be introduced or expanded. And in modern politics, where supporters of reforms can count on support from sensation-hungry and misery-focused media, this is a huge advantage. Two examples will suffice.

First, in the speech just cited, Truman could promise to move further down FDR's course without reservations: "Here in America, we have labored long and hard to achieve a social order worthy of our great heritage. In our time, tremendous progress has been made toward a really democratic way of life. Let me assure the forward-looking people of America that there will be no relaxation in our efforts to improve the lot

107. Melvyn P. Leffler, For the Soul of Mankind (New York: Hill & Wang, 2007), 39.
108. Harry S. Truman, "Address Before a Joint Session of the Congress," (April 16, 1945) *APP*, accessed August 1, 2017, https://www.presidency.ucsb.edu/node/230621.

of the common people."[109] Second, after the Japanese surrender in August 1945, he could call a special session of Congress and present a program that essentially was a liberal bucket list, including improved unemployment insurance, increased minimum wage, and continued price controls. And in both instances, instead of defending his ideas as being in line with exceptionalist orthodoxy, Truman pushed them simply by cuddling Americans' generic penchant for, e.g., exploration: "We must go on. We must widen our horizon even further."[110] After being elected in his own right in 1948, he would also push further left by declaring the U.S. economic system obsolete: "We have abandoned the 'trickledown' concept of national prosperity. Instead, we believe that our economic system should rest on a democratic foundation and that wealth should be created for the benefit of all."[111]

However, nothing politically substantial emerged from this since attention shifted to foreign policy. As noted earlier, the 1917 Russian Revolution had set the stage for a global showdown between communism and capitalism. This was first dulled by Soviet impotence and then Stalin's alliance with the West against Nazi Germany. But, since both are universal ideologies arguing to represent humanity's future, during World War II, the U.S. State Department did predict a conflict between Americanism and communism. And when Hitler was finally defeated, it exploded. Still, while most Americans swiftly realized that the U.S.'s relations with Russia would be troublesome, elites for years turned a blind eye to this new, open-ended ideological battle. Proof positive, the establishments' reactions to Winston Churchill's speech on March 5, 1946, in Fulton,

---

109. Ibid.

110. Harry S. Truman, "Special Message to the Congress Presenting a 21-Point Program for the Reconversion Period," (September 6, 1945) *APP*, accessed August 15, 2017, https://www.presidency.ucsb.edu/node/230568.

111. Harry S. Truman, "Annual Message to the Congress on the State of the Union," (January 5, 1949) *APP*, accessed August 29, 2017, https://www.presidency.ucsb.edu/node/230007.

Missouri, wherein he remarked that the Soviets were building an "Iron Curtain" across Europe, became so harsh that Truman had to make an embarrassing U-turn from private support to public condemnation; an unparalleled snub in "the special relationship" between the two countries.

But a year later, things changed—and fast. After Truman presented only a single complaint that some peace accords were delayed "due partly to the difficulty of reaching an agreement with the Soviet Union" in his State of the Union on January 6, 1947, his administration launched an ideologically charged campaign against the Soviets. And on March 6, the president, enraged by crimes committed by Russian troops in Eastern Europe, publicly emphasized the existence of an unbridgeable political and ideological difference toward the Soviet Union. He also declared the U.S. ready to fight:

> There is one thing that Americans value even more than
> peace. It is freedom. Freedom of worship—freedom of
> speech—freedom of enterprise. It must be true that the first
> two of these freedoms are related to the third. For, through-
> out history, freedom of worship and freedom of speech have
> been most frequently enjoyed in those societies that have
> accorded a considerable measure of freedom to individual
> enterprise. Freedom has flourished where power has been
> dispersed. It has languished where power has been too
> highly centralized. So, our devotion to freedom of enter-
> prise, in the United States, has deeper roots than a desire to
> protect the profits of ownership. It is part and parcel of what
> we call American.[112]

Hence, Truman drew a line in the political sand. And it is especially noticeable that he backpedaled statements made by FDR, himself, and others for over a decade about freedom from want and fear. Instead, he

---

112. Harry S. Truman, "Address on Foreign Economic Policy, Delivered at Baylor University," (March 6, 1947) *APP*, accessed August 26, 2019, https://www.presidency.ucsb.edu/node/232807.

put capitalism back into Americanism.

This was also only the beginning. A week later, in an exceptionalism-laden speech where he promised the U.S. to replace the U.K. as an ally of Greece and Turkey—"to maintain their free institutions and their national integrity against aggressive movements that seek to impose upon them totalitarian regimes"[113]—Truman presented the "containment" doctrine that came to bears his name. Depicting the world as divided between good and evil, he declared that nations at that point had to choose between ways of life. On the one hand, they could side with America and a future marked by the will of "the majority [. . .] distinguished by free institutions, representative government, free elections, guarantees of individual liberty, freedom of speech and religion, and freedom from political oppression." Or, on the other, they could choose a system ruled by "a minority [ruling by] terror and oppression, a controlled press and radio, fixed elections, and the suppression of personal freedoms."[114] And it worked. Americans' support for a hard line against Moscow soared, and even elites understood the gravity of the situation. Therefore, Republicans and Democrats began to speak one language about preserving "the American way of life"[115] with only minor accent differences that would last for decades.

In addition, corresponding policies followed. Among other things, countering fears about communist influence in the U.S. Government, Truman ordered all federal employees to swear "complete and unswerving loyalty to the United States."[116] And as this attitude flowed down the political pyramid, the House Un-American Activities Committee

---

113. Harry S. Truman, "Special Message to the Congress on Greece and Turkey: The Truman Doctrine," (March 12, 1947) *APP*, accessed August 24, 2017, https://www.presidency.ucsb.edu/node/232818.

114. Ibid.

115. Leffler, *Soul of Mankind*, 72.

116. Harry S. Truman, "Executive Order 9835 – Prescribing Procedures for the Administration of an Employees Loyalty Program in the Executive Branch of the Government," (March 21, 1947), *APP*, accessed July 28, 2017, https://www.presidency.ucsb.edu/node/275962.

was revitalized and conducted hearings about people's political views; Attorney General Tom C. Clark was heard saying, "Those who do not believe in the ideology of the United States shall not be allowed to stay in the United States;"[117] and Texas Governor Allen Shivers (D) proposed making membership in the U.S. Communist Party a capital offense. In short, Truman incited a "Second Red Scare." And it would, together with his anti-communist "Cold War liberalism," become handy in 1948 to fend off not only Republican Thomas Dewey but a third-party challenge from FDR's former Vice President Henry Wallace, who, according to both Republicans and Democrats, was a Soviet "useful idiot." However, just as the first scare created by Wilson, its price in the form of intimidation, censorship, and fear would be high—and generally unproductive.

Furthermore, Truman's reaction to the Soviets led to the creation of a national security apparatus outstripping that of World War II. And because of the length of the Cold War, it was to become a most potent and permanent part of the administrative state. The non-civilian part of the U.S. Government was restructured as the armed forces were unified, the defense budget increased, the Central Intelligence Agency (CIA) was created, and much more. Also, U.S. foreign policy began to rely upon formally non-partisan—but regularly far from un-ideological—experts like George Kennan, whose "Long Telegram" in February 1946, about the Soviet Union's fiery merge of nationalism and Marxism, cemented Truman's—and, in the long run, nearly all Americans'—view of the Cold War. Among other things, it contributed to the creation of the Marshall Plan; an aid package aimed to neutralize the breeding ground for communism in Western Europe. And even if its statist policies were New Deal-inspired, the boldness regarding the U.S. economy to shoulder such a burden was squarely exceptionalist. In 1949, Truman boasted:

---

117. Linfield, *Freedom Under Fire*, 80.

I have confidence in the unlimited capacity and in the unlimited opportunities of the American economy and the American people. I have confidence in our ability to master the international problems which confront us and to achieve world peace. I have this confidence because of our achievements in the past and because of the present strength of our institutions. Above all, I am confident because I believe that Almighty God has set before this Nation the greatest task in the history of mankind, and that He will give us the wisdom and the strength to carry it out.[118]

The Marshall Plan is also noticeable for another reason. By turning West Germany into a thriving U.S.-like capitalistic democracy in the heart of Europe—and in the face of the Soviet Union—it became the U.S.' first nation-building project outside the developing world. And with similar makeovers of Austria, Japan, and South Korea, it created a meme indicating that dictatorship could effortlessly be replaced by freedom everywhere. However, these countries were all culturally distinct and marked by traits like a high level of trust in (or at least general obedience to) public institutions and strong work ethics that made democracy and capitalism possible. In societies with less-suitable characteristics, like the autocracies of Eastern Europe, the despotisms of the Middle East, and the tribal communities of Africa, forced modernization was not to work as well. But this fact was, for the moment, for both practical and political reasons obscured (or ignored; take your pick), creating a belief in the universality of freedom—and a foreign policy to implement it—that was to survive into the twenty-first century and lead to nation building fiascos like Afghanistan and Iraq.

This illusion of the primacy of freedom was rubbed in with plenty of

118. Harry S. Truman, "Radio and Television Report to the American People on the State of the National Economy," (July 13, 1949) *APP*, accessed December 17, 2019, https://www.presidency.ucsb.edu/node/229710.

propaganda. For example, on July 4, 1947, Truman gave an Independence Day Address at Thomas Jefferson's *Monticello*. It was broadcast nation-wide and focused on the Declaration as an "expression of democratic philosophy" and the need to make its principles the loadstar of the free world's fight against communism. He also said that all governments should "derive their just powers from the consent of the governed;" show "common respect for basic human rights;" accept "free and full exchange of knowledge, ideas, and information among the peoples of the earth;" and that all "nations shall devise their economic and financial policies to support a world economy."[119] This was, obviously, Americanism in the raw, and as the drumbeat caught on, the country's mood transformed. That fall, U.S. representatives gave up on trying to cooperate with the Soviets, and Americans, as one, began to promote their country's unique character. Hollywood, for instance, started producing hundreds of anti-communist films to refute its reputation as a radical campsite. And in 1949, a privately operated red, white, and blue *Freedom Train* made stops in some three hundred cities displaying Americana accompanied by patri-otic festivities, radio shows, and films.

This kind of public self-promotion became natural during the Cold War. The whole period 1947–1989 can be seen as one long publicity contest wherein Americans and Soviets tried to convert national and international audiences about their merits. And even if the U.S., as a democratic coun-try with often vivid debates raging more about its vices than its virtues, it could never keep up with Soviet hoopla in either volume or pomposity, like no country before, America sold itself to both its citizens and people around the globe through new technologies, art, movies, clothing, food, drinks, etc. As a result, Americans became cockier than ever—and the

---

119. Harry S. Truman, "Independence Day Address Delivered at the Home of Thomas Jefferson," (July 4, 1947) *APP*, accessed August 27, 2017, https://www.presidency.ucsb.edu/node/232015.

spontaneous bottom-up Americanization of other countries that had been going on since the inter-war period now became so intense that even some U.S. allies (read: the French) began to moan about "Coca-colonization." Decades later, a Czechoslovakian would also concur more positively by saying, "Coke equals America. America equals freedom."[120]

However, the most important result of this propaganda war was that presidents from Truman onward could rely on strong public support for a hard line against the Soviets. In fact, Americanism became near-identical to anti-communism in only a few years. When Gallup in 1954 asked if "a man can believe in communism and still be a loyal American," nearly 90 percent answered no. Moreover, Truman continued to drive home this development with speeches in which he portrayed the Cold War as far more than a "normal" conflict:

> This challenge to us is more than a military challenge. It is a challenge to the honesty of our profession of the democratic faith; it is a challenge to the efficiency and stability of our economic system; it is a challenge to the willingness to work with other peoples for world peace and for world prosperity.[121]

Hence, like the world wars, he described the Cold War as an ideological conflict where the winner would decide the future of mankind. Thus, Americans were fostered rather to be "dead than red" and to view the U.S. as a St. George figure, protecting the world and, in particular, the West from the red dragon of communism.

This picture would also steer U.S. foreign policy for four decades. However, the price for it became "to bind [America] to multilateral insti-

---

120. John Kenneth White, *The New Politics of Old Values* (Hanover, NH: University Press of New England, 1988; second edition 1990), 108.

121. Harry S. Truman, "Annual Message to the Congress on the State of the Union," (January 8, 1951) *APP*, accessed September 1, 2017, https://www.presidency.ucsb.edu/node/231403.

tutions that would manifestly limit its historic obsession with unfettered freedom of action."[122] In other words, the U.S. had to abandon its isolationist-protectionist line. This process had begun already with the Bretton Woods Agreement in 1944, laying the foundation for the free world's post-war economy, and was finalized around 1950 by military agreements with European (NATO) and Pacific (ANZUS) allies. In between, the U.S. also initiated the making of the United Nations, and politicians of nearly all brands first paid homage to this organization. As FDR's brainchild, Democrats would for over fifty years celebrate it as the foundation for a new "liberal" era in world affairs based on human rights. As such, it was also attractive to a growing band of internationally-minded "modern" Republicans. And for most others, the U.N. seemed like a reasonable continuation of the Allies' cooperation during the World Wars. So, unlike the League of Nations, not joining it was never a serious alternative. However, the U.N. quickly became handicapped by the Cold War's clash between grand visions and bitter realities.

Moreover, after winning two world wars and with Europe politically, economically, and militarily exhausted, Americans high and low accepted nothing but a leading international role for their country. In January 1950, only five years after the U.N.'s founding, Truman declared the U.S. to be the first among its (un)equal members:

> We have a more productive economic system and a greater
> industrial potential than any other nation on the globe. Our
> standard of living is an inspiration for all other peoples.
> [. . .] Our tremendous strength has brought with it tremen-
> dous responsibilities. We have moved from the outer edge
> to the center of world affairs. Other nations look to us for a
> wise exercise of our economic and military strength, and for

---

122. Borgwardt, *New Deal for the World*, 10.

vigorous support of the ideals of representative government and a free society. We will not fail them.[123]

On June 1 that year, Truman also revealed the thin relationship between words and truths by asking Congress for funding for global U.S. military actions because there was "clear evidence that certain adherents to the [U.N.] Charter will not hesitate to use force and to threaten the integrity of other countries."[124] And only a few weeks later, this resolve was put to the test when North Korea invaded its southern neighbor. Thanks to a temporary Soviet boycott of the Security Council, Truman managed to uphold the ensuing war's image as an international "police operation" under the U.N. flag. But since the president's view was that America was not only militarily capable but morally obliged to act alone, if necessary, he would probably have acted likewise anyway. In a speech to the American people on July 19, he said: "Our country stands before the world as an example of how free men, under God, can build a community of neighbors, working together for the good of all. That is the goal we seek not only for ourselves, but for all people."[125]

Consequently, the U.N. never became the pillar of the post-war international order most people hoped it would be (and many, to this day, still tell themselves it is). Instead, organizations such as NATO, IMF, the World Bank, and OECD, in which membership was exclusive and America's role preeminent, became essential. Moreover, Truman continued to defend the containment of communism, including his action in Korea, until he left office in stark language. For example, in early 1952, he described the Soviets as turning free nations "into colonies" while Americans were

123. Harry S. Truman, "Annual Message to the Congress on the State of the Union," (January 4, 1950) *APP*, accessed August 29, 2017, https://www.presidency.ucsb.edu/node/231027.

124. Harry S. Truman, "Special Message to the Congress on Military Aid," (June 1, 1950) *APP*, accessed September 6, 2017, https://www.presidency.ucsb.edu/node/230716.

125. Harry S. Truman: "Radio and Television Address to the American People on the Situation in Korea," (July 19, 1950) *APP*, accessed August 11, 2017, https://www.presidency.ucsb.edu/node/230990.

"working night and day to bring peace to the world and to spread the democratic ideals of justice and self-government to all people."[126] In his last State of the Union, a year later, he also placed the Cold War in a historical context by calling it "a struggle as old as recorded history; it is freedom versus tyranny."[127] And in his Farewell Address a few weeks after that, he predicted victory in the Cold War not primarily because of U.S. material strengths but spiritual supremacy:

> The Communist world has great resources, and it looks strong. But there is a fatal flaw in their society. Theirs is a godless system, a system of slavery; there is no freedom in it, no consent. The Iron Curtain, the secret police, the constant purges, all these are symptoms of a great basic weakness— the rulers' fear of their own people. In the long run the strength of our free society, and our ideals, will prevail over a system that has respect for neither God nor man.[128]

This torch of freedom was too keenly taken over by his successor.

THE EISENHOWER ADMINISTRATION

There are many similarities between Harry S. Truman and Dwight D. Eisenhower. Both were Midwestern farm boys, sincerely religious, hard workers, and firm believers in Americanism of the "international" kind heralded by Wilson and FDR. However, there are differences between them as well. Most obviously, while Truman became a progressive Democrat, Eisenhower evolved into a Conservative Republican, indicating a fundamental difference in their political imaginations. Also, whereas Truman's

126. Harry S. Truman, "Annual Message to the Congress on the State of the Union," (January 9, 1952), *APP*, accessed September 27, 2017, https://www.presidency.ucsb.edu/documents/annual-message-the-congress-the-state-the-union-17.

127. Harry S. Truman, "Annual Message to the Congress on the State of the Union," (January 7, 1953) *APP*, accessed September 26, 2017, https://www.presidency.ucsb.edu/node/231314.

128. Harry S. Truman, "The President's Farewell Address to the American People," (January 15, 1953) *APP*, accessed September 27, 2017, https://www.presidency.ucsb.edu/node/231372.

strength was to make sense of politics in folkish language, Eisenhower's forte was to talk about it in serious prose. This made for two rhetorically different presidencies, of which Eisenhower's is especially noteworthy because of its dual character. On the one hand, by depicting the Cold War as a "dark chamber of horrors," he emphasized the apocalyptic mood of the 1950s stemming from the risk of nuclear war. On the other, his grandfatherly persona cherished the optimism arising from the decade's strong economic and scientific developments. Each is thus worth a closer look.

Let's start with foreign policy. In 1953, Eisenhower opened his Inaugural Address by inviting people to join him in prayer, asking God to give "us [. . .] the power to discern clearly right from wrong" before devoting his speech near-completely to foreign affairs. He portrayed the world as dire: "We sense with all our faculties that forces of good and evil are massed and armed and opposed as rarely before in history." He also asked how far man had come in his "long pilgrimage from darkness toward the light? Are we nearing the light—a day of freedom and of peace for all mankind? Or are the shadows of another night closing in upon us?" Eisenhower also stressed the righteousness of America's cause, without calling the Soviet Union by name, by outlining the evils of communism: "The enemies of this faith know no god but force, no devotion but its use. They tutor men in treason. They feed upon the hunger of others. Whatever defies them, they torture, especially the truth." Finally, striking a more optimistic tone towards the end of the speech, he turned to the missionary theme of Americanism: "Destiny has laid upon our country the responsibility of the free world's leadership." And among the tasks coming with this role was to respect "the identity and the special heritage of each nation" and not "impress upon other people our own cherished political and economic institutions."[129]

---

129. Dwight D. Eisenhower, "Inaugural Address," (January 20, 1953) *APP*, accessed October 28, 2017, https://www.presidency.ucsb.edu/node/231580.

However, in office, Eisenhower would often behave differently. In fact, by inciting change on a worldwide scale from nation-building projects to making covert operations a standard foreign policy tool, under him, America not only finalized the break with John Quincy Adams' advice not to go abroad in search of monsters to destroy but inverted it. Explicitly, under him, the U.S. embarked on a row of foreign adventures, including inciting regime change in Iran and deploying troops to South Vietnam. Moreover, Eisenhower followed in Truman's footsteps, boosting the country's propaganda efforts to never seen peacetime highs. The prime instrument for this promoting of America's role and virtues became the United States Information Agency (USIA), which—like the CPI during World War I—extensively used both government-funded entities (now including entities like Radio Liberty and Radio Free Europe) and informal "soft power" tools like TV, literature, music, and movies. And with the U.S. economy roaring, describing America as an exciting alternative to the grey shades and blood-red realities marking the Soviet Union was easy work.

Furthermore, in the 1950s, next to Eisenhower, several strong personalities played a critical role in U.S. politics, of which only two will be mentioned here. First, John Foster Dulles, a devout Christian and exceptionalist whose core belief was that the U.S. was God's stand-in on the international scene and the Soviet Union the Devil's. And since the Cold War was a struggle between good and evil, he deemed no price for victory too high and became the main promotor of Eisenhower's New Look strategy; a policy aimed at securing world peace (until communism was defeated) through the threat of massive nuclear retaliation. However, Dulles also believed that America's role as a model and alternative to communism was on the verge of failing because of materialism and "extreme individualism" and that a dual revival of Christian faith and American idealism was the world's only hope. Moreover, as Eisenhower's Secretary of State, he defined America's Cold War policies by giving the country an Athenian rather than Roman global role, meaning that the U.S. relied on treaties and alliances, not occupation and colonization. Nonetheless, rounding and snubbing the pacifism of Europe and other parts of the world, he sent a clear message to the Soviets about not pushing their luck.

Second, Joseph McCarthy was a rough-and-tumble Republican Wisconsin Senator. His way to disrepute was by utilizing Truman's Red Scare to expose alleged infiltration of the U.S. government by Soviet spies and homegrown communists. For example, in a speech in West Virginia in 1950, he both echoed Truman and presaged Eisenhower and Dulles by calling the Cold War a "showdown between the democratic Christian world and the communist atheistic world" and said that America was "losing on every front" because of communist infiltration.[130] Today we also know that quite a few communists did manage to infiltrate the U.S. Government, of which U.S. State Department official Alger Hiss—who, before being exposed in 1948, had been involved in the creation of the United Nations—became the best known. However, being carried away by his own rhetoric, McCarthy became widely detested even by many Republicans, President Eisenhower included, for presenting haphazard mixes of true, false, and unverifiable conspiracy charges. Even so, before his fall, his rhetoric played a vital role in shaping the American public's view of the Cold War and merging anti-communism with Americanism.

Still, the prime actor in this process was Eisenhower. The prime reason for this was the Soviet Union's rise as a similarly exceptionalist-minded superpower. However, a spiritual awakening led by Billy Graham's "evangelical crusades" took place at the same time, and support for traditional institutions like the nuclear family soared. And tying it all together was

---

130. Joseph R. McCarthy, "Enemies from Within" in Bob Blaisdell (ed.), *Infamous Speeches: From Robespierre to Osama bin Laden* (Mineola, NY: Dover Publications, 2011), 142.

Eisenhower's way of arguing not only for a firm policy against the Soviets but for various conservative policies at home. Explicitly, he framed domestic debates as battles between traditional ideals and radical beliefs threatening the U.S.'s exceptional nature. As in his first State of the Union, when he expressed opposition to the New Deal by saying that human society was a primarily spiritual entity: "Happily, our [American] people, though blessed with more material goods than any people in history, have always reserved their first allegiance to the kingdom of the spirit, which is the true source of that freedom we value above all material things."[131] As President, Eisenhower also used exceptionalist language for market reforms, lower taxes, and less bureaucracy; e.g., describing private pension plans as a "new application of [the] old ideas of freedom."[132] And since such arguments so far had seldom been used against reforms, this marks a turning point which made the "new normal" of 1950s America a problematic mix of acute fear regarding nuclear Armageddon, economic affluence, and national unity.

Moreover, as seen, *freedom* had been a central notion in the national story of America since the Founding Period, but *equality* since Lincoln's time has been hailed nearly as consistently. However, because of the threat from the Soviet Union, freedom now gained renewed distinction across the political spectrum and especially on the right. Eisenhower's devotion to this subject is crucial to this development, and he touched upon it in nearly every major speech. For example, in his 1952 RNC Acceptance Speech, he said he resigned himself to become president after being "summoned [. . .] on the behalf of millions [. . .] to lead a great crusade—for

---

131. Dwight D. Eisenhower, "Annual Message to the Congress on the State of the Union," (February 2, 1953) *APP*, accessed October 31, 2017, https://www.presidency.ucsb.edu/node/231684.
132. Ibid.

Freedom in America and Freedom in the world"[133] and his focus on the theme continued after assuming office and he almost always used the traditional "hard" form—freedom *from*—rather than the progressive's "soft"—freedom *to*—definition of it. This also fits with the defining phenomenon of U.S. politics in the 1950s, the rise of the Conservative Movement, to which we will return in the coming chapters.

Finally, three more comments about Eisenhower's domestic policies can be made. First, he became the first modern president to express grave concern for bureaucratization, technocratic influence, and the intimate relations between the administrative state and big businesses. His warning about "the military-industrial complex" is well-known here, but he in the same speech also delivered a warning about "the equal and opposite danger that public policy could itself become the captive of a scientific-technological elite."[134] Thus, Eisenhower presaged that military *and* civilian developments threatened Americans' liberties—a historic break with the positivist-technocratic mindset of the time. Second, when the Soviets launched *Sputnik*, the world's first satellite, in October 1957, Eisenhower acted swiftly on Americans' fears that the Russians had gained the upper hand in technology and that their rockets threatened national security. And his answer became truly American in scale but not in kind by giving massive resources to federal programs like the Defense Advanced Research Project Agency (DARPA), the National Defense Education Act (NDEA), and the National Aeronautics and Space Administration (NASA).

Third, Eisenhower's exceptionalist-laden rhetoric accelerated the phasing out of dislikes between Protestants, Catholics, and Jews. Historically,

133. Dwight D. Eisenhower, "Address Accepting the Presidential Nomination at the Republican National Convention in Chicago," (July 11, 1952) *APP*, accessed October 28, 2017, https://www.presidency.ucsb.edu/node/275894.

134. Dwight D. Eisenhower, "Farewell Radio and Television Address to the American People" (January 17, 1961) APP, accessed November 9, 2017, https://www.presidency.ucsb.edu/node/234856..

the country's Protestant majority had held traditional anti-Catholic biases and anti-Semitic prejudices like Irish being drunks and Jews greedy, but since Americans in the 1930s had been confronted with fascism, a move away from such bigotries had begun. Not least, the Holocaust led to a historic reevaluation of people's views of the Jews. And now, when faced with communism, a further reduction of prejudice took place as Catholics and Jews could use Eisenhower's rhetoric and its anti-communist dimension to achieve complete emancipation. For instance, Cardinal Francis Spellman of New York used Americanism "as if it were some venerable dogma of the Catholic Church,"[135] and continuous ill-treatment of Jews in the Soviet bloc helped dissolve prejudices across the political spectrum. Instead, a new, broader Judeo-Christian identity took a form that already in the 1960–64 election cycle made it possible for one Catholic and one Jew, both running on exceptionalist and anti-communist platforms, to win their respective party's presidential nominations.

---

135. Conor Cruise O'Brien, *God Land: Reflections on Religion and Nationalism* (Cambridge, MA: Harvard University Press, 1988), 34.

"For the first time in world history we have the abundance and the ability to free every man from hopeless want, and to free every person to find fulfillment in the works of his mind or the labor of his hands."

Lyndon B. Johnson | 1964

CHAPTER 5 |

A Defining Decade

As the New Deal increased people's expectations of what Washington, D.C., could offer and World War II and the Cold War made persons in that city aware they were ruling the most powerful nation in history, U.S. politics transformed. However, due to good economic times, cultural lag, and general peace, this did not become evident until the 1960s. Political events, ideological shifts, and technological advances also made this the first "modern" decade as the public was introduced to the lot from jet planes to contraceptives challenging old habits, norms, and values. And as the wealthiest, most commanding people in history, Americans felt more exceptional than ever. Moreover, after the global near-death experience of the 1962 Cuban Missile Crisis eased superpower tensions, attention shifted from foreign to domestic policy, which again became subjugated by confidence in positivist theories and technocratic governance. This relapse had several reasons, including a general—and generational—reaction to the conservative mindset of the 1950s, high economic growth, and a futuristic vouge shaped by happenings like the Space Race, the development of "supercomputers," and the introduction of industrial robots. Also, the renewed trust in political means to reach social, economic, and other goals led to a significant expansion of public bureaucracies as well as private intuitions such as universities, media, and big business—and the people filling all new positions forming a "New Class" that disliked near-everything traditional. Hence, America, after political and economic liberalism, was to be hit by a third wave of radicalism in the form of social and cultural "tolerance."

NEW GATEKEEPERS

All societies have people deciding which ideas, values, and mores should (not) be shared in public. Such "gatekeepers" historically formed tiny cliques of government officials and religious leaders. However, in the 1700s, philosophers, academics, and others began to join the group. In time, the archetype of this extended gatekeeper gang became The Editor, deciding what should be printed in tomorrow's newspaper. Moreover, from the mid-to-late 1800s, nearly all gatekeepers through academic studies became schooled in the positivist-technocratic mindset of the era. And after World War II, as the group was expanded by new scores of administrators, lawyers, engineers, professors, teachers, and others, it swelled into what some scholars have called a New Class, or what's today often talked about as 'the deep state." Next to pre-Civil War plantation owners, this became the closest America has ever been to having an actual leisure class. Its members also see themselves as the modern embodiment of the Founding Fathers' natural aristocracy. However, unlike the Founders, they became guided not by tradition, religion, and common sense but by radical ideas and abstract theories, often of foreign origin.

Furthermore, the first-generation New Classers' belief in America was still strong but limited to the generic view that the U.S. was big, best, and unbeatable. Their ideas and goals instead reflected *managerial liberalism*; a philosophy about "subjugating and controlling the natural world, human nature, and human society by means of scientific technique in particular and rationality generally, while uprooting custom and banishing religion to the wholly private realm."[136] Hence, their liberalism retained the Progressive code of constant change and mentality that when the ideological Map doesn't match Reality, the latter should be changed. Therefore, their belief in the possibility of reaching political goals through bureaucratic means was—and is—absolute. And as they in the 1960s began to take over "commanding heights" like government agencies, media, and universities, they got into positions to start changing stuff. And next to hiring each other, New Classers' primary way to promote change was to field theories within the "iron triangle" of politics, academia, and media and to create new discourses simply by cross-referencing each other and encircling their "bubble" with, e.g., peer-review systems and research grants. This made it all but impossible to challenge their views—or "the scientific consensus," as they call them.

The New Class relied especially on sociology, which became the most renowned academic subject after World War II. The reason for this is simple: it allegedly verifies the core assumption of liberalism that the modern world is so complex that ordinary people need expert guidance. Also, besides cross-referencing and supporting each other with research grants, radicals began to use their own postulates and conclusions as evidence for their ideas being true; that is, circular reasoning. For example, because poor people live in poor neighborhoods, they are poor because they live in poor neighborhoods. And while such theories unquestionably hold some truth, they are perceived as absolute in the meaning that no other explanations can be regarded as equally or more valid. For instance, that people can be poor and live in bad neighborhoods because they actively chose not

---

136. White, *New Politics*, 79.

to work and/or use drugs is often vehemently denied (and to boot, not seldom described as cynical, racist, etc.).

The New Class also learned to use more specific theories and models to prove their points and expand their power, of which only three will be mentioned here. First, Walt Rostow's "modernization theory," which explains modernization as a result of free enterprise and free trade but also upholds government as a natural provider of services like education, infrastructure, and healthcare was used as "proof" of the need for a big, active government at home and "nation-building" in Africa, Latin America, and Asia. Second, economist John Kenneth Galbraith offered a neatly balancing theory. Echoing Marx by asserting economies are not directed by "laws" but by cultural conventions that can be changed, he told elites they could do whatever they wanted, including structuring countries' economies to support welfare states, which he saw as the endpoint of political history. And third, by far, the most influential post-World War II theory was *behaviorism*. It is so completely saturating sociology and many other "soft" academic subjects that it needs a more detailed going-through.

Already the Ancient Greeks noticed that human nature is an essentially fixed mix of virtues and vices. This view also remains dominant in most civilizations until today. However, in the 1700s, some Western thinkers such as Jean-Jacques Rousseau began to see this fact as an obstacle to their ideological schemes and began to argue instead that humans lacked an inborn nature, or that it was so plastic that it could be molded at will. This idea was then accepted by European socialists and left-wing liberals and, in America, by progressives; the latter through their endorsement of a form of Social Darwinism ignoring that evolution is a process involving change *and* rigidity. Precisely, while organisms adapt to their environments on one side, they conserve characteristics with high survival values on the other. And by only taking the first part into account regarding the human mind, progressives saw the opportunities to change society by altering people through manipulating their surroundings as endless. On top of that, after Hitler's atrocities created a biology-hostile political milieu, radicals went to the extreme and completely omitted human biology as a political, economic, and other kind of force. Hence, thousands of years of wisdom about man's character was replaced with the view that humans are born "blank slates" without any innate mental traits, impulses, or other genetic-based behaviors. Thus, *nature* was replaced by *nurture*. And the damage done by this can never—beyond the 100+ million killed by various national and international socialist regimes in their bids to build Utopia—be estimated. To take just one example, the human and other costs imposed by the mantra "It's society's fault" during the post-war era to explain (excuse) criminal, sexual, and other depraved behaviors is confounding.

Moreover, behaviorism, almost needless to say, is the very opposite of the Founding Fathers' view of human nature and its political consequences. Still, the New Class and millions more took over the old progressive view of human nature during the post-World War II era. It lured them to believe that everything from abolishing poverty to landing on the Moon was possible. And while a few things, like the latter, did turn out doable, Reality often turned out to be thornier than Theory. Thus, the number of grand political and bureaucratic failures began to multiply. As we will see, two examples of this are (on the micro level) Defense Secretary Robert McNamara, who convinced himself that the U.S. could win the Vietnam War from Washington, D.C. by "comprehend[ing] what was happening on the ground by staring at a spreadsheet" and producing an accurate "body count."[137] And (on the macro level) Lyndon B. Johnson's

---

137. Kenneth Cukier & Viktor Mayer-Schönberger, "The Dictatorship of Data: Robert McNamara epitomizes the hyper-rational executive led astray by numbers," (May 31, 2013) *MIT Technology Review*, accessed January 18, 2018, https://www.technologyreview.com/s/514591/the-dictatorship-of-data/.

Great Society, which most goals, like poverty reduction, improved housing and education, and the elimination of racism, have not yet been met despite being sixty years running and 25+ trillion dollars spent to date.

What's more, as this born-again positivist brashness throughout the 1960s infused popular culture, it led to a form of "super exceptionalism" and made everything from giant hairdos to big cars to science fiction popular. Real happenings and fictional novelties also often merged and further boosted futuristic themes, tastes, and visions. For example, the first "supercomputers" and the Moon Program left people spellbound by Stanley Kubrick's movie *2001: A Space Odyssey* (1968). And the TV series *Star Trek* (1966–69) became so popular that its fans would get the White House to interlope directly in NASA's space program in the following decade. This series' most popular character also tellingly became the sterilely logical (i.e., positivist) Mr. Spock; an alien from the planet Vulcan who was always correct and endlessly puzzled by his emotion-driven human colleagues' irrational behavior. Indeed, since this worldview clashed with deeply rooted Christian and other sentiments, it remained a marginal phenomenon. Still, because of many believers' important political, economic, and societal roles, their beliefs and arrogance radicalized the Democratic Party and New Classers so far beyond the mainstream that America began to splinter.

A GROWING DIVIDE

Until the end of the nineteenth century, U.S. politics had been marked by a broad consensus concerning the Founders' federalist-minimalist regime only sporadically interrupted by heated debates about specific issues such as the need for a national bank, slavery, and tariffs. All principal actors also agreed that freedom and equality could coexist and were mutually reinforcing. However, when freedom is defined negatively as the absence of force, necessity, and restriction, but equality as parity of outcome, tension occurs between them. And this is precisely what happened from the 1890s onward. As the Democrats started to move left and taxes and regulations intended to help some by "leveling the playing field," they eventually began to hamper success for all (or at least too many). As a result, the American economy began to slow—and social and cultural traits and habits earlier supporting the highly productive American system (high work ethic, honesty, entrepreneurship, risk-taking, etc.) degenerated accordingly. We will return to these effects, but for now, let's note that the U.S. passed a tipping point between tolerable and excessive taxation and regulation roughly at the same time as the Democrats decided to close the gap in statism vis-à-vis Europe and the Vietnam War started to drain the federal budget.

Moreover, postulating that this is more than a coincidence is hardly extreme. We only need to recall that people in Europe have lived with public interference in private life for thousands of years and since the seventeenth century—when heavy taxation and bureaucratization to wage conflicts like the Thirty Years War had been introduced—also grown used to government absolutism. In consequence, beginning with Germany in the 1870s, welfare states could be introduced and instantly become popular. But in America, where views of the government's proper size and role were different, politicians had to overcome numerous political, social, and cultural taboos to expand their power. Moreover, breaking these taboos negatively affects the country's exceptional qualities, people's industriousness and work ethic. Of particular importance is also that even if the Puritan heritage of communitarianism superficially resembles modern collectivism, the concepts are poles apart. Because while the former stresses family, small groups, voluntarism, and personal responsibility, the latter relies on governmental action, top-down management, large-scale operations, and regimentation. Consequently, as Democrats began to adopt radical policies while Republicans stuck with Americanism, not only did the U.S. economy and culture suffer. Ideological differences and party affiliation also began to turn into existential questions, leading forward to a political hatred as grave as the one haunting Europe around 1900.

One early example of this fractioning of America is the Civil Rights Movement. After Reconstruction, as repression returned to the South with Jim Crow and everyday racism continued to mark the North, African Americans' situation remained depressed. Therefore, in the 1950s, the Civil Rights Movement took off. Causes for this timing were many: frustrations with the lack of racial progress during the New Deal era; that racism after World War II became intolerable; and the Cold War turning attention to the conflict between American ideals and societal realities. Also, the Declaration's ideal that "all men are created equal" paired well with President Eisenhower's freedom agenda, and the movement's leader, Martin Luther King, Jr., long showed a solid dedication to the nation's founding principles. In 1955, he said:

> We are here in a general sense because first and foremost we
> are American citizens and we are determined to apply our
> citizenship to the fullness of its meaning. We are here also
> because of our love for democracy, because of our deep-
> seated belief that democracy transformed from thin paper
> to thick action is the greatest form of government on earth
> [. . .] If we are wrong, the Supreme Court of this nation
> is wrong. If we are wrong, the Constitution of the United
> States is wrong. If we are wrong, God Almighty is wrong.[138]

Thus, King's original goal was only to obtain the same freedom from oppression for blacks that the country's whites had declared for themselves

---

138. Martin Luther King Jr., "The Montgomery Bus Boycott," (1955) *BlackPast.org*, accessed February 19, 2018, http://www.blackpast.org/1955-martin-luther-king-jr-montgomery-bus-boycott.

in 1776. He was also at first frank about that full emancipation required self-improvement among blacks—"In this day we are going to compete with white people, not Negro people. So don't set out to do a good Negro job. [. . .] No matter what this job is, you must decide to do it well"[139] —and his early speeches soared with optimism: "The annual income of the Negro is now at about seventeen billion dollars a year, more than the annual income of Canada, and more than all of the exports of the United States. We've come a long, long way."[140] This allowed people of all races to support King's fight. However, when he, on August 28, 1963, held his *I Have a Dream* speech at the Lincoln Memorial in Washington, D.C., he had begun to give a more mixed message. Indeed, what he said there about the Constitution and the Declaration still expressed a strong belief in Americanism. But, frustrated with things not progressing faster, he also told the marchers that "those who hope that the Negro [only] needed to blow off steam and will now be content, will have a rude awakening if the nation returns to business as usual."[141]

Hence, King's most famous speech shows a change in the Civil Rights Movement's focus, from equality of opportunity to demands for political action leading to speedy socioeconomic parity with whites; i.e., demands for positive rights. Given blacks' socioeconomic situation, this was a natural evolution. It was also guided by King's political outlook, which combined Christianity and moralism in ways that made him a social democrat. However, first and foremost, this change fits into the broader ideological arc of the twentieth century toward demands for equality of

---

139. Martin Luther King Jr., "Some Things We Must Do" (December 5, 1957), *Stanford: The Martin Luther King, Jr. Research and Education Institute*, accessed February 19, 2018, http://kingencyclopedia.stanford. edu/encyclopedia/documentsentry/some_things_we_must_do_address_delivered_at_the_second_annual_ institute_on_/index.html.

140. Ibid.

141. Martin Luther King Jr., *A Testament of Hope: The Essential Writings and Speeches of Martin Luther King Jr.*, (ed.) by James M. Washington (New York: Harper One, 1986), 217f.

outcome driven by a belief in reaching political goals through bureau-cratic means. Moreover, this new message led to a de facto politicization of the movement and its message that—in addition to its slide toward violence after King's death—seriously reduced its general appeal. From the late 1960s, its leadership thus ended up in a close relationship with the Democratic Party, advancing its ongoing final turn into a European-type left-wing party.

THE CAMELOT YEARS

Running for the presidency in 1960, John F. Kennedy personified the Democratic Party's slowly but steadily changing nature since 1898. On the one side, like FDR, he was a moderate Northeastern patrician posi-tioning himself as a champion of "normal folk" and an advocate of an active government. On the other, he was a fiscal conservative but also more liberal on social and cultural issues than the party as a whole and not least its Southern faction. In addition, JFK was a firmer believer in Americanism and sturdier anti-communist than FDR, plus an even more captivating orator—when he chose to be. In contrast to today's image of an enchanting speaker (shaped by a handful of highlight film clips), most of his speeches were academic and technocratic in nature. But by at long last finding a way to use exceptionalist oratory to promote liberal domes-tic reforms and policies, a few of them became so inimitable that they deeply affected his party and the nation. Let's start with foreign policy.

JFK's active-inclusive form of Americanism is apparent. For example, when commenting on Latin America during the 1960 campaign, he said: "Our ambassadors must be spokesmen for democracy, not supporters of tyrants, and we must constantly press for free elections in any country where such elections are not held."[142] And in his Inaugural Address, he stated:

> The same revolutionary beliefs for which our forebears fought are still at issue around the globe—the belief that the rights of man come not from the generosity of the state but from the hand of God. We dare not forget today that we are the heirs of that first revolution. Let the word go forth from this time and place, to friend and foe alike, that the torch has been passed to a new generation of Americans [. . .] unwilling to witness or permit the slow undoing of those human rights to which this nation has always been committed, and to which we are committed today at home and around the world.[143]

Hence, JFK made FDR's democratism the goal of his foreign policy. However, his language was firmer, especially when it came to anti-communism. By 1960, this notion had become part of Americanism, and he frequently referred to communism as a given evil. Like in his 1962 State of the Union, when he reassured Americans that they were fighting the same principled fight in the Cold War as they had done during the World Wars: "Since the close of the Second World War, a global civil war has divided and tormented mankind. [. . .] It is our belief that the state is the servant of the citizen and not his master."[144] On communism, JFK also delivered during the 1962 Cuban Missile Crisis, by forming the Green Berets to fight communism in the Third World, and turning Eisenhower's nuclear strategy into a formal policy of mutually assured destruction (MAD).

Still, even if JFK's anti-communism resembled Truman's and Eisen-

142. Theodore C. Sorensen (ed.), *Let the Word Go Forth: The Speeches, Statements, and Writings of John F. Kennedy 1947 to 1963* (New York: Dell Publishing, 1988), 114.

143. John F. Kennedy, "Inaugural Address," (January 20, 1961) *APP*, accessed March 23, 2018, https://www.presidency.ucsb.edu/node/234470.

144. John F. Kennedy, "Annual Message to the Congress on the State of the Union," (January 11, 1962) *APP*, accessed March 22, 2018, https://www.presidency.ucsb.edu/node/236917.

hower's more than FDR's, it was more delicate than theirs. In particular, he saw the Cold War as an economic as much as an ideological conflict. This mirrored his progressive belief in a linear relationship between material wealth and peace and made him prone to praising groups such as USAID, whose "programs help people, and, by helping people, they help freedom."[145] To improve the U.S.' international standing, he also launched projects like the Peace Corps, which was to carry "American idealism [to] the far corners of the earth,"[146] and the Alliance for Progress, "a Marshall Plan for Latin America." However, the principal aspect of JFK's laxer tone is that it nourished a group of "anti-anti-communist" Democrats sharing the European left's idealist-pacifist view of world affairs. Among these was Senator William Fulbright; a maverick from Arkansas who, besides opposing civil rights and supporting segregation, in the 1960s would harass JFK's successor for his Vietnam policy and make headlines by refuting the whole post-1898 exceptionalist mindset. Moreover, he was for airing a naïve view of communism, holding a revisionist opinion on the Cold War, and calling to replace foreign aid with an international welfare system, called "Senator Halfbright" by ex-president Truman but became a hero for a spectrum of people stretching from remaining U.S. isolationists, via European peace activists, to Soviet propaganda officers.

Therefore, to look slightly ahead, the salient effect of Fulbright's passive form of Americanism was that it—in tandem with the Vietnam War—was to swamp the Democratic Party. And the speed with which this happened after JFK's death indicates that the characteristic American and uncompromising form of Cold War liberalism had never enjoyed—or by then had lost—the support of most elite Democrats. As a result, in front of the 1968 election, the party plank would begin to refute Wilson, FDR,

---

145. Dallek, *An Unfinished Life*, 346.
146. Dearborn, *Exceptionalist-In-Chief*, 186.

Truman, and others' active forms of exceptionalist-tinted international liberalism, promising instead to "resist the temptation to try to mold the world, or any part of it, in our own image, or to become the self-appointed policeman of the world."[147] The party's anti-communism would in the next decade also turn into a fig leaf, unable to hide many liberals if not direct support for socialist principles so their unwillingness to play hardball with Moscow.

Beyond this development, another critical difference between JFK and Eisenhower and Truman was their view of what the Cold War demanded of Americans. And here, the progressive tying and blending of domestic and foreign policies finally became complete. Because even if JFK's immediate predecessors had seen communism as a significant threat and accepted that the Cold War required great sacrifices, they had never said that the U.S., its people, or its values needed to change. On the contrary, according to them, the only chance to beat Uncle Joe (Stalin) had been for Uncle Sam to stick to his guns. However, in his Inaugural Address, JFK told Americans that the U.S. would "pay any price, bear any burden, meet any hardship, support any friend, oppose any foe to assure the survival and the success of liberty" to fulfill its mission. And if these words are read ideologically, they are nothing more than a variant of the old progressive-now-liberal mantra that the U.S. needed to change. What makes them notable is that they helped JFK to be remarkably successfully driving that message home—and break many Americans' enduring opposition to more radical political reforms.

This quality of JFK's rhetoric should be carefully considered. Because since the Cold War extended Americans' acceptance of collective policies prompted by the Great Depression and World War II even further, he could exploit the general recoil against the conservative mindset of

---

147. Johnson & Porter (ed.), *National Party Platforms*, 723.

the 1950s. And what he devised was a simple but effective three-point checklist for liberal talk. First, assure Americans through exceptionalist jargon that they can achieve anything by combining the country's endless resources with determination and hard work. Second, rally support for reforms by stroking people's support for equality (without mentioning the "of outcome" qualifier). Third, depict reforms as so self-evidently smart and desirable—so "common sense"—that only cold-hearted reactionaries can oppose them. JFK's best-known tweaking of collectivism to fit America's political heritage is his Inaugural Address line about "ask not what your country can do for you—ask what you can do for your country."[148] However, a more elaborate example is his 1960 DNC Acceptance Speech. He began by talking conventionally about the Frontier as a place where "the pioneers of old gave up their safety, their comfort and sometimes their lives to build a new world." But he then inversed this iconic theme by saying that the redeeming of the West had been a result of collective more than individual efforts and that the pioneer's motto had been "not 'every man for himself'—but 'all for the common cause.' "[149] And he then added:

> Today, some would say that those struggles [of the old West] are all over—that all the horizons have been explored—that all the battles have been won—that there is no longer an American frontier. But [. . .] the problems are not all solved and the battles are not all won—and we stand today on the edge of a *New Frontier*—the frontier of the 1960's—a frontier of unknown opportunities and perils—a frontier of unfulfilled hopes and threats.[150]

148. Kennedy, "Inaugural Address," (January 20, 1961).

149. John F. Kennedy, "Address of Senator John F. Kennedy Accepting the Democratic Party Nomination for the Presidency of the United States - Memorial Coliseum, Los Angeles," (July 15, 1960) *APP*, accessed March 14, 2018, https://www.presidency.ucsb.edu/node/274679.

150. Ibid. Emphasis added.

Thus, by adding the adjective "new" to the noun, JFK transformed the Frontier from a physical place in space and time into a state of mind. That is, he turned it into a futuristic topic by giving up Wilson, FDR, and others' attempts to declare the Frontier period over and used it instead as an argument for abandoning the policies of "old" America. Hence, he tied victory in the Cold War directly to the core objective of progressivism: perpetual reforms at home. This fitted perfectly with the avant-gardist mentality of the day at the same time as it continued to appeal to most people's traditional fondness for destiny, exploration, and hard work. Thus, JFK offered Americans a chance to continue the historic journey begun by their ancestors. And they better take it because . . .

> The New Frontier is here, whether we seek it or not. Beyond
> that frontier are the uncharted areas of science and space,
> unsolved problems of peace and war, unconquered pockets
> of ignorance and prejudice, unanswered questions of poverty
> and surplus. It would be easier to shrink back from that
> frontier, to look to the safe mediocrity of the past, to be
> lulled by good intentions and high rhetoric—and those who
> prefer that course should not cast their votes for me, regard-
> less of party.[151]

Later in this speech, to tighten his case further, JFK also talked about America's destiny to support freedom in a modern form of standing up against totalitarianism: "We must prove all over again whether this nation—or any nation so conceived—can long endure—whether our society—with its freedom of choice, its breadth of opportunity, its range of alternatives—can compete with the single-minded advance of the communist system."[152]

---

151. Ibid.
152. Ibid.

Three more things should be noted about the impact of JFK's political style. First, he created a new form of presidential rhetoric through multiple addresses. Explicitly, by offering a vision of America's future more daring than anyone before, his presidency became the point in U.S. history where the boldness of European idealists like Rousseau at last overpowered the realist wisdom of the Founders. And by doing so, JFK's rhetoric not only neutralized much remaining resistance to domestic reforms. In conjunction with his dramatic fate, it also put pressure on others to offer their own, even grander visions of America's future. Or bluntly, he made tall talk as vital for presidential wannabes as their ability to present concrete policies. Second, it was JFK who, on January 9, 1961, introduced the exceptionalist phrase par excellence into American discourse:

> I have been guided by the standard John Winthrop set
> before his shipmates on the flagship Arbella three hundred
> and thirty-one years ago, as they, too, faced the task of
> building a new government on a perilous frontier. 'We must
> always consider,' he said, 'that we shall be as *a city upon a
> hill*—the eyes of all people are upon us.'[153]

Third, taking note of Eisenhower's rhetoric, JFK tried to recapture "freedom" from conservatives. However, in this effort, he failed since he was often forced to use the term in its positive "rights" format to make it fit his agenda. And one result of this was that the division between radicals and conservatives would under his replacement deepen to a point where it opened a political civil war.

EMPIRE OF EQUALITY

Metaphorically, if Woodrow Wilson tilled the ground for modern liberalism, FDR planted its intellectual seeds, and JFK fertilized the field with

---

153. Sorensen (ed.), *Let the Word Go Forth*, 57. Emphasis added.

rhetorical ingenuity, Lyndon B. Johnson became the one who could reap its fruits and stage a harvest fest. This backwater school teacher had a dazing drive to get ahead, making him the closest thing to a full-blooded Machiavellian ever to occupy the Oval Office. LBJ also gained extensive political experience, e.g., as Democratic leader in the Senate, making him a very effective politician. He also had a mega-American, Texan attitude about doing all things bigger, better, and faster that meant only one absolute—no half-measures! During his tenure, he would indeed use both his persona and skills to upend the nature and function of U.S. politics from bottom-up, local, and communitarian to top-down, national, and collective. However, since he, like many influential leaders, seldom brooded over details, mapping the worldview and painting his ideological profile demands some puzzle work.

To start, LBJ's view of human nature needs to be noted. He seems to have shared the Founding Fathers' view of it as a fixed mix of virtues and vices. Hence, he held a different perspective than most radicals, which made him a political moderate in many ways. As we will see, this also goes for some of his specific views. However, since he differed from the Founders in many other ways, his goals and actions were all but restrained. Most importantly, he didn't believe that constitutional arrangements could compensate for human depravities enough to allow bottom-up republican governments and thought that political wisdom generally had to come from above. Moreover, LBJ's view of history was that mankind moved forward, upward, and toward more freedom, welfare, and equality. But he did not see this growth as deterministic, destiny bound, or driven by any spiritual, material, or other impersonal forces: "History is not made by nameless forces. History is made by men and women, by their governments and their nations."[154] And since he shared JFK's confidence that America was blessed with endless resources, he naturally deemed it America's—and more specifically, her government's—duty to take care of the downtrodden at home and to engage in nation-building abroad.

Furthermore, LBJ thought that there was something special with Americans. Once he said, "They came here—the exile and the stranger, brave but frightened—to find a place where a man could be his own man. They made a covenant with this land."[155] He also believed that U.S. greatness depended upon Americans being the world's most moral people. Their task was "to show that freedom from the control of other nations offers the surest road to progress, that history and experience testify to this truth." Moreover, being an example wasn't sufficient: "It is not enough to call upon reason or point to examples. We must show it through action and we must show it through accomplishment."[156] Still, in a liberal fashion, LBJ did not believe that America's political, social, and economic order was suited to meet present challenges. And he did not feel sentimental about it: "Is our world gone? We say farewell. Is a new world coming? We welcome it, and we will bend it to the hopes of man."[157] This unsentimental approach colored his whole attitude in both life and politics. For example, he saw economic growth simply as a means to political ends. He could hail a tax cut by saying, "By placing maximum reliance on the initiative and the creative energies of individual businessmen and workers,

154. Lyndon B. Johnson, "'Two Threats to World Peace' - Remarks in Omaha on the Occasion of the Sending of the Five-Millionth Ton of Grain to India," (June 30, 1966) *APP*, accessed May 12, 2018, https://www.presidency.ucsb.edu/node/238575.

155. Lyndon B. Johnson, "The President's Inaugural Address," (January 20, 1965) *APP*, https://www.presidency.ucsb.edu/documents/the-presidents-inaugural-address, accessed September 2, 2022.

156. Lyndon B. Johnson, "Address to Members of the Association of American Editorial Cartoonists: The Challenge of Human Need in Viet-Nam," (May 13, 1965) *APP*, accessed May 16, 2018, https://www.presidency.ucsb.edu/node/241577.

157. Ibid.

we have created here in our land the most prosperous nation in the history of the world," only to clarify that if it didn't create desirable results, "the federal Government will have to do for the economy what the economy should do for itself."[158]

In all, LBJ's self-esteem and belief in man-made destinies, American greatness, and ordinary folks' feebleness gave him an almost unqualified confidence in the power of politics. All needed for great things to happen was for him, as president, to take the lead, push legislation through Congress, and funnel resources to bureaucrats to resolve whatever issue was at hand. Clearly, this view did not match the Founders' vision of America as an ordered arena of freedom set to allow for individual self-realization. Nor did he respect their view of the U.S. as only a model for others to follow at will. For him personally, the result of this became a dual ambition to trump FDR as the greatest reformer in U.S. history and to match JFK's internationalism. In other words, LBJ wanted to go further, run faster, and aim higher than any other president. To do so, he decided to move on from FDR's basic welfare system toward equality of outcome and alter America from a prosperous and free republic to a world police. Let's begin at home.

LBJ's persona made him a perfect candidate for the historic act of turning Thomas Jefferson's Empire of Freedom into an Empire of Equality. On his first day in office, he singled out two issues to maximize his political prospects: a tax cut and civil rights. JFK had taken initiatives on both, but Midwestern Republicans and Southern Democrats blocked the bills in Congress; the former because they were fiscally conservative, the latter because they were racists. Therefore, within a week of JFK's death, LBJ told Congress that it was time for "the ideals which [JFK] so nobly

---

158. Lyndon B. Johnson, "Radio and Television Remarks Upon Signing the Civil Rights Bill" (July 2, 1964) *APP*, accessed May 12, 2018, https://www.presidency.ucsb.edu/node/239092.

represented [to] be translated into effective action" and that they should "fulfill the destiny that history has set for us."[159] And because of the shock the murder had brought, this point in U.S. history became what one scholar calls "a Promethean moment when everything seemed possible: the abolition of poverty, the overnight elimination of prejudice, unending economic expansion."[160] Or, in short, the time for limited government was definitively over.

Still, grasping that this mood was temporary, LBJ knew that he, to keep the reform train going long-term, had to rely on well-established arguments to persuade people that his managerial liberalism would bring "redemption without sacrifice [and] fulfillment of moral sensibilities without personal pain."[161] And to do this, he took JFK's rhetoric and ran with it. In his speech to Congress cited above, he revealed that he wanted more reforms beyond his predecessor's tax and civil rights bills, many of which progressives had sought for decades. Six weeks later, in his 1964 State of the Union, he also defined himself—plus gave his presidency a purpose of its own—by declaring "unconditional war on poverty in America." And he challenged Congress to go ahead before that year's General Election and turn itself into "the best in the Nation's history."

> [Be] known as the session which did more for civil rights
> than the last hundred sessions combined; as the session
> which enacted the most far-reaching tax cut of our time; as
> the session which declared all-out war on human poverty
> and unemployment in these United States; as the session
> which finally recognized the health needs of all our older
> citizens; as the session which reformed our tangled transpor-
> tation and transit policies; as the session which achieved the

---

159. Lyndon B. Johnson, "Address Before a Joint Session of the Congress," (November 27, 1963) *APP*, accessed May 1, 2018, https://www.presidency.ucsb.edu/node/238734.

160. Frum, *How We Got Here*, xxii.

161. Andrew, *Lyndon Johnson*, 9.

most effective, efficient foreign aid program ever; and as the session which helped to build more homes, more schools, more libraries, and more hospitals than any single session of Congress in the history of our Republic.[162]

He also added, "All this and more can and must be done [. . .] by this summer, and it can be done without any increase in spending" and that it would make America "free from want and a world that is free from hate—a world of peace and justice, and freedom and abundance, for our time and for all time to come."

Hence, not only did LBJ reintroduce FDR's freedom from want into his version of Americanism, but he added the eradication of "hate" and several other pledges to the list. By turning speech like this into facsimiles of the endless catalogs of Utopian promises characterizing Soviet five-year plans, he also irresponsibly inflated people's expectations of what was to come. However, to make all these things happen, he first had to push JFK's bills through Congress—and get elected in his own right. However, while the tax cut was popular among both politicians and voters and easy to get through, the Civil Rights bill demanded broad Republican support to get around the big block of racist Southern Democrats in the Senate. The problem was that even if the GOP wanted reform, the language of JFK's bill was so vague that many feared it would open doors for federal power grabs far beyond racial issues. Nevertheless, in the political haze descending over the country after JFK's murder, this was not noted by some and ignored by others. And with plenty of LBJ's notorious political arm-twisting, it was enough for most Republicans to vote yes.

Here, let's pause and note two things. First, the 1964 Civil Rights Act, however well intended it was, did indeed become the wrecking ball sub-

162. Lyndon B. Johnson, "Annual Message to the Congress on the State of the Union," (January 8, 1964) *APP*, accessed May 10, 2018, https://www.presidency.ucsb.edu/node/242292.

duing the Constitution's limitations upon the federal government critics presaged. As an example, Democratic Minnesota Senator and LBJ's Vice President-to-be Hubert Humphry promised both to "eat my hat if [the bill] leads to racial quotas" and the appropriate pages if its language led to forced busing between schools (a reform that allegedly would improve educational opportunities for black children but so-far had been blocked by constitutional concerns). And he didn't need to go hungry. It took liberal activists—and the Supreme Court—only a few years to construe the bill in such ways. Liberal advocates and judges at all levels have since then also used the spirit of the 1964 Civil Rights Act to (re)interpret the Constitution to, e.g., take away prayer in schools, liberalize pornography, and—in a move that certainly infected the political climate—legalize abortions. Thus, the Act has contributed directly to an overall expansion of federal powers on the one side and curtailed individual and state rights on the other in ways that in earlier eras would have been seen as not only wrong but obscene.

Second, whether or not the language allowing for this historic weakening of the Constitution was deliberate, it also broke many elitists' respect for the document and created a political-judicial environment that quickly became increasingly alien. Case in point, when LBJ the following year spoke to Congress in favor of the subsequent Voting Rights Act, he said that the right to vote "is no issue of States rights or national rights. There is only the struggle for human rights."[163] That is, what the U.S. president told the U.S. Congress was that human rights were superior to the U.S. Constitution and that this document had to be reinterpreted simply because "the time for waiting is gone."[164] Hence, in a liberal fashion, LBJ hinged his position on the Declaration's idealism, not the realism

---

163. Lyndon B. Johnson, "Special Message to the Congress: The American Promise," (March 15, 1965) in *APP*, https://www.presidency.ucsb.edu/node/242211, accessed May 12, 2018.
164. Ibid

of the Constitution, which was the ordering opposite of the Founders. George Washington made this clear by saying that the Constitution as it "at any time exists till changed by an explicit and authentic act of the whole people [must be] sacredly obligatory upon all."[165] Thus, the 1964 Civil Rights Act symbolizes the final divorce (in the liberal mind) of the Declaration from the Constitution and the final move toward "a living constitution." Or, in judicial mumbo-jumbo, it signifies a shift in jurisprudence from "liberal restraint" to the "loose constructionism" of the Warren and Burger Courts. The proof for this is that since the 1960s, the U.S. has changed more than it did between 1789 and 1964, without politicians bothering to change the Constitution.

To move on, while waiting for the Civil Rights Act to be approved, LBJ laid down the premise for his "war on poverty" and declared that "the richest nation on earth can afford to win it."[166] He also named it the Great Society, which is fitting because the program would demand a scale of political intrusion never seen west of the Mid-Atlantic Ridge. In a customary American style, he also considered victory as given and no cost as too high. Many operations were hence taken to move on from FDR's limited welfare programs, aimed to fix temporary ills, toward a full-sized welfare state aspiring to achieve more permanent equality of outcome. Central to this was replacing the concept of absolute poverty—being unable to meet your immediate survival needs—with a relative measurement. Thus, poverty was henceforth to be defined in the sense of a millionaire being poor next to a billionaire, meaning that (despite many "poor" Americans already living on material levels equating to or exceeding middle-income Europeans) 10–15–20 percent of the U.S. voting population would forever be considered entitled to tax-funded support.

165. Washington, "Farewell Address" (September 19, 1796).

166. Lyndon B. Johnson, "Annual Message to the Congress on the State of the Union," (January 8, 1964) *APP*, accessed May 3, 2018, https://www.presidency.ucsb.edu/node/242292.

Moreover, after introducing the term Great Society in January 1964, LBJ at the University of Michigan gave a more profound meaning to the term in May. In the time-honored left-wing fashion to depict the present as so different from the past that a break with the original American order was necessary, he crooned the same tune as FDR had done in his Commonwealth speech:

> For a century we labored to settle and to subdue a
> continent. For half a century we called upon unbounded
> invention and untiring industry to create an order of plenty
> for all of our people. The challenge of the next half century
> is whether we have the wisdom to use that wealth to enrich
> and elevate our national life, and to advance the quality of
> our American civilization. [. . .] For in your time we have
> the opportunity to move not only toward the rich society
> and the powerful society, but upward to the Great Society.[167]

And on June 4 of the following year, with the Civil Rights Act in the bank and himself reelected, LBJ came out full monty. At Howard University, he echoed the Martin Luther King Jr. "dream" speech by saying that traditional negative freedoms were insufficient for African Americans: "We seek not just legal equity but human ability, not just equality as a right and a theory but equality as a fact and *equality as a result*." And he didn't shun what this meant in terms of government responsibilities:

> Jobs are part of the answer. They bring the income which
> permits a man to provide for his family. Decent homes
> in decent surroundings and a chance to learn—an equal
> chance to learn—are part of the answer. Welfare and social
> programs better designed to hold families together are part
> of the answer. Care for the sick is part of the answer. An

---

167. Lyndon B. Johnson, "Remarks at the University of Michigan," (May 22, 1964) *APP*, accessed May 3, 2018, https://www.presidency.ucsb.edu/node/239689.

understanding heart by all Americans is another big part
of the answer. And to all of these fronts—and a dozen
more—I will dedicate the expanding efforts of the Johnson
administration.[168]

Hence, by making Great Society "an open-ended commitment to growth in government,"[169] LBJ made it a turning point beyond which no significant roadblocks were left for making America a "normal" welfare state. This naturally thrilled liberals. Still, knowing that he needed to sell his plans to ordinary Americans, he often stuffed his speech about Great Society with exceptionalist themes and phrases. For example, in his UofM speech, next to a typical technocratic-positivist promise to make Great Society programs work by gathering "the best thought and the broadest knowledge from all over the world," he stroked Americans' communitarian sensibility by promising to make use of "new concepts of cooperation, a creative federalism, between the National Capital and the leaders of local communities."[170] However, LBJ had to break that promise. Because by funneling federal funds to grassroots organizations rather than to established state and local entities, Great Society programs quickly became so riddled with waste, fraud, and corruption that they speedily had to be replaced with more traditional top-down structures. For instance, Medicare and Medicaid, created in 1965, were made standard federal programs from the start.

Furthermore, the most important—and, for the American system, devastating—effect of adding Great Society flesh onto the New Deal skeleton was that countless decisions previously made on local and state levels, or by people themselves, were relocated to federal bureaucrats

168. Lyndon B. Johnson, "Commencement Address at Howard University: 'To Fulfill These Rights'," (June 4, 1965) *APP*, accessed May 12, 2018, https://www.presidency.ucsb.edu/node/241312. Emphasis added.

169. Sven R. Larson, *The Rise of Big Government: How Egalitarianism Conquered America* (London: Routledge, 2018), 11.

170. Johnson, "Remarks at the University of Michigan," (May 22, 1964).

and doomed to be decided by courts ultimately. Both New Classers and (liberal) judges thus got a historic chance to increase their power, which added trouble to worry as they soon learned how to create rules and regulations more in line with their own, extra radical likings than LBJ's—as many of them saw it—outdated social and cultural views. This led the president to mumble about "kooks and sociologists"[171] and to a distressing dissonance between programs' intentions and workings, but when such problems were discovered, they were usually too far gone to be fixed. And even more importantly, solving problems by federal political-bureaucratic means, rather than looking for state, local, or private solutions, became a kneejerk reaction deeply embedded in the New Class's and parts of the judicial branch's DNA.

To finish this part, the Great Society became a manifestation of LBJ's megalomaniac character. As he made the program a central theme of the 1964 election campaign, he, as already noted, stuffed speeches with exceptionalist talk and hints at the country's millennial and think-big traditions in its defense. To offer one more example:

> We stand at the edge of the greatest era in the life of any
> nation. For the first time in world history we have the abun-
> dance and the ability to free every man from hopeless want,
> and to free every person to find fulfillment in the works of
> his mind or the labor of his hands. Even the greatest of all
> past civilizations existed on the exploitation of the misery
> of the many. This Nation, this people, this generation, has
> man's first chance to create a Great Society: a society of
> success without squalor, beauty without barrenness, works of
> genius without the wretchedness of poverty.[172]

171. Kesler, *I Am the Change*, 156.
172. Lyndon B. Johnson, "Remarks at a Fundraising Dinner in Detroit," (June 26, 1964) *APP*, accessed May 7, 2018, https://www.presidency.ucsb.edu/node/239191.

As the election loomed, LBJ also tried to square the Great Society with the country's intellectual heritage. However, this failed rather miserably. In his DNC Acceptance Speech, he made the same old mistake of using the positive, right-based form of freedom to defend his plans: "The man who is hungry, who cannot find work or educate his children, who are bowed by want [. . .] is not fully free." When he tried to put the Great Society into the span of U.S. history, he thus ended up just adding it to the shorter annals of progressivism: "For more than thirty years, from social security to the war against poverty, we have diligently worked to enlarge the freedom of man."[173] And for many Americans, this was still not enough for them to accept more radical policies.

Even so, LBJ won a landslide victory. And even if this was mostly a post-humous vote for JFK, he became so blinded by the event that he claimed it was a mandate for Great Society. In his 1965 Inaugural Address, he outlined the story of America as a contract that was still valid but, because of the present's "rapid and fantastic change,"[174] in need of an update. It was also just a few months later that he, in a Howard University address, threw his support behind King's budding demand for more than negative freedoms in the quest to achieve full racial equality promptly. Obviously, he wanted to seem in step with the times. However, things were changing so fast that he became obsolete as he spoke. For example, he still believed in capitalism, a balanced budget, and lower taxes to spur economic growth. I.e., what "real" liberals would soon scorn as "trickle-down" economics. He also held on to an old-style belief in opportunity and hard work that made his "welfarism" a curate's egg compared to the full-fledged social democracy embraced by many others. And such discords were only minor

173. Lyndon B. Johnson, "Remarks Before the National Convention Upon Accepting the Nomination," (August 27, 1964), *APP*, accessed May 15, 2018, https://www.presidency.ucsb.edu/node/241812.

174. Lyndon B. Johnson, "The President's Inaugural Address," (January 20, 1965) *APP*, accessed May 2018, https://www.presidency.ucsb.edu/documents/the-presidents-inaugural-address.

inconveniences compared to what was to come. The U.S. had namely "embarked on a series of ventures that bespoke a conviction of limitless power at home as well as abroad."[175] And besides Great Society, the main part was a new war.

APOCALYPSE NOW

To distance himself from the far left, LBJ had early in life branded himself a Cold War liberal. Ahead of the 1964 election, though, he described his foreign policy goals as limited to those "in Washington's time, to protect the life of our Nation, to preserve the liberty of our citizens, and to pursue the happiness of our people."[176] And since his focus was domestic policy, and his overriding ambition to become a "great" president, this was probably an honest declaration. It also fitted his strategy to run as a "peace candidate" against his hard-nosed Republican rival Berry Goldwater. Be this as it may, LBJ was still acutely aware that his standing hung on not being perceived as soft on communism. He consequently left nothing to chance and planned for an escalation of the country's limited engagement in Vietnam—after the election. Before Election Day 1964, he only hinted about what was coming occasionally. Like when he said that "no negotiated settlement in Viet-Nam is possible, as long as the communists hope to achieve victory by force."[177] And for voters still in the process of learning to know LBJ's true persona, this sounded harmless.

After the election, though, few could remain in doubt for long. Between November 1964 and March 1965, LBJ began escalating U.S. involvement in Vietnam. And in his Inaugural Address in January 1965, he came out as an activist liberal internationalist who shared JFK's view of America's

---

175. John A. Andrew III, *Lyndon Johnson and the Great Society* (Chicago: American Ways Series, 1999), 83f.

176. Lyndon B. Johnson, "Remarks on Foreign Affairs at the Associated Press Luncheon in New York City," (April 20, 1964) *APP*, accessed June 14, 2018, https://www.presidency.ucsb.edu/node/239272.

177. Ibid.

role in the world with a sharp Wilsonian edge: "If American lives must end, and American treasure be spilled, in countries that we barely know, then that is the price that change has demanded of conviction and of our enduring covenant."[178] And a few months after that, he added that it was the U.S.' "task to show that freedom from the control of other nations offers the surest road to progress [and that] it is not enough to call upon reason or point to examples. We must show it through action, and we must show it through accomplishment."[179] Moreover, even if LBJ first described Vietnam as a quick fix, he made it clear, like Wilson about World War I, that the U.S. would never surrender. Until the independence of South Vietnam was secured, he told the press, "We are going to continue to persist, if persist we must, until death and desolation have led to the same conference table where others could now join us at a much smaller cost."[180]

This didn't go down well among radicals, students, young men facing the draft, or the Baby Boomer generation, which in those years was entering the '60s era of peace, love, and exotic cigarettes. Yet, LBJ had chosen a path from which he couldn't deviate since, besides political reasons, diplomatic pride, and military considerations, his ego was now on the line. On at least one occasion, he revealed that the war was as much about keeping the U.S. (read: his own) anti-communist credentials unspoiled as about helping the South Vietnamese. In May 1965, LBJ also depicted the war as crucial because China stood behind the Việt Cộng and wanted "to discredit America's ability to help prevent Chinese domination over all of Asia."[181] On top, that spring he sent U.S. troops to quell a left-wing revolt

178. Johnson, "The President's Inaugural Address, (January 20, 1965).

179. Johnson: "Address to Members . . ." (May 13, 1965).

180. Lyndon B. Johnson, "The President's News Conference," (July 28, 1965), *APP*, accessed May 19, 2023, https://www.presidency.ucsb.edu/documents/the-presidents-news-conference-1038.

181. Johnson: "Address to Members . . ." (May 13, 1965).

in the Dominican Republic where "communist leaders, many of them trained in Cuba, seeing a chance to increase disorder, to gain a foothold, joined the revolution."[182] Thus, because he saw America's role in the world as a mission, not a choice, his Vietnam rhetoric became pompous, self-righteous, arrogant—and long-term disastrous.

Nevertheless, LBJ was forced to change his tone as the war began to drag out. He started by giving longer speeches in which the themes of freedom and America's moral cause often vanished in clouds of details. That is, he began to echo the flow of telemetric data fed to him by Defense Secretary McNamara, apparently confirming that all was going well. Over time, to show that the war was inevitable *and* honorable, he also paid greater attention to historical context and tried to use exceptionalist themes to prove it. He, e.g., compared it with the Revolutionary War: "Americans and Asians are dying for a world where each people may choose its own path to change. This is the principle for which our ancestors fought in the valleys of Pennsylvania."[183] And after a visit to Andrew Jackson's home in Tennessee, he said: "In our time, as in Jackson's time, courage and vision, and the willingness to sacrifice, will sustain the cause of freedom. This generation of Americans is making its imprint on history. It is making it in the fierce hills and the sweltering jungles of Vietnam."[184]

Also, as Vietnam became a quagmire and its cost began to limit LBJ's ability to pursue his domestic agenda, he began to whine. In 1966, he said, "Because of Vietnam, we cannot do all that we should or all that we would like to do," even though he also said that "we can continue the

---

182. Lyndon B. Johnson, "Radio and Television Report to the American People on the Situation in the Dominican Republic," (May 2, 1965), *APP*, accessed June 16, 2018, https://www.presidency.ucsb.edu/node/241737.

183. Ibid.

184. Lyndon B. Johnson, "Address on U.S. Policy in Vietnam Delivered Before a Joint Session of the Tennessee State Legislature," (March 15, 1967) *APP*, accessed June 14, 2018, https://www.presidency.ucsb.edu/node/237953.

Great Society while we fight in Vietnam."[185] Thus, there was no room in his mind that the U.S. wasn't rich, strong, and right enough to fight and win Vietnam *and* the war on poverty. However, the following year, when forced to ask Congress for a partial repeal of the 1964 tax reduction, his wariness turned into bitterness, and toward the end of his presidency, his defense of Vietnam began to collapse. In 1967, he tried to blame the war on the presidents of the Philippines and South Korea, the prime ministers of Malaysia, New Zealand, and Singapore, and the foreign minister of Thailand.[186] And in January 1969, he even charged the U.S. political system: "No one man or group of men made these commitments alone. Congress and the executive branch, with their checks and balances, reasoned together and finally wrote them into the law of the land."[187]

To summarize. Given Americans' exceptionalist self-image, consolidated by more than half a century of successes like winning two world wars and holding communism at bay in the Cold War, it is only logical that LBJ decided to go full force into Vietnam parallel with rolling out the Great Society. His domestic and foreign policies are thus textbook examples of how boundless belief in Americanism can gravely affect policy formation. Moreover, because of LBJ's excessive talk about American greatness to sell both the Great Society and the Vietnam War, the many failures of the first and the inability to win the latter led to dangerous public distress. And the long-term political effect of this was that Americanism began losing appeal. Indeed, in 1970, Americans would still cheer the opening of Francis Ford Coppola's movie *Patton*, where the World War II general, on the eve of the 1944 Normandy landing, tells his troops that "Americans love a winner. [. . .] That's why Americans have never lost nor will ever

185. Johnson, "Annual Message to the Congress . . .," (January 12, 1966).

186. Lyndon B. Johnson, "Address on Vietnam Before the National Legislative Conference, San Antonio, Texas," (September 29, 1967) *APP*, accessed June 14, 2018, https://www.presidency.ucsb.edu/node/237536.

187. Lyndon B. Johnson, "Annual Message to the Congress on the State of the Union," (January 14, 1969) *APP*, Accessed June 13, 2018, https://www.presidency.ucsb.edu/node/236130.

lose a war; for the very idea of losing is hateful to an American."[188] But their support for the Vietnam War had since long fallen below 50 percent, and LBJ himself was gone. On March 3, 1968, he had chickened out, unexpectedly ending a speech about Vietnam by saying: "I shall not seek and I will not accept the nomination of my party for another term as your president."[189]

---

188. Charles M. Province, "The Famous Patton Speech," (June 5, 1944) *The Patton Society*, accessed June 17, 2018, http://www.pattonhq.com/speech.html.

189. Lyndon B. Johnson, "The President's Address to the Nation Announcing Steps To Limit the War in Vietnam and Reporting His Decision Not To Seek Reelection," (March 31, 1968) *APP*, accessed June 14, 2018, https://www.presidency.ucsb.edu/node/238065.

> *"The American spirit [. . .] is not the visitation of some*
> *ghost of the past; rather it is the affirmation of a deep*
> *national yearning that all of us feel today."*
>
> Richard Nixon | 1968

CHAPTER 6 |

Turning the Tide

A round 1970, the dual nature of modern America showed itself in stark colors. While Neil Armstrong demonstrated the country's technological preeminence by walking on the Moon, disorders were on display back home in the form of race riots, war protests, and drug epidemics. Thus, the U.S. was experiencing its first national crisis— besides the War of 1812 and the Civil War—not conditioned by economic matters. In fact, the difference from the picture of the U.S. just a few years earlier was so stark that many Americans' belief in their republic crumbled. The reason for this seemed to be the Vietnam War. However, beyond this disaster, a much more complex crisis was brewing. The constitutional framework adopted in 1789 had been designed to serve a politically decentralized, economically laissez-faire, and sociocultural agrarian Union, but the costs and structural weights of the modern welfare-warfare state had just been thrown on top of it. And even if some developments, like that of an "Imperial" presidency much stronger than the Founding Fathers intended, happened to fit the needs of a superpower, the tension between American's traditional view of a small U.S. Government and liberal's endless push to expand it led to problems, mistrust, and disorder.

Americans beginning to lose faith in "the System" also led to a reaction against the old liberal paradigm. However, the Democratic Party and the New Class empire struck back, and an ideological Civil War between people who embraced more of the same and those who wanted America to return to her basics began that has raged ever since.

THE CULTURE WARS

In the 1960s, as the federal government and corporations grew and the first-generation New Classers began to take over bureaucracies, big businesses, universities, and media, cohorts of college graduate Baby Boomers, drenched by positivist thinking and "alternative" political views, poured in from below to fill all new positions. Thus, the New Class was at the same time inflated and radicalized. Moreover, its members—as elites tend to do due to titles, pay, and power—became increasingly isolated and lost touch with public wishes, tastes, and wisdom. Accordingly, New Classers began to cling to flawed and evermore outdated theories about the economy, the origin of and solution to social woes, and more. This mechanism became extra strong in guild-like and discourse-making professions like academia and media, whose members interact mainly with—or at least only really trust—each other and, therefore, are extra prone to crippling groupthink. Hence, the distance between "normal folks" and the political, bureaucratic, and media "iron triangle" increased to novel levels, arousing Americans' age-old suspicion against elites to new highs. And since these developments all pointed in the same (leftward) direction, the division between high and low and between Democrats and Republicans would ultimately become destructive.

At the same time, Americans' self-image started to undergo a momentous shift. This happened because of a combination of current political, cultural, and other trends and long-standing "modernist" developments.

And the most critical change concerned the core question of what being an American actually means. Since 1776, "being a proud American" had been the norm and assimilation of minorities and immigrants was both an ideal and a reality. However, the confidence in the sameness of all people assimilation required was challenged first by African Americans when swift improvements in their situation did not follow the 1964 Civil Rights Act. Explicitly, as they joined the Democratic Party as a pressure group to enforce equality of outcome, many turned away from Americanism in favor of cultural tribalism and rejected further integration into mainstream America. Indeed, "going white" became a slur. Blacks were also soon followed by American Indians, Chicanos, Italians, Irish, and others, plus people who began to define themselves first by gender, age, sexual orientation, etc. This turned the U.S. from a "melting pot" into a "salad bowl" of minorities wherein all—except middle-aged white males—were thought (and taught) to lack a national sense beyond the mere fact of being born within the geographical borders of the U.S.

Another dimension of this sundering of modern America stemmed from the Fourth Great Awakening; a theological complex demanding a bit more exhaustive explanation. This is an umbrella term comprising three interrelated trends: rising support for public secularism, including demands for a stringent "firewall" between state and church; weakening support for traditional Protestant denominations and the subsequent growth of fundamentalist congregations; and a growing interest in non-Western beliefs such as Buddhism, Wicca, and Hari Krishna fitting the broader New Age label. Of these changes, the two first had common roots in the liberalization of Protestantism triggered by the Progressive Movement. The core difference is that while traditionalists view the Bible as the direct words of God that must be taken literally, reformists argue that since humans have been writing and editing its texts, they can, to a certain extent, be dealt with figuratively. Hence, traditionalists and reformists' views on the Bible (and, in the case of Jews, the Thora) created "separate and competing moral galax[ies]"[190] driven apart by dogmas. For example, while most reformists have no problem with trusting both that Jesus died for their sins and Darwin's theory of evolution, many traditionalists have a hard time accepting the Biblical story of Noah's Ark and the geological fact that the Earth is 4.8 billion years old.

Moreover, even if most people fall between these religious extremes, their moral and ethical attitudes shape their views not only on topics like sex, abortion, and Darwinism but also on purely political issues. As traditional Protestantism began to wane after World War II, it thus lost its role as the lowest common denominator for being "a real American" as well. Instead, the importance of "believing in America," valuing the Constitution, endorsing various exceptionalism notions, and acts like swearing the Pledge of Allegiance increased. During the Cold War, this broadening of Americanness first strengthened national unity but shortly started to weaken it instead. Because, even if Republicans and Democrats continued to say—and certainly also to believe—that they supported both freedom and equality, the former came to increasingly uphold freedom as America's prime virtue, and the latter to put so much emphasis on equality (of outcome), that people effectively had to choose. And since the importance of which concept they valued the most grew parallel with the scale, scope, and intrusiveness of the political sphere, the differences finally reached a level where they began viewing each other not only as wrong but malicious.

Three further sidenotes on U.S. politics and religion should be made. The first is that Americans' robust religiosity made the split between traditionalists and reformists more pronounced in the U.S. and, in turn, made

---

190. Hunter, *Culture Wars*, 128.

political debates on issues like the nuclear family and abortions more heated but also more balanced than in most other Western countries. The second is that this created a market for "polipastors" like Jesse Jackson and Al Sharpton on the left and Jerry Farwell and Pat Robertson to the right. As professional preachers, they could express their opinions with a spark most politicians could not. For instance, Robertson once thundered: "Either we will return to the moral integrity and original dreams of the founders of this nation [. . .] or we will give ourselves over more and more to hedonism, to all forms of destructive anti-social behavior, to political apathy, and ultimately to the forces of anarchy and disintegration that have throughout history gripped great empires and nations in their tragic and declining years."[191] And because such talk nurtured a picture of there being "no middle ground,"[192] Americans' propensity for perfection led U.S. politics to take "a moral turn" that drove increasing numbers toward not only theological but political extremes, adding to the already ongoing rise in partisanship and polarization.

The third note is that while the first two trends pushed people on the left away from traditional values, institutions, and routines toward beliefs and lifestyles oblivious or even hostile to traditional American ideals, a parallel "reddening of America" took place to the right. This was a broad sociocultural development with profound political ramifications. Besides traditionalists switching from Democrat to Republican, especially in the South, its most crucial effect was to enhance the impact of the country's economic center shifting from the Northeast/Midwest to "the Sunbelt" and the corresponding growth in the South's—and to a lesser degree also the West's—political and cultural importance. In a word, as people and enterprises moved in, bringing electoral votes, congressional seats, and tax

191. Ibid, 112f.

192. Andrew Hartman, *A War for the Soul of America: A History of the Culture Wars* (Chicago: The University of Chicago Press, 2015), 10.

revenues with them, Southern and Southwestern mannerisms like country music, cowboy boots, pickup trucks, and foods spread out. This meant the growth of "a new kind of conservatism [. . .] more populist, more middle class, more antiestablishment"[193] than the old Country Club-based northeastern form and cultivated "a distinct southern republicanism, which opposed the Leviathan state and determined to concentrate power as close to home as possible."[194]

As a result, around 1970, the political landscape started to change, and the bottom line of U.S. politics became "Who is most American? Republicans, who prioritize freedom, or Democrats, who advocate equality?" And because the latter's answer came at the expense of ideas such as individual freedom and states' rights, at the same time as academics, journalists, and others because of the Vietnam War started to treat patriotic language and idols (including the military) as subjects of hate and ridicule, Americanism in effect began to turn into an ever more politically conservative theme. This also led to a split between a naïve "my country right or wrong" nationalism on the right and a "critical patriotism" on the left, often crossing the line of anti-Americanism. And as this meshed with the split between religious traditionalists and reformists, debates on issues like abortion, school prayer, and flag burning fostered new generations of more confrontational-minded Republicans and Democrats. Thus, the political theater began to form a triangle drama with a small but mighty, self-venerated, and secluded elite of liberals at the top and a "silent majority" of conservative/traditionalist Americans, plus a small cluster of counter-culture groups, at the base. And since neither group—because of small size, lack of organizing, and nuttiness, respectively—could fully

193. Bruce J. Schulman, *The Seventies: The Great Shift in American Culture, Society, and Politics* (New York: The Free Press, 2001), 114.

194. Eugene D. Genovese, *The Southern Tradition: The Achievement and Limitations of an American Conservatism* (Cambridge: Harvard University Press, 1994), 56.

dominate the public scene, politics changed into a cynical game defined by posturing and empty talk arranged to appeal to all and intimidate none that annoyed everybody.

MODERN CONSERVATISM

As noted, LBJ's expansion of the New Deal into a full-sized federal welfare state made the ideological conflict lines clear. For the Democrats, this development followed gradually as party bodies and voter blocks continued to radicalize along the overall "more equality of outcome" line. In contrast, after losing the White House in 1960, centrist Republicans lost their historic hold over the party to the Conservative Movement. This was a conglomerate of people that challenged the postwar consensus about the New Deal, the Cold War, and other issues and wanted the GOP to offer "a choice, not an echo." And even if the policy difference between Country Club and "New Right" Republicanism is often exaggerated, it was rhetorically stark. For example, in 1968, William F. Buckley Jr., one of the movement's founders, declared:

> I will not cede more power to the state. I will not willingly
> cede more power to anyone, not to the state, not to General
> Motors, not to the CIO. I will hoard my power like a miser,
> resisting every effort to drain it away from me. I will then
> use my power, as I see fit. I mean to live my life an obedient
> man, but obedient to God, subservient to the wisdom of my
> ancestors; never to the authority of political truths arrived at
> yesterday at the voting booth. That is a program of sorts, is
> it not? It is certainly program enough to keep conservatives
> busy, and Liberals at bay. And the nation free.[195]

195. William F. Buckley Jr., *Up From Liberalism* (Toronto: Bantam Books, reprint 1968), 175f. The CIO stands for Congress of Industrial Organizations; a federation of industrial unions that in 1955 merged with the American Federation of Labor into today's AFL–CIO.

Hence, the Conservative Movement formed as a counterpoint to Modern Liberalism. The 1960s is also, as already indicated, the point in U.S. history where defenders of freedom and agents of equality decisively, for many reasons, went separate ways. Thus, on top of religious and partisan rifts, an ever-widening split opened between people supporting a European-like welfare state and those who emphasized free markets, low taxes, and other policies that can be derived from Americanism. As this movement began to affect the GOP, three things happened. One, conservative rhetoric became crisper and clearer. Two, the party's voter base began to shift from moderate New England and protectionist-isolationist Midwestern states toward the traditionalist South and free-spirited West. Three, the GOP turned from being a politically and socially comparatively consistent alliance of farmers, small-town dwellers, and businessmen into a cacophonic "Leave me alone!" coalition of traditionalists, libertarians, and anti-communists held together mainly by people's belief in Americanism. Still, in 1964, this coalition became headed by a man who knew how to unite and animate its disparate parts.

Barry Goldwater was not an archetypal Republican. He was of Jewish descent, a hard-nosed ideologue, a political maverick, and—since Arizona at his birth was still a territory—America's last prominent frontier politician. After joining the Senate in 1952, he criticized President Eisenhower for being too liberal, called the U.N. "a discussion forum" and "sacred cow," and labeled LBJ "the Santa Claus of the free lunch [and] the government handout." However, Goldwater's most striking move came when he, running for the GOP's 1964 presidential nomination, opposed the Great Society and the Civil Rights Act not because he (like Sothern Democrats) was racist, but for judging it threatening state's rights. Thus, for the first time in decades, a major party's presidential candidate was challenging not only parts but the whole idea of a federal welfare state. This also concluded the state rights issue's historic move from a Democratic to a Republican pet issue—and it ensured him the epithet "Mr. Conservative."

Unsurprisingly, Goldwater used deeply ideological and plenty of exceptionalist and religious rhetoric. In his 1964 RNC Acceptance Speech, he declared statism to be the time's foremost challenge to America's character and her freedoms:

> The good Lord raised this mighty Republic to be a home for the brave and to flourish as the land of the free—*not* to stagnate in the swampland of collectivism—*not* to cringe before the bullying of Communism. The tide has been running against freedom. Our people have followed false prophets. We must and we *shall* return to proven ways—*not* because they are old, but because they are *true*. We must and we shall set the tides running again in the cause of freedom.[196]

He also took Eisenhower's freedom agenda to its logical extreme by stating that freedoms dwindling at home had a broader meaning because the U.S.'s mission was to guide the world: "We Americans understand freedom. We have earned it, lived for it, and died for it. This nation and its people *are* freedom's model in a doubting world. We *can* be freedom's missionaries in a doubting world." However, Goldwater did not believe in any overriding human longing for freedom: "I know that freedom is not the fruit of every soil. I know that our own freedom was achieved through centuries by the unremitting efforts of brave and wise men."[197] Accordingly, except for standing firm against communism, he did not call for ideologically inspired invasions and nation-building abroad.

Furthermore, Goldwater said that modern Americans at home were guided by a false view of equality, which "rightly understood, as our

---

196. Barry Goldwater, *Where I Stand* (New York: McGraw-Hill, 1964), 9.
197. Ibid, 10.

founding fathers understood it, leads to liberty and to the emancipation of creative differences [but] wrongly understood, as it has been so tragically in our time, it leads first to conformity and then to despotism." Thus, if anything but conservative, he expressed libertarian sentiments. Still, after closing with, "I would remind you that extremism in the defense of liberty is no vice [and] that moderation in the pursuit of justice is no virtue,"[198] Goldwater was written off as an extremist. And given the political atmosphere at that moment in time, he was one. Yet, he only spelled out the post-1898 difference between traditional freedom and equality of outcome and so presaged the level of ideological polarization to come. His focus on freedom also struck a chord with millions who felt that something was off base, and even after his massive loss against LBJ that November, the GOP establishment would fail to stifle his ideological line.

Moreover, toward the end of Goldwater's campaign, a former FDR liberal gave his message a second and genuinely captivating voice. On October 27, 1964, Ronald Reagan, a fading movie star, gave a televised speech to support his campaign. He began by criticizing the Great Society, especially the tax burden it imposed, and told Americans that "it's time we ask ourselves if we still know the freedoms that were intended for us by the Founding Fathers." He then attacked the liberal definition of equality (of outcome) head-on: "We have so many people who can't see a fat man standing beside a thin one without coming to the conclusion that the fat man got that way by taking advantage of the thin one." Reagan also employed Biblical language to underline that modern society was threatened by moral decay and cowardness. When alluding to the communist threat, he panned people wanting "peace at any price" for being prepared to "live on [their] knees [rather] than die on [their] feet." And he continued:

---

198. Ibid.

If nothing in life is worth dying for, when did this begin—
just in the face of this enemy? Or should Moses have told
the children of Israel to live in slavery under the pharaohs?
Should Christ have refused the cross? Should the patriots at
Concord Bridge have thrown down their guns and refused
to fire the shot heard 'round the world'? The martyrs of
history were not fools, and our honored dead who gave their
lives to stop the advance of the Nazis didn't die in vain.
Where, then, is the road to peace?"[199]

Finally, he roused the viewers by borrowing a phrase from FDR: "You and I have a rendezvous with destiny. We will preserve for our children this, the last best hope of man on Earth, or we will sentence them to take the last step into a thousand years of darkness."[200]

Reagan's performance that night made him Goldwater's "ideological heir," and after the election, he took on a leading role in keeping the Conservative Movement going. And after 30+ years of progressive and liberal supremacy, the time was finally ripe. First, in the 1966 midterms, the GOP made significant gains not only as a natural rebound after its 1964 losses but because many candidates ran on Goldwater-inspired platforms. Among these were Reagan himself being elected Governor of California; Spiro Agnew becoming Governor of Maryland; and George Bush a House representative from Texas. Moreover, Eisenhower's former VP Richard Nixon campaigned widely for conservative Republicans and positioned himself as the front-runner for a second presidential run in 1968. Before getting to him, however, any outline of the "new" GOP taking form in the 1960s must be completed by mentioning one more group that would first stiffen, then warp, and finally corrupt the party's conservative soul.

---

199. Ronald Reagan, "Address on Behalf of Senator Barry Goldwater: 'A Time for Choosing'," (October 27, 1964) *APP*, accessed December 3, 2018, https://www.presidency.ucsb.edu/node/276336.
200. Ibid.

From the 1940s, as Stalin's and Mao's crimes began to be exposed, a few extreme left-wingers became so distressed that they reconsidered their ideological beliefs, turned into liberals, and joined the Democratic Party. However, youthful ideals tend to create thought patterns that can survive the most drastic ideological conversions. As some of these substituted class struggle and proletarian doctorship for the notions of Americanism, they began to loathe socialism in general and the Soviet Union with the same fieriness they had earlier despised "bourgeoisie democracy" and capitalism. And after becoming dismayed by the 1960s "counter-culture" and the Democrat's new "soft" foreign policy, they took one more step, joined the GOP, and, still with the zeal of converts, tried to outdo everybody by parking themselves as far to the right as possible. They did so, e.g., by branding themselves "neoconservatives" and picking up a thick right-wing accent, but their basic worldview remained radical.

Four things must be mentioned here. First, even if most "neocons" seem to accept the notion of a flawed human nature, they think that people's longing for freedom overrides other inborn desires for security, family, community, etc. Second, while actual conservatives believe in natural laws and eternal truths but that these can only be partially understood by humans, neocons, like Plato and modern positivists, believe that they can be fully revealed by the superior logic of a select few (read: themselves). Third, while conservatives believe that every society's historical, social, and cultural forms and values are unique and perpetually refined over generations in the form of evolving laws, customs, and mores, neocons mistrust traditions because they adapt and change. Hence, since traditions are not identical to the eternal Truths and Values they seek, they deem them useless and, like Marxists, instead have one complete blueprint in mind for all societies. Fourth, neocons are elitists who prefer clear-cut theories, reason in the abstract, and—in a peculiar fashion for self-proclaimed freedom lovers—believe they can use government to put all things right.

These fundamentally different viewpoints also lead to some key policy differences. Most importantly, neocons believe in an overriding human longing for freedom that makes them blind to historical, cultural, and other obstacles to the democratization of other countries. This view—together with a Trotskyist meme about how the world can be changed swiftly through military means—makes them ready to implement democracy with force. However, this gun-ho passion would not become pronounced until the 1990s. First-generation neocons such as Jeane Kirkpatrick, in the meantime, instead become "ultra-realists" like John Foster Dulles, accepting, e.g., alliances with anti-communist Third World dictators. Moreover, in the domestic arena, while conservatives think constitutionalism, gentlemanliness, and "ordered liberty" are necessary for a sustainable economy, neocons believe in the "magic" of the market, free trade, and tax cuts. When "the godfather of neoconservatism," Irving Kristol, discussed the economy in 1977, for example, he rebuked Keynesianism and instead backed "supply-side fiscal policy." The cardinal idea of this policy is that tax cuts can stimulate the economy enough to cover subsequent deficits. However, in developed economies supporting welfare states, tax cuts must be paired with budget cuts. Kristol, though, ignored this and declared that tax cuts would fix everything, including the welfare state dilemma: "Simply to reduce government expenditures [. . .] creates too many problems. (And a ruthless dismantling of the welfare state is, in any case, unthinkable.)"[201] Hence, neocons tend to be "big government conservatives." Even so, in the late 1960s, this was still in the future, and the dribble of neocons joining the GOP only seemed to strengthen the anti-liberal coalition.

---

201. Irving Kristol, *The Neoconservative Persuasion. Selected Essays, 1942-2009* (New York: Basic Books, 2011), 154.

THE JANUS PRESIDENCY

Richard Nixon entered politics to serve his country and win social veneration, but his byzantine persona contained a mix of virtues and vices. He vacillated between being personally charming and ill-mannered, politically smooth and brutal, ideologically weak and persistent, academically brilliant and anti-intellectual. Sadly, he lacked an antipode to the distrustful streak that would eventually get him into the worst distress ever faced by a sitting U.S. president. Moreover, Nixon was no stranger to playing political hardball, and his rhetorical weapon of choice was anti-communism. During his Senate campaign in 1950, he had been dubbed "Tricky Dick" for depicting his opponent as having the voting record of a communist. But since this also earned him a national reputation, two years later, as Eisenhower's vice-presidential "attack dog," he delivered jabs like Democratic candidate Adlai Stevenson holding a "Ph.D. from Dean Acheson's College of Cowardly Communist Containment."[202] To boot, Nixon was a master of reading voters' moods and could, when deeming it expedient, turn on a dime politically. As in 1971, when he moved from resisting to embracing wage and price controls to combat inflation in two weeks.

Like his personality, Nixon's philosophical principles are elusive, but a few things stand out. First, like LBJ, he saw history as steered by "great men" rather than spiritual forces or material structures. Second, he held a traditional view of Man having a dual nature of good qualities and bad impulses that needed to be cultivated and restrained, respectively. Third, he believed in timeless values as revealed in Christianity and Western culture. Fourth, he saw politics (including the Cold War) as a clash of values that could be won only in the realm of ideas. Fifth, his Quaker upbringing

---

202. Richard Nixon, *Richard Nixon: Speeches, Writings, Documents* (Princeton: Princeton University Press, edited and introduced by Rick Perlstein), xxvii.

made his principal political priority "peace for America and the world."[203] More specifically, Nixon believed peace required a U.S. foreign policy based on a partnership with like-minded countries, military superiority, and a readiness to negotiate with enemies; i.e., a form of nineteenth-century European *Realpolitik*. Yet, his belief in Americanism shines through in his trust in a rapport between peace and freedom: "When the people are free to choose their choice is more likely to be peace among nations; and because man yearns for freedom, when peace is secure the thrust of social evolution is toward greater freedom within nations."[204]

Moreover, even if Nixon saw peace and freedom as dominant human urges, the influence of exceptionalist thinking upon his foreign policy was modest. Because, even if he every so often talked in terms of America's "destiny," his actions were checked by the view that the U.S.'s role in world affairs was given by its size and military strength, not a divine mission. Also, regarding national security, Nixon always used exceptionalist jargon sensibly. In 1950, for example, when as a member of the House, he gave a speech accounting for his role in exposing Alger Hiss a Soviet spy, he talked firmly but not gaudily:

> America today stands alone between communism and the
> free nations of the world. We owe a solemn duty, not only to
> our own people but to free peoples everywhere on both sides
> of the iron curtain, to expose this sinister conspiracy for
> what it is, to roll back the Red tide which to date has swept
> everything before it, and to prove to people everywhere that
> the hope the world lies not in turning toward totalitarian

---

203. Richard Nixon, "Annual Message to the Congress on the State of the Union," (January 22, 1970) *APP*, accessed July 5, 2018, https://www.presidency.ucsb.edu/node/241063.

204. Richard Nixon, "First Annual Report to the Congress on United States Foreign Policy for the 1970's," (February 18, 1970) *APP*, accessed June 29, 2018, https://www.presidency.ucsb.edu/node/240665.

dictatorship but in developing a strong, free, and intelligent democracy.[205]

Nixon's rhetoric also tended to be didactic. For instance, when he as president called the Statue of Liberty a symbol of what America meant to the world, he said: "[It] is not its wealth, and not its power, but its spirit and purpose—a land that enshrines liberty and opportunity, and that has held out a hand of welcome to millions in search of a better and a fuller and, above all, a freer life."[206]

One illustration of Nixon's dual political personality is from October 1967. He was then positioning himself for his second presidential run and published two articles that showcased his talent to move freely between populism and sophistication. The first was a *Readers Digest* piece in which he opined that the U.S., because of rising crime and disorderly Vietnam War and Civil Rights protests, was suffering through an "armed insurrection." He blamed the situation on disdain for traditional values and the elites' dedication to social engineering and behaviorist theories on crime:

> The shocking crime and disorder in American life today
> flow in large measure from two fundamental changes that
> have occurred in the attitudes of many Americans. First,
> there is the permissiveness toward violation of the law and
> public order by those who agree with the cause in ques-
> tion. Second, there is the indulgence of crime because of
> sympathy for the past grievances of those who have become
> criminals."[207]

He then also condemned liberals' lack of response: "Any system that fashions its safeguards for the innocent so broadly and haphazardly that they

205. Nixon, *Richard Nixon*, 59. .

206. Richard Nixon, "Address on the State of the Union Delivered Before a Joint Session of the Congress," (January 20, 1972) *APP*, accessed July 9, 2018, https://www.presidency.ucsb.edu/node/254749.

207. Rick Perlstein (ed.), *Richard Nixon: Speeches, Writings, Documents* (Princeton, NJ: Princeton University Press, 2008), 122.

also provide a haven from punishment for uncounted thousands of the guilty is a failure—an indictment, not an adornment, of a free society."[208]

In *Foreign Affairs*, Nixon's second article addressed a different audience and applied a very different tone. A solid scholarly analysis of East Asia's situation outlined an alternative to the Manichean Cold War view of world affairs. He began by arguing that LBJ's Vietnam policy was bankrupt since East Asia, apart from China and Vietnam, was economically moving in the right direction. And after predicting that "the United States [role] as a world policeman is likely to be limited in the future," he delivered his main point:

> Americans must recognize that [their] highly sophisticated, highly advanced political system, which required many centuries to develop in the West, may not be the best for other nations which have far different traditions and still are in an earlier stage of development. What matters is that these governments are consciously, deliberately and programmatically developing in the direction of greater liberty, greater abundance, broader choice and increased popular involvement in the process of government.[209]

Thus, Nixon asked for a more nuanced approach to democratization and a limit on U.S. involvement overseas. And this was not a hindsight cry produced by LBJ's failed Vietnam policy but a view based upon a lifetime of reflection. He had made similar statements before America entered the Vietnam War, including during his first presidential run in 1960 when he had run as a moderate and Eisenhower's heir. But Americans then had not yet experienced the fuller costs of the country's military might or a federal welfare state and instead voted for JFK's more daring style.

---

208. Ibid, 125.
209. Ibid, 138.

However, in 1968, both Nixon and the electorate had learned many lessons, and he managed to conduct one of America's most well-disciplined presidential campaigns during the apex of the nation's sociocultural upheaval. Adjusting his speaking style and message to the popular mood, he fed voters well-cut pieces of populist and exceptionalist red meat. His RNC Acceptance Speech, for example, became one of his best speeches ever. It is of triple significance. First, it reflects how Americanism had moved to the center of U.S. political discourse. Second, it broke with more than half a century of positivist-technocratic political tradition by addressing complex issues in partly populist language. Third, by doing so, it altered many Republican policies and partly reframed public debates on both foreign and domestic issues for years to come. Moreover, by stepping forward as a tribune for ordinary Americans, he upended the familiar order of U.S. politics:

> [They] give drive to the spirit of America. They give a lift
> to the American Dream. They give steel to the backbone
> of America. They are good people, they are decent people;
> they work, and they save, and they pay their taxes, and they
> care. [. . .] America is a great nation. And America is great
> because her people are great.[210]

Hence, by appealing to "the silent majority," Nixon broke with the old picture of the Democrats being the party of the people. And he made a good case for this being more than just fancy words. Effortlessly, given the ongoing civil unrest, he also challenged present political correctness by declaring that society's first obligation was to punish, not "reform" criminals. He too echoed Martin Luther King Jr.'s "dream" speech by stressing links between race, crime, and urban development in ways Democrats, now being the "black" party, no longer could do:

---

210. Richard Nixon, "Address Accepting the Presidential Nomination at the Republican National Convention in Miami Beach, Florida," (August 8, 1968) *APP*, accessed July 8, 2018, https://www.presidency.ucsb.edu/node/256650.

For too long, white America has sought to buy off the
Negro—and to buy off its own sense of guilt—with ever
more programs of welfare, of public housing, of payments
to the poor, but not for anything except for keeping out
of sight: payments that perpetuated poverty, and that kept
the endless, dismal cycle of dependency spinning from
generation to generation. Our task—our challenge—is to
break this cycle of dependency, and the time to begin is
now. The way to do it is not with more of the same, but by
helping bring to the ghetto the light of hope and pride and
self-respect.[211]

With this, Nixon finalized the GOP's takeover as the country's populist
party. At the same time, his populism always remained moderate, calcu-
lated, and deep in the meaning of focusing on real problems and based
upon serious thought. For example, he ended one speech on legal issues
by saying that it was necessary to return to the country's communitarian
roots:

If violence is met with indifference or appeasement, if the
individual is no longer responsible for his actions, if a fog of
permissiveness blurs our moral vision, if there has been an
erosion of respect and decency, if there is too little concern
about the social causes of disorder—then fundamental
sources of order bear some of the responsibility. And so, I
say—In every family let us renew our commitment to the
traditional American standards.[212]

Such language was at one go sufficient to stand out from the time's PC
murmur and mild enough to avoid, contrary to Goldwater four years earlier, being accused of right-wing extremism. In fact, many would probably

211. Richard Nixon, "Remarks on the CBS Radio Network: "Bridges to Human Dignity, The Concept,' "
(April 25, 1968) *APP*, accessed October 13, 2018, https://www.presidency.ucsb.edu/node/326763.
212. Richard Nixon, "Remarks on the Mutual Broadcasting System: 'Order and Justice Under Law,' "
(September 29, 1968) *APP*, accessed October 13, 2018, https://www.presidency.ucsb.edu/node/326774.

have welcomed harsher language because, outside the stadium of politics, things in 1968 were so rough that when the Chicago police beat violent protesters outside the International Amphitheater (where that year's DNC took place) bloody, most people applauded.

However, Nixon needed a more "serious" image and vision for his presidency than simply talking tough on crime and criticizing hippies. He, therefore, delivered more highbrow orations also. Like in October, when he gave a speech on the theme "The American Spirit" at William and Mary University in Williamsburg, Virginia. Standing in the Great Hall, where George Washington and Thomas Jefferson had taken meals as students, he talked about his favorite theme of freedom's role in domestic and international peace:

> When we recall the days of our Revolution, we think of the
> phrase "the spirit of '76." That is not just a slogan; there was
> a real "spirit of '76." That spirit was the driving force within
> most Americans of that revolutionary era. I believe that a
> nation, like a person, has a spirit. I believe that a national
> spirit comes to the fore in times of national crisis. I believe
> that each time a national spirit makes itself felt, it speaks
> to its own time with a different message directed to the
> problems of that time. That is why a searching look at the
> American spirit is needed today.[213]

Next, he also listed events such as the Civil War when this spirit had stirred the nation and declared the present a similar moment, remarking that the "underlying reason for the feeling of emptiness in so many hearts today" was a loss of personal freedom. However, Nixon also declared the days for principled opposition to welfare to be over and said that he only wanted to mend what liberals had wrecked: "We are going to change our

213. Richard Nixon, "Remarks in Williamsburg, Virginia: 'The American Spirit,' " (October 2, 1968) *APP*, accessed October 7, 2018, https://www.presidency.ucsb.edu/node/326737.

welfare system to make it fit the American system, to provide each person with a means of escape from welfare into dignity. This is not an impossible dream."[214]

This mixed image of populism and seriousness worked, and as President, Nixon would try to deliver. He started by proposing to replace the whole New Deal-Great Society apparatus with a minimum income system, not sparing his words about the present system by calling it "a colossal failure," "a welfare quagmire," "a monster," "morally wrong," and said that "if we take the route of the permanent handout, the American character will itself be impoverished."[215] Moreover, underlying this Titanic plan was *New Federalism*; a model for transferring, since the 1930s, federalized issues back to the state and local levels and—by doing so—"shifting money and support from the northeastern elites to the nation's heartland."[216] And even if it was primarily a way to defederalize welfare policies, Nixon tried to use it in policy areas like cultural appropriations, where the goal became to shift endowments from modern to popular art forms. So, even if Nixon failed to overhaul the federal government, his ambition had a significant impact by creating partly new political discourses and furthering conservative views.

However, by doing so, New Federalism also produced one distressing effect. By showing that reducing the size of the federal level was not an ideological pipe dream but a viable alternative, many Americans became born-again believers in lower taxes, less bureaucracy, and more freedom at the same time as they became forced to base their retirement on Social Security, cherished national endeavors like the Space Program, etc. In addition, tens of millions had become dependent on food stamps;

214. Ibid.
215. Richard Nixon, "Address to the Nation on Domestic Programs," (August 8, 1969) *APP*, accessed June 29, 2018, https://www.presidency.ucsb.edu/node/239998.
216. Schulman, *Seventies*, 32ff.

three million worked directly for the federal government, many more for state and local political bodies, and uncountable others for private military and other companies dependent upon federal orders and subsidies. Thus, Democrats and the New Class could quickly put a halt not only to Nixon's plan for the welfare system but to all kinds of changes. In fact, the "consensus" remained so strong that spending within existing welfare systems under him increased by $80 billion. Thus, just as Eisenhower had consolidated the New Deal, Nixon made the Great Society permanent.

Nevertheless, the nation passed a breaking point, and the 1972 presidential campaign already reflected rapidly deepening ideological differences. Running on a more conservative platform than four years earlier, Nixon branded his opponent a "New Class candidate" who wanted amnesty for draft dodgers, legalized abortions, and Senator Fulbright's foreign policy. Also, in his RNC Acceptance Speech, Nixon again reached out to all citizens to join him to form "a new American majority [. . .] not on the basis of the party label you wear in your lapel, but on the basis of what you believe in your hearts." He also turned on what he saw as detractors of the U.S.:

> It has become fashionable in recent years to point up what is wrong with what is called the American system. The critics contend it is so unfair, so corrupt, so unjust, that we should tear it down and substitute something else in its place. I totally disagree. I believe in the American system. I have traveled to 80 countries in the past 25 years, and I have seen Communist systems, I have seen Socialist systems, I have seen systems that are half Socialist and half free. Every time I come home to America, I realize how fortunate we are to live in this great and good country.[217]

217. Richard Nixon, "Remarks on Accepting the Presidential Nomination of the Republican National Convention," (August 23, 1972) *APP*, accessed August 8, 2018, https://www.presidency.ucsb.edu/node/254755.

On his side, Democrat candidate George McGovern took the opposite route. In his DNC Acceptance Speech, he also tried to sound populist, e.g., by describing his primary win as "the people's nomination." However, he spent most of the time pledging new, free stuff. He said that to bring on "a new period of important and hopeful change in America,"[218] new welfare programs, including national health insurance, were needed. He also talked about ending a "system of economic controls in which labor is depressed but prices and corporate profit run sky-high."[219]

For this, the voters rejected McGovern in a landslide for Nixon. However, they also told the latter to hold back his horses by sending huge Democratic majorities, hell-bent on continuing the progressive-liberal project, back to Congress. Hence, in the clearest choice between left and right, radicalism and conservatism, since 1932, voters pulled both levers. Therefore, to partisanship, ideological polarization, religious tensions, and the Cultural Wars was added divided government. This truly turned "D.C." into a political swamp. Because to maneuver in this environment, both politicians and bureaucrats in that city were now doomed to engage deliberately in doublespeak. The cynic may say this was nothing new, but voters' active demand for liberal goods and conservative ends now added difficulty to hardship. Specifically, while Democrats were forced to ensure that new reforms could be carried out without raising taxes, Republicans had to guarantee that lower taxes and high defense spending did not threaten existing welfare systems.

Another example of modern doublespeak in Washington, D.C., is environmental policy. In the 1960s, pollution and other problems had become critical subjects. This was partly because some issues did demand

---

218. George McGovern, "Address Accepting the Presidential Nomination at the Democratic National Convention in Miami Beach, Florida," (July 14, 1972) *APP*, accessed August 8, 2018, https://www. presidency.ucsb.edu/node/216662.
219. Ibid.

attention, partly because some touched upon emotional themes central to national mythology such as fertile soil, grand rivers, virgin woods, and flourishing wildlife; including the possible extinction of the bald eagle. Sensing the opportunity, LBJ had therefore turned the environment into a full-fledged federal policy arena dominated by bureaucrats transfixed by government action. Thus, Nixon now had to try to walk the walk by balancing ecological concerns with economic needs while talking the talk. However, his typically American, optimistic tone rather than dystopian prophecies about modern society's "unnatural" ways were botched. Even significant victories, like the creation of the Environmental Protection Agency (EPA), were depicted as too small and too late. And forevermore extreme environmental demands—tapping into Americans' fondness for perfectionist talk and confidence in technocratic methods—have remained the norm.

Moreover, the only way to resolve (read: pay for) these new requirements was through permanent deficit spending. Case in point, 1968 became the last year the federal budget was balanced (except for a few years during the dot-com bubble in the late 1990s). As these costs were thrown on top of the already crippling economic and regular expenses of the Great Society and the Vietnam War, the U.S. economy soon entered not a traditional economic slump but a prolonged period of low growth, high unemployment, and runaway inflation, or "stagflation." And since the root cause of this mess was not economic but partisan, both left and right chose to spend more time blaming each other (and frequently promising even higher federal expenditures) than solving the problem. After his reelection, Nixon thus decided to abandon his role as a conservative discourse shaper and stay within the economic paradigm by saying things like, "We are all Keynesians now."[220]

---

220. Richard Nixon, "Annual Message to the Congress on the State of the Union," (January 22, 1971) *APP*, accessed July 10, 2018, https://www.presidency.ucsb.edu/node/240562.

Two more comments about Nixon's presidency should be made. First, since he, like LBJ, was convinced that a one-sided U.S. withdrawal from Vietnam would be used against him as being soft on communism, he continued the war. For years, he made his main argument for it to achieve "peace with honor" and said things like, "a nation cannot remain great if it betrays its allies and lets down its friends."[221] However, talking about national honor didn't arouse Americans anymore, or at least not so regarding such a clearly lost cause. Second, Nixon never seems to have used Americanism and exceptionalist arguments to defend himself during the Watergate scandal. The nearest was when he said it was "the [American] system that has brought the facts to light and that will bring those guilty to justice."[222] His adversaries, though, quite frequently used such language. A Democratic House Representative remarked: "Some say this is a sad day in America's history. I think it could perhaps be one of our brightest days. It could be really a test of the strength of our Constitution, because what I think it means to most Americans is that when this or any other president violates his sacred oath of office, the people are not left helpless."[223] Also, after Nixon's resignation, his successor used patriotism and exceptionalist language in his attempts to heal the nation.

"A FORD, NOT A LINCOLN"

Republican Michigan House representative Gerald R. Ford was a down-to-earth and soft-spoken former football player, lawyer, and "Middle American at ease with himself and the enduring values of our Constitution."[224] As mentioned earlier, he had also been an American

221. Richard Nixon, "Address to the Nation on the War in Vietnam," (November 3, 1969), *APP*, accessed June 29, 2018, https://www.presidency.ucsb.edu/node/240027.
222. Richard Nixon, "Address to the Nation About the Watergate Investigations," (April 30, 1973) *APP*, accessed July 16, 2018, https://www.presidency.ucsb.edu/node/255385.
223. Joan E. Greve, "What Richard Nixon's Impeachment Looked Like" (August 5, 2014) *Time Magazine*, accessed July 26, 2018, http://time.com/3063704/nixon-impeachment/.
224. Douglas Brinkley, *Gerald R. Ford* (New York: Times Books, 2007), 1.

Firster before World War II but became an internationalist "modern Republican" and an "Eisenhower conservative" in the 1950s. That is, he was exactly what the country needed after the twin trauma of Vietnam and Watergate and was elected to replace Nixon's Vice President Spiro Agnew after he was forced to resign in 1973. Moreover, ideologically nearly a Nixon clone, Ford would continue his predecessor's policies at home and abroad. However, as a more amiable person, more religious, and a more emotional believer in Americanism than Nixon, he would manage to reconcile the country by, e.g., reminding Americans that they still, despite war, scandal, and economically challenging times, had much in common and to be proud of.

After assuming office on August 9, 1974, Ford began his Inaugural Address by referencing U.S. history to legitimize his "accidental" presidency: "The oath that I have taken is the same oath that was taken by George Washington and by every President under the Constitution." He also said that America had survived Watergate thanks to a combination of earthly strength and divine grace: "My fellow Americans, our long national nightmare is over. Our Constitution works; our great Republic is a government of laws and not of men. Here the people rule. But there is a higher Power, by whatever name we honor Him, who ordains not only righteousness but love, not only justice but mercy."[225] A month later, Ford too turned to both the Constitution and God when he decided to spare the nation a potential nightmarish Nixon criminal trial by pardoning him:

> I have promised to uphold the Constitution, to do what is
> right as God gives me to see the right, and to do the very
> best that I can for America. I have asked your help and your
> prayers, not only when I became president but many times
> since. The Constitution is the supreme law of our land and

---

225. Gerald R. Ford: "Remarks on Taking the Oath of Office," (August 9, 1974) *APP*, accessed July 18, 2018), https://www.presidency.ucsb.edu/node/255838.

it governs our actions as citizens. Only the laws of God, which govern our consciences, are superior to it. As we are a nation under God, so I am sworn to uphold our laws with the help of God.[226]

Such intensive religious-exceptionalist language had probably not been heard from a U.S. president since the 1800s, at least during peacetime. Still, serious damage had been done.

One example is from the following October, when Ford attempted to launch a Whip Inflation Now (WIN) campaign. It failed miserably. Only a few years earlier, when Nixon had asked people to conserve energy, over 90 percent of the country's gas stations had voluntarily stopped selling gas on weekends. Now, Ford's drive became a theme of sarcasm, with some wearing WIN buttons upside down saying that NIM meant "No Immediate Miracles." Clearly, this was at least partly dependent upon people's trust in the presidency being damaged by Watergate. But it is important to note that American's long-term turn toward atomistic individualism had by now also begun to affect politics. Specifically, communitarian views had been declining since the late 1800s. And even if this development had been temporarily reversed by the world wars, the Great Depression, and the Cold War, it had increased again in the 1960s and now formally exploded during "The Great Rebellion" of the 1970s. This meant that millions lived out bohemian fantasies and joined in on secular, hedonist requests for a society where people could do whatever they wanted, including ignoring distressing government edicts. Notes one scholar: "Somewhere after World War II it seemed the nation had lost its capacity for self-sacrifice in the broader interest, no matter how worthy and smart the cause—and effects—might be."[227]

226. Gerald R. Ford, "Remarks on Signing a Proclamation Granting Pardon to Richard Nixon," (September 8, 1974) *APP*, accessed July 19, 2018, https://www.presidency.ucsb.edu/node/256490.
227. Brinkley, *Gerald R. Ford*, 77.

Nevertheless, despite taking a blow in the polls for his pardon of Nixon and the WIN failure, Ford managed to rebuild trust in himself and the office over time, and his presidency became successful. One specific reason for this was his belief in the power of words. For example, when Ford in 1975, despite many fearing that the so-called Helsinki Accords sanctification of post-World War II borders would cement the Soviet's grip over Eastern Europe, he signed it anyway and said: "When two centuries ago the United States of America issued a declaration of high principles, the cynics and doubters of that day jeered and scoffed. Yet eleven long years later, our independence was won and the stability of our Republic was really achieved through the incorporation of the same principles in our Constitution."[228] And his optimism was proper. As the Accords' subsequent language on human rights became a rallying point for dissidents in communist countries, the Soviet system finally became measured according to Western standards—and propaganda about it as a form of democracy and "human alternative" to capitalism exposed as the clean lies they were.

Another example of how Ford successfully used language and Americanism is the 1976 Bicentennial Celebration of the American Revolution. He declared he wanted to use the event to "make America once again and for centuries more to come what it has so long been—a stronghold and a beacon-light of liberty for the whole world."[229] And on July 4, at Valley Forge, Pennsylvania, where George Washington's army had endured the most testing circumstances during the Revolutionary War, Ford hailed the founding principles of the country and declared that the Pioneers' experiences were still essential to the body politic of America:

228. Gerald R. Ford, "Address in Helsinki Before the Conference on Security and Cooperation in Europe," (August 1, 1975) *APP*, accessed July 27, 2018, https://www.presidency.ucsb.edu/node/256556.

229. Gerald R. Ford, "Address Before a Joint Session of the Congress Reporting on the State of the Union," (January 15, 1975) *APP*, accessed December 20, 2019, https://www.presidency.ucsb.edu/node/256753.

The American pioneers knew that in their wilderness homes they could not be colonials ruled by a distant government. They had assurance that in due course they could govern themselves as full citizens of equal States. This political guarantee made all the risks and all the sacrifices worthwhile. Their children and future generations would have all the rights of Washington, Jackson, and Lincoln. So do we, and more so.[230]

Overall, the Bicentennial allowed for a much-needed patriotic extravaganza in the form of, e.g., parades, fireworks, and even a new *Freedom Train*; this time carrying items ranging from George Washington's draft of the Constitution to Moon rocks.

Moreover, since 1976 was an election year, Ford also used it to forward his own agenda. In that year's State of the Union, he used exceptionalist language and sounded the tone of the Conservative Movement: "We thought we could transform the country through massive national programs, but often, the programs did not work. Too often they only made things worse. In our rush to accomplish great deeds quickly, we trampled on sound principles of restraint and endangered the rights of individuals."[231] This speech helped set a new standard for Republican critique of Democrats as earlier detailed-oriented criticisms were increasingly succeeded by jeremiads blaming the U.S.'s problems not only on the effects but also on the ambitions of liberal policies. And because Ford and Republicans now aggressively demanded both more personal freedom and limited government, Ford came close to winning four full years in the White House. According to one estimate, a switch of 3,687 votes in Hawaii and 5,559 in Ohio would have been enough. But, a Democrat,

230. Gerald R. Ford, "Remarks in Valley Forge, Pennsylvania," (July 4, 1976) *APP*, accessed July 31, 2018, https://www.presidency.ucsb.edu/node/257824.

231. Gerald R. Ford, "Address Before a Joint Session of the Congress Reporting on the State of the Union," (January 19, 1976) *APP*, accessed July 29, 2018, https://www.presidency.ucsb.edu/node/257493.

removed from his party's radical wing enough to still articulate conservative sentiments, beat him at the finish line.

THE CARTER ADMINISTRATION

That Jimmy Carter won the Democratic Party's nomination in 1976 mainly depended on the nation's need for an "anti-Nixon" who could tell Americans that he—like George Washington in the Cherry Tree Tale— would never tell them a lie. He also turned out to be a sincere politician who often did not hesitate to tell harsh truths, even to his disadvantage. But most importantly, stemming from a traditional Southern family and being a fiscal conservative and a born-again Christian, he was still deemed electable by Southerners. And this was enough to give him a small victory. However, whether he was a liberal or a conservative, Carter said, "I'm a more complicated person than that."[232] Like Wilson, he was also overly confident in his intellectual abilities, and as an engineer, like Hoover, a technocrat viewing the world through theoretical filters more than political lenses. This qualified his Americanism, which seems unreserved only when it comes to the nation's origin:

> America's birth opened a new chapter in mankind's history.
> Ours was the first nation to dedicate itself clearly to basic
> moral and philosophical principles: that all people are
> created equal and endowed with inalienable rights to life,
> liberty, and the pursuit of happiness, and that the power of
> government is derived from the consent of the governed.
> This national commitment was a singular act of wisdom and
> courage, and it brought the best and the bravest from other
> nations to our shores. It was a revolutionary development
> that captured the imagination of mankind.[233]

232. Julian E. Zelizer, *Jimmy Carter* (New York: Times Books, 2019), 19.
233. Carter, "Our Nation's Past and Future," (July 15, 1976).

Beyond this, Carter seldom spoke in exceptionalist terms about America without qualifying caveats like "we cannot dwell upon remembered glory."[234]

Carter's mechanical mindset also profoundly affected his policies. To start with foreign policy, he said he wanted to restore its "moral compass" by basing it upon America's founding principles and on a "firm commitment to human rights."[235] Or, more precisely, the country's origin made it "a pioneer in shaping more decent and just relations among people and among societies." He, therefore, wanted to promote democracy abroad without military interventions and believed in "a sustained architectural effort to shape an international framework of peace within which our own ideals gradually can become a global reality."[236] Thus, Carter sought Wilson's and FDR's visions of the world to come true through JFK's "soft" policies. And even if this was a naïve desire, it was a timely one since human rights by the end of the 1970s had not only gained a central role in world politics through institutions like the U.N. and treaties such as the Helsinki Accords. Compliance and appeasement toward the Soviets were now also in demand on an influential spectrum stretching from Democrats to media to "peace activists" filling the streets. But despite this promising starting point, Carter would score only two successes: the Panama Canal Treaty and the Camp David Agreement, which had nothing to do with human rights.

The reasons for this failure were many. One is that the Soviet Union saw the "Western form" of human rights as part of a plot to subvert its empire, so it blatantly ignored them. A big problem was also that Carter

234. "Jimmy Carter, Inaugural Address," (January 20, 1977) *APP*, accessed November 2, 2018, https://www.presidency.ucsb.edu/node/241475
235. Jimmy Carter, "The State of the Union Address," (January 19, 1978) APP, accessed August 19, 2018, http://www.presidency.ucsb.edu/node/245063.
236. Ibid.

hampered himself by trying to promote human rights *and* following his pragmatic instincts. Examples abound. To support Iran, he censured his critique of the Shah's human rights record, only to see this policy contributing to the Islamic Revolution in 1979. While he to secure *détente* with the Soviets muted criticism of "internal affairs" in communist countries, he fiercely criticized such crimes in U.S.-friendly countries like Chile and South Africa. And like Wilson, he arrogantly declared the U.S. the world's natural umpire of human rights: "We do not seek to intimidate, but it is clear that a world which others can dominate with impunity would be inhospitable to decency and a threat to the well-being of all people."[237] In addition, Carter's foreign policy had two huge domestic effects. First, his human rights focus completed the Democratic Party's turning from "hawkish" Cold War liberalism toward a "dovish" foreign policy, making it a virtually clear-cut left-right policy field. Second, his foreign policy failures and the hostage crisis following the Iranian revolution specifically convinced millions, including many Democrats, that softness in dealing with thugs did not work.

Yet, it was not foreign policy that eventually caused the bottom to fall out of Carter's presidency. It was his handling of domestic affairs and, most of all, his attempt to take some of Americans most holy cows to slaughter. As noted, since the early 1970s, the burdens of the Great Society, the Vietnam War, and skyrocketing energy costs had led to stagflation. This continued to be a haunting phenomenon throughout the decade, and since high unemployment and high inflation—according to Keynesian dogma—could not co-occur, in July 1979, Carter, the technocrat, decided to retreat to Camp David with a group of experts to analyze why Reality so stubbornly refused to align with the Map. After a ten-day conclave, Carter, the president, then appeared on TV delivering a *malaise*

---

237. Jimmy Carter, "Inaugural Address," (January 20, 1977).

speech laying out a case for why America, this time, seemed unable to lift itself by the bootstraps.

The impact of this speech can only be fully appreciated in the context of Americans for over two hundred years being told that their country is exceptional. In short, this belief had only a few years earlier literally taken Americans to the Moon and back again, but Carter now told them that the U.S. suffered from "a crisis that strikes at the very heart and soul and spirit of our national will" and that the cause was not economic but spiritual:

> In a nation that was proud of hard work, strong families, close-knit communities, and our faith in God, too many of us now tend to worship self-indulgence and consumption. Human identity is no longer defined by what one does, but by what one owns. But we've discovered that owning things and consuming things does not satisfy our longing for meaning. We've learned that piling up material goods cannot fill the emptiness of lives which have no confidence or purpose.[238]

Also, Carter said that this threatened not only Americans' well-being but the country's mission: "We always believed that we were part of a great movement of humanity itself called democracy, involved in the search for freedom, and that belief has always strengthened us in our purpose. But just as we are losing our confidence in the future, we are also beginning to close the door on our past."[239]

Hence, Carter's speech snubbed Americans' self-image on all levels—individually, communally, nationally, and internationally. Still, since his analysis sounded ideologically conservative and implied that the lib-

---

238. Jimmy Carter, "Address to the Nation on Energy and National Goals: The Malaise Speech," (July 15, 1979) *APP*, accessed August 30, 2018, https://www.presidency.ucsb.edu/node/249458.
239. Ibid.

eral project to remake the U.S. had failed, it, at first, was well received. However, questioning Americans' view of personal freedom as the liberty to pursue individual success and blaming them collectively for the nation's despair was not popular. So was not telling the people that they, by turning into egotists, had tattered the republican ethos and wrecked the balance between material whips and spiritual carrots so prudently comprised by the Founding Fathers. And by questioning if the nation was still "the best country in the world," Carter had defied the very essence of Americanism. A powerful backlash accordingly began after two days when he asked his whole Cabinet to resign, which naturally brought back the feeling of disarray and caused many to lose whatever confidence they had left in the president's ability to lead the nation. All in all, the lasting result of Carter's *malaise* speech became a permanent downturn in his poll numbers and a matching decline in Americans' already record-low trust in politicians.

> *"Freedom leads to prosperity. Freedom replaces the ancient hatreds among the nations with comity and peace. Freedom is the victor."*
>
> Ronald Reagan | 1987

CHAPTER 7 |
An Exceptionalist Presidency

The 1980s became marked by ideas, moods, and developments opposite those of the two previous decades. While good economic times removed the gloom and doom of the 1970s and created an optimism rivaling the 1920s, new goods and habits like fax machines, cell phones, and "eating out" made business easier and transformed private life. Lower taxes and deregulations made it possible for millions to seek fortunes as entrepreneurs and invest in real estate and the stock market. And novelties like cable TV, the VCR, and video games detached people from old, collective media such as cinema, radio, and the "big three" television networks, turning Americans into more fearless individualists. Thus, the decade offered a culturally broad but—as we will see—politically thin reaction against the post-war era's collectivist policies. Moreover, the flickering globalization of news and pop culture brought on by CNN and MTV merely foretold the looming information explosion of the 1990s. Indeed, the influx of foreign goods and ideas was still so limited that "the '80s" became the last decade when most Americans still belonged to one mainstream culture. Still, mass immigration from Latin America did begin to challenge the nation's traditional

WASP culture at the same time as crime, drugs, and AIDS plagued the country's big cities, and deindustrialization created a Rustbelt stretching from Boston to Chicago. Clearsighted observers could thus predict that, even if most acute problems went away, America would never be the same. Still, by voting for the most conservative president since Calvin Coolidge, Americans at least tried to say, "Not so fast."

AN AMERICAN LIFE

Author, journalist, and Nixon speechwriter William Safire once called Ronald Reagan a life-size Norman Rockwell painting. And there is plenty of truth to this statement. After growing up in a low-income Midwestern home with an alcoholic father drifting between towns looking for jobs, for him to make consecutive and successful careers as a radio sports commentator, movie star, TV host, and governor before becoming one of America's most influential presidents ever is a truly remarkable—and quintessentially American—story. Next to George Washington, Abraham Lincoln, and Franklin D. Roosevelt, he is also one of the most studied U.S. presidents. Moreover, friends and foes alike today agree that his background, personality, and careers, plus his unshakable belief in Americanism, are inseparable from his ideological beliefs and political skills to a much higher degree than most other presidents. Three parts of his life story stand out.

First, the Reagan family's struggles during the Great Depression made young Ronald a "Roosevelt liberal." However, his upbringing in small, socially and culturally tight-knit towns frontloaded his mind with traditionalist views and values that—together with his encounter with communists in Hollywood and the insight that he as an actor was "living in a tinsel factory"—put him on track to become a conservative. Also, as Reagan in the 1940s began to view his rise from rags to riches as proof of the U.S. model's supremacy, he concluded that making the New Deal permanent was as grave a threat to freedom at home as communism was abroad. Thus, Reagan's reaction to LBJ's Great Society became harsh and his political transformation mirrors the distancing of modern liberalism from Americanism. After finally formally changing parties in 1962, he would forever insist that "I didn't leave the Democratic Party, the Democratic Party left me."

A second key to Reagan is his religiosity. Raised in the Disciples of Christ church (whose founder, among other things, had already talked about America as a world savior in the 1830s), he became a steadfast believer in a generic form of Christianity. And amongst the memes inserted in his childhood mind was one about Godless communism being an evil system. Like Dwight Eisenhower, John Foster Dulles, and many others, Reagan thus came to view the post-WWII world as a drama wherein America was God's agent, Russia the Devil's, and the Cold War a holy war between them. In 1957, he defined it as a struggle "between those who believe in the sanctity of individual freedom and those who believe in the supremacy of the state."[240] What's more, Reagan's Christianity blended with his exceptionalist beliefs so completely that he, in due course, became convinced that God had fated him to save the American spirit and help the West "transcend communism."

The third aspect is Reagan's radio, movie, and TV experiences. They trained him to talk smoothly in a mix of highbrow prose and a down-to-earth vernacular and to drive home his talking points with humor and edifying stories. Together with a for many modern discourses' atypical inductive style of reasoning, this led some to think that he was an "amiable dunce" who assumed things without processing them rationally. However, even if Reagan was not a political philosopher, he was a deeply reflective per-

---

240. Ronald Reagan, "Remarks at a Spirit of America Festival in Decatur, Alabama," (July 4, 1984) *APP*, accessed April 12, 2019, https://www.presidency.ucsb.edu/node/261171.

son who was well-read in many historical, theological, and other subjects. Moreover, as an actor, a promoter for War Bonds during World War II, and a PR envoy for General Electric in the 1950s, he became a first-rate stump speaker and debater. For example, in 1984, he would wave off whether he was too old to seek a second term with an ill-concealed smile and the comment: "I will not make age an issue of this campaign. I am not going to exploit, for political purposes, my opponent's youth and inexperience."[241]

Moving on to Reagan's worldview, realizing that his imagination included several dissonant—or at least intricate—parts is crucial. Mentioning five will have to suffice. One, as a Christian, he accepted human nature's "ethical duality" but presumed its virtuous side (especially a longing for freedom) to be dominant. Two, because he saw freedom as God's gift to man, anything restricting it was dubious, and democracy was "just a political reading of the Bible."[242] Three, on the following question, if God, History, or something else directs man's pace toward the future, Reagan talked endlessly about "America's destiny" but sounded different when reasoning about the underlying dynamic: "History is no captive of some inevitable force. History is made by men and women of vision and courage."[243] Four, he thought that people everywhere were the same and that freedom leads to peace. In fact, his whole worldview largely hinged on these two assumptions. In 1982, he told the British Parliament, "It would be cultural condescension, or worse, to say that any people prefer dictatorship to democracy."[244] Fifth, Reagan had a futuristic mindset that

241. Ronald Reagan, "Debate Between the President and Former Vice President Walter F. Mondale in Kansas City, Missouri," October 21, 1984) *APP*, accessed November 17, 2018, https://www.presidency.ucsb.edu/documents/debate-between-the-president-and-former-vice-president-walter-f-mondale-kansas-city.

242. Ronald Reagan, "Remarks at a Spirit of America Festival in Decatur, Alabama," (July 4, 1984) *APP*, accessed December 14, 2018, https://www.presidency.ucsb.edu/node/261171.

243. Ronald Reagan, "Address Before a Joint Session of Congress on the State of the Union," (February 4, 1986) *APP*, accessed April 18, 2019, https://www.presidency.ucsb.edu/node/254269.

244. Ronald Reagan, "Address to Members of the British Parliament," (June 8, 1982) *APP*, accessed November 29, 2018, https://www.presidency.ucsb.edu/documents/address-members-the-british-parliament.

made him a jarring optimist: "There are no constraints on the human mind, no walls around the human spirit, no barriers to our progress except those we ourselves erect."[245] Specifically, he viewed technical, medical, and other advances as highways to a near-utopian future where people would live longer, better, and freer lives both on Earth and in Space (which was also one of his favorite topics).

Combined, Reagan's views and the tendency for daydreaming they created make it possible to question his status as a true conservative, for which, above all, moderation and realism are key. One analyst has instead called him "a rightwing liberal, indeed a progressive."[246] Indeed, his positions of man and the world's political functioning come close to the "mature" form of neoconservatism that would flourish in the 1990s and beyond. However, even if Reagan's views of human nature, the primacy of freedom, and progress must be deemed radical in nature, they don't seem to have been so in origin. Explicitly, his optimism stemmed more from the Reformation's idea about humans' ability to achieve earthly progress through hard work than the Enlightenment's ideal of man as a freedom-seeking *Homo libertas*. Also, two more things should be noted. First, the optimism of Reagan, as well as FDR, JFK, and many others, can be deemed more of a side quality of Americanism than an intellectual weakness. Two, even if Reagan often allowed himself to be carried away by his own rhetoric, he rarely let his political decisions be decided by wishful thinking.

A swift outline of Reagan's early political career reveals this last point. After studying the dynamics leading up to LBJ's 1964 landslide, he moderated the fervor marking his Goldwater speech but continued to give ideological speeches filled with optimism. In other words, he chose mod-

245. Ronald Reagan, "Address Before a Joint Session of the Congress on the State of the Union," (February 6, 1985) *APP*, accessed January 25, 2019, https://www.presidency.ucsb.edu/node/258923.
246. Genovese, *Southern Tradition*, 82.

eration over zealotry without giving in to "consensus" and political correctness. And in the late 1970s, this style became unbeatable. In a word, Reagan could transcend the feeling of *malaise* both by style and by policies that would get "government off our backs, out of our pockets, and back to the standards of excellence once envisioned by the Founding Fathers."[247] Also, since his political imagination was as vivid as his belief in America was strong, his use of exceptionalist themes continued to go further and be classier than anyone's, including JFK's. When announcing his candidacy in November 1979, he said: "To me our country is a living, breathing presence, unimpressed by what others say is impossible, proud of its own success, generous, yes and naive, sometimes wrong, never mean, and always impatient to provide a better life for its people in a framework of a basic fairness and freedom."[248] In addition, Reagan was running at a time when liberal policies were failing on nearly all fronts and the Democrats had a lackluster mouthpiece in Jimmy Carter. So, if pundits had been writing horoscopes, they would have concluded that in front of the 1980 election, all planets lined up favorably for Reagan while Carter's Mercury was in retrograde.

Nevertheless, after winning the primaries, many expected Reagan to scale back his rhetoric and go for independents in the middle. Instead, he made his RNC Acceptance Speech decisively conservative and filled it with so much patriotic language that he effectually turned the election into a referendum on America's past *and* future. After blaming Carter and the Democrats for the "unprecedented calamity which has befallen us," he said:

---

247. Ronald Reagan, "Remarks at a Montana Republican Party Rally in Great Falls," (October 28, 1982) *APP*, accessed December 7, 2018, https://www.presidency.ucsb.edu/node/245075.

248. Ronald Reagan, "Remarks Announcing Candidacy for the Republican Presidential Nomination," (November 13, 1979) *APP*, accessed April 10, 2019, https://www.presidency.ucsb.edu/node/255827.

They say that the United States has had its day in the sun;
that our nation has passed its zenith. They expect you to
tell your children that the American people no longer have
the will to cope with their problems; that the future will be
one of sacrifice and few opportunities. My fellow citizens,
I utterly reject that view. The American people, the most
generous on earth, who created the highest standard of
living, are not going to accept the notion that we can only
make a better world for others by moving backwards ourselves. Those who believe we can have no business leading
the nation.[249]

Reagan then turned to history to show that Americans had handled earlier
challenges by standing firm in the country's original values. Toward the
end, he also promised to restore the Founders' economic system that "for
more than two hundred years helped us master a continent, create a previously undreamed-of prosperity for our people," and invited Americans
"who have abandoned hope" to join him in a "great national crusade to
make America great again!"[250]

During the fall, Reagan continued to "speak American" by expressing belief in Americanism and policies derived from its specific notions;
primarily tax cuts and deregulations. He also never stopped hammering
Carter for mishandling the economy and foreign policy. Additionally, as
a former actor, Reagan excelled in picking the right settings and attuning
his message to given surroundings. Such as holding a Labor Day rally in
Liberty Park on the Jersey side of New York with the Statue of Liberty as
a backdrop. There he mused:

---

249. Ronald Reagan, "Address Accepting the Presidential Nomination at the Republican National
Convention in Detroit," (July 17, 1980) *APP*, accessed February 7, 2019, https://www.presidency.ucsb.edu/
node/251302.
250. Ibid.

> Through this "Golden Door," under the gaze of that
> "Mother of Exiles," have come millions of men and women,
> who first stepped foot on American soil right there, on Ellis
> Island, so close to the Statue of Liberty. These families came
> here to work. They came to build. Others came to America
> in different ways, from other lands, under different, often
> harrowing conditions, but this place symbolizes what they
> all managed to build, no matter where they came from or
> how they came or how much they suffered.[251]

Reagan had, at this point, led Carter by a wide margin in most opinion polls since May. However, after the conventions, his lead shrunk and between late August and late October stayed roughly around 5 percent. But, after beating Carter in a debate on October 28 by simply asking voters, "Are you better off than you were four years ago?" he pulled ahead again.

In his Election Eve Address, Reagan made his final argument: "Americans today, just as they did two hundred years ago, feel burdened, stifled and sometimes even oppressed by government that has grown too large, too bureaucratic, too wasteful, too unresponsive, too uncaring about people and their problems." He also used two of his rhetorical specialties. First, as he had done for over a decade, he applied the "city on a hill" metaphor for America and its God-given mission:

> I know I have told before of the moment in 1630 when
> the tiny ship Arabella bearing settlers to the New World
> lay off the Massachusetts coast. To the little bank of settlers
> gathered on the deck John Winthrop said: "We shall be a
> city upon a hill. The eyes of all people are upon us, so that
> if we shall deal falsely with our God in this work we have

---

251. Ronald Reagan, "Remarks at Liberty State Park, Jersey City, New Jersey," (September 1, 1980) *APP*, accessed March 12, 2019, https://www.presidency.ucsb.edu/node/285596.

undertaken and so cause him to withdraw his present help from us, we shall be made a story and a byword through the world."[252]

Second, he demonstrated his understanding of the imaginary power of the Wild West:

> Last year I lost a friend who was more than a symbol of the Hollywood dream industry; to millions he was a symbol of our country itself. And when he died, the headlines seemed to convey all the doubt about America, all the nostalgia for a seemingly lost past. "The Last American Hero," said one headline, "Mr. America dies," said another. Well, I knew John Wayne well, and no one would have been angrier at being called the "last American hero." Just before his death, he said in his own blunt way, "Just give the American people a good cause, and there's nothing they can't lick." Duke Wayne did not believe that our country was ready for the dust bin of history, and if we'll just think about it, we too will know it isn't.[253]

For younger readers, this last anecdote perhaps needs an explanation. Through over eighty Western movies, in which John "The Duke" Wayne usually played a terse but honest and upright hero, he had become synonymous with the Frontier and everything good it represented: manhood, bravery, heroism, optimism, hope, sweet success for the diligent, and harsh justice for the deprived. Thus, Reagan here not only punctured JFK's collective take on the Wild West. By evoking Wayne as a friend, he also drew his posthumous endorsement. And he knew exactly what he was doing. When he, a few years later, as president, would open an exhibition on the American cowboy, he explained:

252. Ronald Reagan, "Election Eve Address 'A Vision for America,' " (November 3, 1980) *APP*, accessed March 12, 2019, https://www.presidency.ucsb.edu/node/285591.
253. Ibid.

This exhibit explores both the reality and the myth of the American West. And both are important. Here are more than the bits and pieces of a rough and gritty life, but the tangible remnants of a national legend. Among the horsehair lassoes and Remington sculptures and Gene Autry songs is a part of our national identity. Tails of Wild West men and women from Kit Carson to Wild Bill Hickok to Calamity Jane to Annie Oakley are woven into the dreams of our youths and the standards we aim to live by in our adult lives. Ideals of courageous and self-reliant heroes, both men and women, are the stuff of Western lore.[254]

To finish, even though the economy and foreign policy were the decisive factors in the 1980 election campaign, Reagan's optimism and exceptionalist rhetoric made him a stronger and, in the end, unbeatable candidate. Proof of this lies in his strong showing among three previously sturdy Democratic but equally sternly patriotic groups: blue-collar workers, Catholics, and evangelicals. The emergence of these "Reagan Democrats" and the partial collapse of FDR's New Deal coalition they created by breaking decisively in Reagan's favor is undoubtedly complex, but that he spoke their political, religious, and emotional jargon better than Carter is clear. Also, Reagan's persona and message made his electoral coattails long. That night, beside the White House, the GOP won thirty-three new seats in the House, twelve new seats in the Senate (flipping the chamber for the first time since 1954), and hundreds of state and local seats and offices across the country.

---

254. Ronald Reagan, "Remarks at the Opening of 'The American Cowboy' Exhibit at the Library of Congress," (March 24, 1983) *APP*, accessed February 9, 2019, https://www.presidency.ucsb.edu/node/262135.

THE REAGAN REVOLUTION

After the election, Reagan again surprised pundits by sticking to his homey speaking style. He also continued to utilize impressive, patriotic settings. Being the first president to be sworn in at the West Front of the Capitol, overlooking the National Mall, he opened his Inaugural Address with a historic, exceptionalist walk-through of the scene in front of him:

> Directly in front of me, the monument to a monumental man, George Washington, father of our country. A man of humility who came to greatness reluctantly. He led America out of revolutionary victory into infant nationhood. Off to one side, the stately memorial to Thomas Jefferson. The Declaration of Independence flames with his eloquence. And then, beyond the Reflecting Pool, the dignified columns of the Lincoln Memorial. Whoever would understand in his heart the meaning of America will find it in the life of Abraham Lincoln. Beyond those monuments to heroism is the Potomac River, and on the far shore the sloping hills of Arlington National Cemetery, with its row upon row of simple white markers bearing crosses or Stars of David.[255]

This was, of course, a storyteller's (and former radio presenter's) way to invite those who could not attend in person to join in on the occasion. He then turned the whole speech into a patriotic ode by stroking, e.g., what he saw as the ideological carrier wave of U.S. history:

> If we look to the answer as to why for so many years we achieved so much, prospered as no other people on Earth, it was because here in this land we unleashed the energy and individual genius of man to a greater extent than has ever been done before. *Freedom and the dignity of the individual*

---

255. Ronald Reagan, "Inaugural Address (January 20, 1981) *APP*, accessed January 30, 2019, https://www.presidency.ucsb.edu/node/246336.

have been more available and assured here than in any other place on Earth. [. . .] It is time for us to realize that we're too great a nation to limit ourselves to small dreams.[256]

As president, Reagan also—to most commentators' snarky disgust—continued his habit of telling stories and cracking jokes. And even if they frequently sounded to be delivered off the cuff, he often used them purposely to expose and ridicule his enemies. For example, he told Soviet jokes like, "A man puts down money to buy a car and is told that he can take delivery of his automobile in exactly ten years. 'Morning or afternoon?' the purchaser asks. 'Ten years from now, what difference does it make?' replies the clerk. 'Well, I have plumbers coming in the morning.' " And on the home front, he assisted in giving "the L-word" a negative connotation with pokes like, "We could say [liberals] spend money like drunken sailors, but that would be unfair to drunken sailors because the sailors are spending their own money,"[257] and that Democrats" are going so far left, they've left America."[258] What effect Reagan's jokes had on the Soviets is hard to tell, but at home, his jabs helped turning "liberal" into a political mark of Cain. Toward the end of his tenure, the term had become associated with "profligacy, spinelessness, malevolence, masochism, elitism, fantasy, anarchy, idealism, softness, irresponsibility, and sanctimoniousness."[259]

On a higher level of political import, President Reagan spent much time explaining complex political issues. For example, in his Inaugural Address, he alluded to the inherent tension between freedom and political

256. Ibid. Emphasis added.

257. Ronald Reagan, "Remarks Accepting the Presidential Nomination at the Republican National Convention in Dallas, Texas," (August 23, 1984) APP, accessed March 29, 2019, https://www.presidency.ucsb.edu/node/261945.

258. Paul R. Abramson, John H. Aldrich & David W. Rohde, Change and Continuity in the 1984 Elections: Revised Edition (Washington, D.C.: CQ Press, 1987), 56.

259. Michael Kazin, The Populist Persuasion: An American History (Ithaca: NY: Cornell University Press, 1995; reprint with a new preface 2017), 246.

power in layman's terms by saying that "government is not the solution to our problem; government is the problem," and "the Federal Government did not create the States; the States created the Federal Government."[260] Wary about Nixon's failure to roll back federal powers, he also applied a dual strategy of reforms and nominations of conservative judges, of which the latter's job—if the former failed to pass—was to contest the "living constitution" and overturn liberal rulings on issues such as busing, affirmative action, and abortions. And in support of both reforms and judges, Reagan delivered rows of speeches hailing the Founding Fathers. He venerated them as saints whose deeds were so far unsurpassed in human history:

> This Nation was born when a band of men, the Founding
> Fathers, a group so unique we've never seen their like since,
> rose to such selfless heights. Lawyers, tradesmen, merchants,
> farmers—56 men achieved security and standing in life
> but valued freedom more. They pledged their lives, their
> fortunes, and their sacred honor.[261]

As could be expected, Reagan showed a special appreciation for George Washington. In 1982, when celebrating the 250th anniversary of his birth at Mount Vernon, he said: "We come filled with pride and gratitude to honor George Washington, Father of our Country, knowing that because of what he did, we're free and we're Americans. [. . .] His love was liberty, and his trust was in the people. He believed they were dependable and right-minded and he believed that a leader's responsibility is to bring out their best qualities."[262]

---

260. Reagan, "Inaugural Address (January 20, 1981).

261. Ronald Reagan, "Address at Commencement Exercises at the University of Notre Dame," (May 17, 1981) *APP*, accessed January 26, 2019, https://www.presidency.ucsb.edu/node/247548.

262. Ronald Reagan, "Remarks at a Mount Vernon, Virginia, Ceremony Commemorating the 250th Anniversary of the Birth of George Washington," (February 22, 1982) *APP*, accessed January 26, 2019, https://www.presidency.ucsb.edu/node/245206.

However, because Washington, a Federalist, had been less vocal about limiting the federal government, Reagan most frequently cited Thomas Jefferson. In 1982, for example, he depicted him as an advocate of his own effort to strengthen states' rights and the independence of counties, school districts, churches, and families: "Jefferson said, 'I know no safe depository of the ultimate powers of the society but the people themselves . . .' "[263] Likewise, Reagan persistently evoked the Declaration, the Constitution, and the Bill of Rights, among other things, to mock attempts to exclude religion from public schools: "The first amendment of the Constitution was not written to protect the people of this country from religious values—it was written to protect religious values from government tyranny."[264] And it worked, sort of. In 1981, 83 percent of Americans agreed with the statement that the U.S. Government should be curbed, and two years later, 79 percent expressed support for Reagan's form of New Federalism. And even if Democrats and the New Class would stop most reforms of the New Deal/Great Society system, he did manage to stage one revolution.

Since only general optimism could break the paralyzing atmosphere of *malaise*, Reagan knew he had to change not only Carter's economic policy but also the public mood. He thus sold his economic reform package as a plan that the Founding Fathers would have approved of. However, even if tax cuts and deregulations aligned with their general view, Reagan's support for "supply-side" theory and free trade stood contrary to Hamilton's budget discipline and neomercantilism. He could thus rarely define or defend these policies with hard historical examples and was instead forced to use the progressives trick to discuss his goals in broad terms empty

263. Ronald Reagan, "Address Before a Joint Session of the Alabama State Legislature in Montgomery," (March 15, 1982) *APP*, accessed December 11, 2018, https://www.presidency.ucsb.edu/node/245688.

264. Ronald Reagan, "Remarks at the Annual Meeting of the United States Chamber of Commerce," (April 26, 1982) *APP*, accessed January 25, 2019, https://www.presidency.ucsb.edu/node/245327.

of details. For instance, Reagan stretched his rhetoric thin by associating *laissez-faire* with most people's vague schoolbook image of early America as a low-tax/free-market heaven:

> We are changing the direction of America. We're putting her back on the course of hope that was charted by our Founding Fathers. We've begun to handcuff the big spenders, to get the Federal Government off your backs, promote economic recovery, and put you, the people, back in charge of your country again. With your support [. . .] we're clearing away the economic wreckage that was dumped in our laps.[265]

Reagan also leaned on Americans' optimism, aptness for experimentation, and large-scale thinking, reassuring them that his economic plan let "the American spirit" loose: "As surely as America's pioneer spirit made us the industrial giant of the twentieth century, the same pioneer spirit today is opening up on another vast front of opportunity, the frontier of high technology."[266]

In time, this strategy would work. However, his decision to combat inflation by first cutting back the money supply led to a recession that hurt millions. For two years, Reagan could therefore only offer cheerleading: "Send away the handwringers and doubting Thomases and bring on the capitalists and entrepreneurs. Once again, free enterprise is breathing life into our economy and we will not tolerate a return to the old ways of profligate spending and taxing that threatened to snuff it out."[267] However, this was not enough since Americans had grown accustomed to govern-

---

265. Ronald Reagan, "Remarks at a North Carolina Republican Party Rally in Raleigh," (October 26, 1982) *APP*, accessed February 20, 2019, https://www.presidency.ucsb.edu/node/245014.

266. Ronald Reagan, "Address Before a Joint Session of the Congress on the State of the Union," (January 25, 1983) *APP*, accessed February 11, 2019, https://www.presidency.ucsb.edu/node/26310.

267. Ronald Reagan, Remarks at a Meeting of the National Association of Home Builders," (May 16, 1983) *APP*, accessed February 7, 2019, https://www.presidency.ucsb.edu/node/262137.

mental handouts and perks such as federal unemployment benefits and job training programs. In the 1982 midterms, coinciding with the bottom of the recession, the GOP was delivered a hard blow. And just a few months later, Reagan's 35 percent personal approval rating hit not too far above Carter's all-time low in 1979. At that point, the Reagan Revolution appeared doomed; particularly since the world situation seemed, if possible, even worse.

By 1980, Reagan had spoken blatantly about the Soviet Union for decades. For example, in 1963, he predicted that head-on economic and technological competition with the Soviets would mean victory over communism "based on the belief (supported so far by all evidence) that in an all-out race, our system is stronger, and eventually the enemy gives up the race as a hopeless cause."[268] He had also long dismissed established views of the Cold War with puns like, "Détente—isn't that what a farmer has with his turkey—until Thanksgiving Day?"[269] and dismissed socialism as a form of mental illness: "Communism is neither an eco[nomic] or pol[itical system]—it is a form of insanity—a temporary aberration which will one day disappear from the earth because it is contrary to human nature."[270] Thus, when Carter's foreign policy collapsed in 1979 due to the Iranian hostage crisis and a Soviet invasion of Afghanistan, Reagan looked vindicated. In 1980, he could accuse Carter of "weakness, indecision, mediocrity, and incompetence"[271] and demand a new foreign policy.

Furthermore, after Reagan, in his Inaugural Address, only said things

---

268. Heclo, "Ronald Reagan," in W. Elliot Brownlee, & Graham Huge Davis (ed.), *The Reagan Presidency: Pragmatic Conservatism & Its Legacies* (Lawrence, KS: University Press of Kansas, 2003), 27.

269. Jim Mann, *The Rebellion of Ronald Reagan: A History of the End of the Cold War* (New York: Viking, 2009), 23.

270. Kiron K. Skinner, Annelise Anderson & Martin Anderson (ed.), *Reagan, In his Own Hand* (New York: The Free Press, 2001), 134.

271. Ronald Reagan, "Address Accepting the Presidential Nomination at the Republican National Convention in Detroit," (July 17, 1980) *APP*, accessed March 27, 2019, https://www.presidency.ucsb.edu/node/251302.

like "the will and moral courage of free men and women [. . .] is a weapon our adversaries in today's world do not have,"[272] many assumed that he in foreign policy would "play the game" and curtail his anti-communism. However, a week later, he shocked foreign policy experts, academics, journalists, Democrats, and even Republicans when answering a question about his view of the objectives of the Soviets:

> I know of no leader of the Soviet Union since the revolu-
> tion, and including the present leadership, that has not more
> than once repeated in the various Communist congresses
> they hold their determination that their goal must be the
> promotion of world revolution and a one-world Socialist or
> Communist state, whichever word you want to use. Now,
> as long as they do that and as long as they, at the same time,
> have openly and publicly declared that the only morality
> they recognize is what will further their cause, meaning they
> reserve unto themselves the right to commit any crime, to
> lie, to cheat, in order to attain that, and that is moral, not
> immoral, and we operate on a different set of standards, I
> think when you do business with them, even at a detente,
> you keep that in mind.[273]

And Reagan had not misspoken. After recovering from an assassination attempt on March 30, 1981, he embarked on a three-year-long verbal crusade against communism, paralleled by a blitz of crisp anti-Soviet propaganda. During his first term, he also underwrote his image as an unbending anti-communist by raising the defense budget and sending troops to oust a Marxist regime in the Caribbean nation of Grenada.[274]

---

272. Reagan, "Inaugural Address," (January 20, 1981).

273. Ronald Reagan, "The President's News Conference," (January 29, 1981) *APP*, accessed April 1, 2019, https://www.presidency.ucsb.edu/node/246569.

274. Ronald Reagan, "Remarks of the President and Prime Minister Eugenia Charles of Dominica Announcing the Deployment of United States Forces in Grenada," (October 25, 1983) *APP*, accessed March 28, 2019, https://www.presidency.ucsb.edu/node/261906.

However, Reagan's primary weapon against the Soviets was speeches, and he delivered a first historic one in June 1982 when he—symbolically as the leader of a breakaway colony—in an address to the British Parliament asked the West to aim for political victory in the Cold War. Forecasting that a "democratic revolution was gathering new strength" around the world, he said the present was a historic opportunity "to foster the infrastructure of democracy, the system of a free press, unions, political parties, and universities, which allows a people to choose their own way to develop their own culture, to reconcile their own differences through peaceful means." At heart, this was no harsher than what every U.S. president since Wilson had said. However, Reagan also concluded that the "march of freedom and democracy [. . .] will leave Marxism-Leninism on the ash heap of history."[275] And because many now deemed blunt talk about the Soviets needlessly provocative (as many today shun criticism of Islam), the political, diplomatic, academic, and media worlds gasped.

Reagan had also only started. In March 1983, he again talked about the world situation, this time before the Convention of National Evangelicals. And he this time worried about that so many evangelicals were expressing support for one-sided Western disarmament:

> Let us pray for the salvation of all of those who live in that totalitarian darkness-pray they will discover the joy of knowing God. But until they do, let us be aware that while they preach the supremacy of the state, declare its omnipotence over individual man, and predict its eventual domination of all peoples on the Earth, they are the focus of evil in the modern world.[276]

---

275. Reagan, "Address to Members of the British Parliament" (June 8, 1982), 2018, https://www.presidency.ucsb.edu/documents/address-members-the-british-parliament.

276. Ronald Reagan, "Remarks at the Annual Convention of the National Association of Evangelicals in Orlando, Florida," (March 8, 1983) *APP*, accessed March 29, 2019, https://www.presidency.ucsb.edu/node/262885.

Given the setting, this escalation of rhetoric from the political categories of free and unfree into the religious realm of good and evil should not have shocked anybody. Nevertheless, it did. After his remark was cabled around the world, an overwhelmingly negative body of reactions—"the worst presidential speech ever;" "outrageous;" "primitive"[277]—started to pore back in. This showed how much political discourse had changed since the 1950s, when such language had been commonplace.

And Reagan was now on a roll. Only two weeks later, he upped the ante with Moscow even further, all the way into space, with his Strategic Defense Initiative (SDI). Missile defense was not a new concept, but after Nixon signed the Anti-Ballistic Missile (ABM) treaty in 1972, such systems had been banned and the idea faded from the public's mind. However, Reagan never gave up on it. Viewing missile defense as a moral and not a military or juridical matter, he considered every idea, however far-fetched, about defending America and other free countries from nuclear blackmail as an ethical responsibility worth exploring. What's more, SDI added to the arms race and Reagan's verbal crusade an economic and technical challenge that he (and the Kremlin) knew that the Soviet's rheumatoid economic and industrial system could never meet. How much its economic and psychological costs eventually contributed to the collapse of communism is debated, but his message was clear:

> I know this is a formidable, technical task, one that may
> not be accomplished before the end of this century. Yet,
> current technology has attained a level of sophistication
> where it's reasonable for us to begin this effort. It will take
> years, probably decades of effort on many fronts. There will
> be failures and setbacks, just as there will be successes and
> breakthroughs. And as we proceed, we must remain constant

277. Stephen F. Hayward, *The Age of Reagan: The Conservative Counterrevolution 1980-1989* (New York: Crown Forum, 2009), 288f.

in preserving the nuclear deterrent and maintaining a solid capability for flexible response. But isn't it worth every investment necessary to free the world from the threat of nuclear war? We know it is.[278]

And this time, his words really hit the political fan.

Since the Soviet Union was still perceived as a permanent entity, people foresaw the future either as a forever edgy state of world affairs threatening human extinction by nuclear Holocaust, or a place where atomic weapons were abandoned or controlled by some form of world government (effectively meaning the U.N.). Consequently, for political blockheads, SDI appeared to be what Democratic Massachusetts Senator Ted Kennedy called a "reckless Star Wars scheme," and an extraordinarily long lineup of detractors both at home and abroad exploded in a litany of criticisms like "a delusion," "a pipe dream," and "a crackpot scheme." And, since nearly all Democrats now wanted a "soft" foreign policy, SDI instantly became a partisan affair. However, Reagan's idea not only tickled Americans' attitude of "If anyone can do it, it is us!" It also offered an alternative to the Damoclean sword of Soviet nukes under which Americans had lived since the 1950s. When polled, Americans thus tended to support it. Also, the conventional picture of dovish Democrats and hawkish Republicans was overturned as conservative SDI supporters now appeared as peace-minded visionaries next to hang-tough liberals arguing for sticking with the MAD doctrine.

Furthermore, Reagan's unforgiving speeches, for a couple of years, seemingly did not affect the Soviets. On the contrary, they ignited what some historians call a Second Cold War. Still, as a master strategist, Reagan knew what he was doing: boxing in the enemy. Moreover,

278. Ronald Reagan, "Address to the Nation on Defense and National Security," (March 23, 1983) *APP*, accessed April 3, 2019, https://www.presidency.ucsb.edu/node/262125.

he never deliberately risked war, and in his January 1984 State of the Union, he eventually changed his tone toward Moscow. There were several reasons for this turn. One is that it was an election year, and another is that he had armed the U.S. into a powerful enough barging position by then. So, if only Nixon could go to China, Reagan could now go to Moscow! To boot, all he needed to do rhetorically was to move focus from what divided the superpowers politically to what he supposed unified all people: freedom. And after a comparable shift in Moscow the following year when Mikhail Gorbachev became the Soviet Premier, the tensions between East and West began to ease. But even as Reagan's strategy began to pay off, his attitude remained firm. Before traveling to his first meeting with Gorbachev in 1985, he said that superpower cooperation would not come through appeasement. And these were now weighty words since his firmness the year before had helped him win the most overwhelming reelection victory in U.S. history.

"MORNING IN AMERICA"

In 1984, Reagan's prime achievement was the economy. For as historically flawed as his sale of supply-side economics and free trade as original parts of American political philosophy was, these policies paid off in the end. After two decades of war, scandal, and misery, as the recession ended and markets went into overdrive, America laced back. And the relief was as much mental as it was material. One scholar writes that "a patriotic hurricane" formed, and since it made landfall just in time for that year's election, Reagan could hit the campaign trail boasting things like: "We came together in a national crusade to make America great again, and to make a new beginning. Well, now it's all coming together."[279] Appearing

279. Ronald Reagan, "Remarks Accepting the Presidential Nomination at the Republican National Convention in Dallas, Texas," (August 23, 1984) *APP*, accessed April 15, 2019, https://www.presidency.ucsb.edu/node/261945.

in front of cheering crowds, he could also ignore attacks upon him for being a heartless capitalist and dangerous warmonger and deliver comforting patriotic talks. When visiting Abraham Lincoln's hometown of Springfield, Illinois, he said:

> In 1861, just before beginning the long train journey east
> to become President, Abraham Lincoln stood near this
> spot and spoke to the people of this good town. He said,
> "A duty devolves upon me which is perhaps greater than
> that which is devolved upon any other man since the days
> of Washington." It was the duty of making certain, as Mr.
> Lincoln would later say at Gettysburg, that this nation
> under God shall have a new birth of freedom, and a govern-
> ment of the people, by the people, for the people, shall not
> perish from the Earth. Well, ever since taking office, we've
> worked hard to restore government of the people, to give
> this blessed land a new birth of freedom and opportunity.[280]

This "rebirth of America" was also made the theme of one of the Reagan campaign's 1984 TV ads. It was part of a series of commercials describing how the U.S. had improved under his leadership and became known as "It's Morning Again in America!" To maudlin music, it shows images of people going to work, a farmer on a tractor, a newspaper boy on his bike, people moving into a new house, a couple getting married, and a man raising the Stars and Stripes at the same time as the narrator explains softly how America was now roaring back:

> It's morning again in America. Today more men and women
> will go to work than ever before in our country's history.
> With interest rates at about half the record highs of 1980,
> nearly 2,000 families today will buy new homes, more than
> at any time in the past four years. This afternoon 6,500

---

280. Ronald Reagan, "Remarks at a Reagan-Bush Rally in Springfield, Illinois," (November 2, 1984) *APP*, accessed February 13, 2019, https://www.presidency.ucsb.edu/node/260652.

young men and women will be married, and with inflation
at less than half of what it was just four years ago, they can
look forward with confidence to the future. It's morning
again in America, and under the leadership of President
Reagan, our country is prouder and stronger and better.
Why would we ever want to return to where we were less
than four short years ago?[281]

This ad became a hit, but not so much because of its pictures and words
as its subtext. Which was that Reagan had returned America to its roots
and the serenity of the 1950s; a time when, in popular memory, the country had been at peace with itself, wealthy, well-functioning—and Baby
Boomers (by 1984 one of the country's most crucial voter blocks) had
been young and happy.

Hence, most people felt that America was great again—and so because
its proper order instituted by the Founding Fathers had been restored.
Their appreciation of Reagan and his policies can be traced in polls and
occurrences. For instance, his approval ratings soared to nearly 60 percent,
and the 1984 Summer Olympics in Los Angeles became a national pag-
eant as "the colors of this Olympics became red, white, and blue [and] the
American flag often upstaged the legendary five overlapping rings."[282] The
power of Reagan's rhetoric also showed in that Democrats tried to steal
his thunder. As when New York Governor Mario Cuomo, in a keynote
address to that year's DNC, tried to refute the president's use of the "city
on a hill" thesis by depicting his America instead as a "Tale of Two Cities."
However, this attempt to breathe new life into JFK's old refrain about
frontier life as a communal endeavor by stating that "the Republicans
believe that the wagon train will not make it to the frontier unless some of

281. https://www.youtube.com/watch?v=fa8Qupc4PnQ
282. Gil Troy, *Morning In America: How Ronald Reagan Invented the 1980s* (Princeton, NJ: Princeton
University Press, 2005), 152.

the old, some of the young, some of the weak are left behind by the side of the trail"[283] quickly vanished in the patriotic hurricane.

Furthermore, by winning 59 percent of the popular vote and 525 to 13 electoral votes, Reagan seemed to have ended the political experiment started by the Progressive Movement. That night, he gave a lyric victory speech:

> We began to carry a message to every corner of the Nation, a simple message. The message is: Here in America, the people are in charge. And that's why we're here tonight. This electoral victory belongs to you and the principles that you cling to—principles struck by the brilliance and bravery of patriots more than 200 years ago. They set forth the course of liberty and hope that makes our country special in the world.[284]

And in his second Inaugural Address, he continued in even more high-brow verse:

> We see and hear again the echoes of our past: a general falls to his knees in the hard snow of Valley Forge; a lonely President paces the darkened halls and ponders his struggle to preserve the Union; the men of the Alamo call out encouragement to each other; a settler pushes west and sings a song, and the song echoes out forever and fills the unknowing air. It is the American sound. It is hopeful, big-hearted, idealistic, daring, decent, and fair. That's our heritage, that's our song. We sing it still. For all our problems, our differences, we are together as of old. We raise our voices to the God who is the Author of this most tender

283. Mario Matthew Cuomo, "1984 Democratic National Convention Keynote Address," (July 16, 1984) *American Rhetoric*, accessed April 11, 2019, https://www.americanrhetoric.com/speeches/mariocuomo1984dnc.htm.

284. Ronald Reagan, "Remarks at a Reelection Celebration in Los Angeles, California," (November 6, 1984) *APP*, accessed May 31, 2020, https://www.presidency.ucsb.edu/node/260741.

music. And may He continue to hold us close as we fill the
world with our sound—in unity, affection, and love—one
people under God, dedicated to the dream of freedom that
He has placed in the human heart, called upon now to pass
that dream on to a waiting and hopeful world. God bless
you, and God bless America.[285]

Unquestionably, these are only a politician's puffing words after a great victory. However, they did reflect a widely held opinion that America had beaten the odds and resurrected itself. There were many signs from both politics and popular culture that could be interpreted this way. For example, the following year, movies like *Back to the Future* and *Rocky IV* would vault in patriotism and boost the feel-good of the nation even further. As the scale of Reagan's victory began to sink into the minds of analytics, there were also those posing that this second landslide proved that Americans were finally ready to return to the country's original socioeconomic system. Even many Democrats saw it this way and began to abandon liberal rhetoric and look for ways to pursue liberal goals through conservative means. In his Farewell Address four years later, Reagan would therefore be able to look back and point toward a bright future for America:

> And how stands the city on this winter night? More prosper-
> ous, more secure, and happier than it was 8 years ago. But
> more than that: After 200 years, two centuries, she still
> stands strong and true on the granite ridge, and her glow has
> held steady no matter what storm. And she's still a beacon,
> still a magnet for all who must have freedom, for all the
> pilgrims from all the lost places who are hurtling through
> the darkness, toward home.[286]

285. Ronald Reagan, "Inaugural Address," (January 21, 1985) *APP*, accessed January 30, 2019, https://www.presidency.ucsb.edu/node/259910.

286. Ronald Reagan, "Farewell Address to the Nation," (January 11, 1989) *APP*, accessed April 15, 2019, https://www.presidency.ucsb.edu/documents/farewell-address-the-nation.

However, besides revitalizing America's economy and reviving its patriotic spirit, Reagan failed in his for the future most significant task—to reverse the "modernizing" of U.S. society at large. In fact, the whole New Deal/Great Society welfare state remained untouched. And it was on Reagan's watch that the mental rot pushing the country away from republican, communitarian, and religious values toward materialism and atomistic individualism really began to undermine American culture. A decade after he left office, a bi-partisan report would reflect on the effects of this process:

> We fret about the weakness of our families, but will not
> make the personal commitments needed to preserve them.
> We worry about the consequences of out-of-wedlock births,
> but refuse to condemn them. We deplore the performance of
> our public schools, but somehow we can't find time the time
> to join parents associations, attend school board meetings,
> or even help our children with their homework. We com-
> plain about the influence of popular culture on our young
> people, but as parents we do not try very hard to monitor
> the programs our children watch and the music they hear.
> We desert neighborhood associations, and then lament the
> fraying of community. We elect, and then reelect, leaders
> for whom we profess mistrust. We say we do not have time
> for civic life. But, in fact, we enjoy more leisure than ever
> before. And too many of us spend it watching television.[287]

So, even if Reagan's presidency marked the end of the post-World War II era, it did not become a break with the past. On the contrary, after the Cold War, as the federal welfare state's roots grew thicker and deeper, the U.S. would also step up, not down, its international role. In other words, the welfare-warfare state would not only survive but thrive. And its credit card bill continue to grow.

---

287. John Kenneth White, *The Values Divide: American Politics and Culture in Transition* (Washington, D.C.: CQ Press, 2002) 11.

"Our hopes, our hearts, our hands are with those on every continent who are building democracy and freedom. Their cause is America's cause."

Bill Clinton | 1993

CHAPTER 8

Bridge Presidents

As the 1980s drew to a close, the fall of communism appeared to mean a final victory for democracy and capitalism. However, freedom would not take proper hold in Russia, never even being tested in China, and in the West, because of a recession, the pendulum shortly swung back toward a "new left" promising to defend the welfare state. Moreover, the end of the Cold War meant the resurfacing of old conflict patterns like territorial claims, separatism, and ethnic-religious quarrels. Case in point, within a year after the fall of the Berlin Wall, Iraq invaded Kuwait, in Italy, Lega Nord began arguing for splitting the country, and Yugoslavia descended into a civil war between Orthodox Serbs, Catholic Croats, and Muslim Bosnians. Even so, the number of democracies did increase, and talk about a New World Order thrived to the extent that it looked like a chance for the U.S. to remake the world in its image had arrived. But, even if Americans felt proud about winning the Cold War, most thought other people should now take care of themselves. Subsequently, they elected a new president that promised to focus on domestic issues. And as the world at the same time entered a computer-driven "third industrial revolution," the economy soon boomed again.

However, because Americans now wanted both high-quality European and Japanese goods and cheap consumer products from Third World countries like China, the good times did this time not benefit the mass of workers and producers. Instead, people in high-skill sectors keeping up with educational demands prospered while low- and middle-class people were doomed to unemployment or low-paying "McJobs."

BUSH 41

As Baby Boomers began stepping forward as political leaders, business executives, and cultural gurus, they brought to the fore the ooze of narcissism, anti-traditionalism, loosening of social standards, and stressed secularization of their youth in the 1960s. However, many subsequent behaviors—public swearing, drug use, promiscuousness, display of homosexual affection, and abortions on demand—were still accepted only by minorities, so their use on TV, in films, and other media escalated the Cultural Wars. Signs that America was undergoing fundamental political and sociocultural change were now all over. For example, while traditional crime shrunk, violence in the form of mass shootings, like the Columbine massacre, and incidents of domestic terrorism, like the Oklahoma City bombing, started to occur. As well, an explosion of new TV channels and the coming of the Internet blew apart the old "one America" culture into a debris field of ever smaller and odder tastes, trends, and subcultures. Moreover, after the Soviet Union disappeared, Americans' bent for conspiracy thinking turned inward, toward the U.S. Government, creating markets for movies like Oliver Stone's *JFK* and the TV series *X-files*. Too, *preppers*, folks preparing for the end of days by stockpiling foods and other necessities, and *militias*, groups organizing for a forthcoming fight against "the Feds" became news staples. In a word, America began to fall apart slowly, in trickles and twists rather than spurts and jumps.

However, when Americans went to the polls in November 1988, most of this was still in the future. And with the Cold War fresh in their memory, people valued both traditional values and competence enough to vote for Vice President George Bush. He was the last World War II veteran elected president and, spare JFK's interlude, the first Northeastern patrician to win the White House since FDR. This background made him ambitious, honest, and politically pragmatic—or ideologically unprincipled, depending upon one's view. His political history was also a bit all over. After first running for office as a Goldwater man in 1966, Bush had then, like Reagan, qualified his beliefs and moved toward the middle by allying himself with Nixon before being named chairman of the RNC, Ambassador to the U.N. and China, and Director of the CIA. Hence, he seemed destined for a bureaucratic career. However, in 1980, he decided to run again, this time for the presidency. And he did it as a moderate, e.g., calling supply-side theory "voodoo economics," before turning right again when offered to become Reagan's vice president.

Still, the position as VP put Bush in an excellent place to seek the GOP's presidential nomination in 1988. But the role turned into a mixed blessing. Because while Reagan's appeal and the economic boom rubbed off, it was hard for him to step forward as his own man. Also, being more of a glimmer of the old, centrist GOP than a fighting spirit of the Conservative Movement, New Right people and neoconservatives did not trust him. Indeed, Bush differed from Reagan—who after his eight years in the White House had turned into a touchstone of conservatism—on several key points, especially communitarianism. In short, while Reagan had focused on the individual, Bush emphasized families, neighborhoods, churches, and other communal bodies. And he felt so strongly about this that he, in his RNC Acceptance Speech, drew lines about it not only to the left . . .

> The idea of community—a beautiful word with a big mean-
> ing, though liberal Democrats have an odd view of it. They
> see community as a limited cluster of interest groups, locked
> in odd conformity. And, in this view, the country waits
> passive while Washington sets the rules. But that's not what
> community means, not to me. For we're a nation of commu-
> nity, of thousands and tens of thousands of ethnic, religious,
> social, business, labor union, neighborhood, regional and
> other organizations, all of them varied, voluntary and
> unique.

. . . but to the right: "Does government have a place? Yes. Government is part of the nation of communities, not the whole, just a part. And I don't hate government. A government that remembers that the people are its master is a good and needed thing."[288]

The reason for this last statement, which could so easily have been omitted, must have been that Bush felt that under the glamorous crust of the 1980s, perversions were running counter to American values and virtues. And indeed, there was no shortage of such. Most of these stemmed from deep wells, including the sexual promiscuity and ethnic tribalism of the 1960s, the hedonism of the 1970s, and the amoral outlook of "modernity" at large. However, some vices—like greed and self-indulgence and the unhinged individuality of the 1980s—drew energy from Reagan's policies, so criticizing them was politically tricky. Even so, he said:

> I wonder sometimes if we've forgotten who we are. We're the
> people who sundered a nation rather than allow a sin called
> slavery. And we're the people who rose from the ghettos and
> the deserts. And we weren't saints, but we lived by standards.
> We celebrated the individual, but we weren't self-centered.

288. George Bush, "Address Accepting the Presidential Nomination at the Republican National Convention in New Orleans," (August 18, 1988) *APP*, accessed June 27, 2019, https://www.presidency.ucsb.edu/node/268235.

> We were practical, but we didn't live only for material
> things. We believed in getting ahead, but blind ambition
> wasn't our way. The fact is: Prosperity has a purpose. It's to
> allow us to pursue "the better angels," [sic!] to give us time
> to think and grow. Prosperity with a purpose means taking
> your idealism and making it concrete by certain acts of
> goodness. [. . .] I want a kinder and gentler nation.[289]

And after eight years of effective but square materialistic policies, voters
desired a more nuanced message. The problem for Bush was that he was
not alone in offering one.

As a second-generation immigrant, Democratic candidate Massachusetts
Governor Michael Dukakis was good at talking about America's many
merits. Picking up on Reagan's reinvigorated feeling of national pride,
he spoke about himself as a product of the American Dream, called the
Democrats "America's Party," used pro-business language, and talked about
the need for compassion and inclusion. Still, because his party's shift right
since 1984 had mainly been linguistic, not political, Dukakis could not
help but offer just a slightly different brand of liberalism. He filled his
DNC Acceptance Speech with references to JFK's portrayal of the U.S. as
a communal rather than individualistic endeavor, invoked John Winthrop
by saying that the Puritans had wanted "a country where each of us asks
not only what's in it for some of us, but what's good and what's right for
all of us," and delivered sound bites such as "Opportunity for some isn't
good enough for America;" "college education is a right;" and "wage war
on hunger and pollution and infant mortality."[290] Even so, as he opened a
substantial post-convention lead over Bush, it seemed to work.

---

289. Bush, "Address Accepting the Presidential Nomination . . ." (August 18, 1988).

290. Michael S. Dukakis, "Address Accepting the Presidential Nomination at the Democratic National
Convention in Atlanta," (July 21, 1988) *APP*, accessed June 27, 2019, https://www.presidency.ucsb.edu/
node/216671.

Contrariwise, Bush's task became to depict Dukakis as a standard liberal ideologue far from the mainstream. And even if he was a lackluster speaker who could only offer a faint echo of Reagan's poetic-visionary style, this was, after decades of conservative stamping of all things left-of-center as un-American, not difficult. In his RNC Acceptance Speech, Bush did his best to sound himself like Reagan, e.g., by hitting hard upon themes such as the death penalty, the right to bear arms, and abortions. He also now paid absolute homage to Reaganomics: "My opponent won't rule out raising taxes, but I will [. . .] Read my lips: no new taxes!" [291] And throughout the fall campaign, Bush stuck the "L-word" on his opponent's forehead at every given turn. And as this message stuck, he regained the lead. In addition, Dukakis turned out to be a terrible campaigner, refusing, among other things, to throw "red meat to the Yahoos" by supporting the death penalty even when asked if someone killed his own wife. An observer thus noted: "The premise of the Bush campaign is that many people west of the Berkshires think that only two things come from Massachusetts, liberals and lobsters, and pretty soon they're going to wake up and say that's not a lobster." [292]

In the end, Bush connected better with voters and won a landslide—or rather a smaller tremor—with 53 percent of the vote and 426 to 111 electors. But, even if Americans in this way finally turned their back on raw 1960s radicalism, a critical eye could notice that Bush's win was as broad as Reagan's socio-cultural impact had been thin. And since the Democrats still dominated Congress, his political situation was weak. Bush was from day one also forced to reaffirm his conservative bona fides. However, nei-

291. George Bush, "Address Accepting the Presidential Nomination at the Republican National Convention in New Orleans," (August 18, 1988) *APP*, accessed June 27, 2019, https://www.presidency.ucsb.edu/node/268235.
292. Maureen Dowd, "Bush and Dukakis Spar Over Issue Of Who Is the Better Conservative," (June 8, 1988) *New York Times*, accessed March 15, 2022, https://www.nytimes.com/1988/06/08/us/bush-and-dukakis-spar-over-issue-of-who-is-the-better-conservative.html.

ther his speaking skills nor his actions matched that task. In his Inaugural Address, for example, he said lamely: "We know what works: Freedom works. We know what's right: Freedom is right. We know how to secure a more just and prosperous life for man on Earth: through free markets, free speech, free elections, and the exercise of free will unhampered by the state."[293] In 1990, Bush would also burn what ideological reliability he had with the now completely dominating New Right/neoconservative wing of the GOP by breaking his "read my lips" promise on taxes in a move aimed to reduce the federal deficit (a decision that, for the record, together with the looming dot-com boom, would actually work).

To make things even worse for himself, Bush limited his rhetorical use of Americanism to occasions like State of the Union addresses; i.e., speeches that were, to a significant degree, written by others. Positively, all modern presidents use speechwriters, but good ones develop a feeling for their patron's style, views, and wishes. That Bush's dittos did not fill his daily speeches with more patriotic language thus indicates that it did not come naturally to him. Even one of his boldest speeches, from May 1989, given just months before the fall of the Berlin Wall, sounded tedious:

> For 40 years, the world has waited for the Cold War to end. And decade after decade, time after time, the flowering human spirit withered from the chill of conflict and oppression; and again, the world waited. But the passion for freedom cannot be denied forever. The world has waited long enough. The time is right. Let Europe be whole and free.[294]

And two years later, in August 1991, when Soviet republics began to join

293. George Bush, "Inaugural Address," (January 20, 1989) *APP*, accessed June 27, 2019, https://www.presidency.ucsb.edu/node/247448.

294. George Bush, "Remarks to the Citizens in Mainz, Federal Republic of Germany," (May 31, 1989) *APP*, accessed July 1, 2019, https://www.presidency.ucsb.edu/node/262786.

a chorus line demanding independence, his moderation got him in trouble. When invited to give remarks to the Ukrainian parliament, he said: "Freedom is not the same as independence. Americans will not support those who seek independence in order to replace a far-off tyranny with a local despotism. They will not aid those who promote a suicidal nationalism based upon ethnic hatred."[295]

Now, since all knew that Bush, at this moment, was tiptoeing around a political powder keg, moderation was clearly understandable. But to hear from a U.S. president that freedom did not necessarily equate to national independence was hard for many to stomach. While a Ukrainian nationalist huffed that Bush "sounded less radical than our Communist politicians on the issue of state sovereignty for Ukraine,"[296] a conservative pundit at home puffed about him giving a "Chicken Kiev speech."[297] And even if Bush later explained his tameness as a deliberate strategy not to provoke backlashes in Eastern Europe, there's reason to believe the speech did reflect his genuine opinion, because five months later, the day the Soviet Union ceased to exist, he expressed only relief. It was first in his 1992 State of the Union four weeks later he sounded jubilant: "In the past 12 months, the world has known changes of almost Biblical proportions. And even now, months after the failed coup that doomed a failed system, I'm not sure we've absorbed the full impact, the full import of what happened. But communism died this year. [...] By the grace of God, America won the cold war."[298]

---

295. George Bush, "Remarks to the Supreme Soviet of the Republic of the Ukraine in Kiev, Soviet Union," (August 1, 1991) *APP*, accessed July 1, 2019, https://www.presidency.ucsb.edu/node/265653.

296. Ann Devroy & Michael Dobbs, "Bush Warns Ukraine on Independence: President Supports Gorbachev's Union Treaty in Kiev Speech," (August 2, 1991) *The Washington Post*, accessed July 1, 2019, https://web.archive.org/web/20140611082257/http://www.highbeam.com/doc/1P2-1077882.html.

297. William Safire, "After the Fall," (29 August 1991) *New York Times*, accessed July 1, 2019, https://www.nytimes.com/1991/08/29/opinion/essay-after-the-fall.html.

298. George Bush, "Address Before a Joint Session of the Congress on the State of the Union," (January 28, 1992) *APP*, accessed July 1, 2019, https://www.presidency.ucsb.edu/node/266921.

Consequently, to finish this first section of Bush, since he always cared more about not doing the wrong thing in the long run than making the right moves in the short, we can say that he was a brilliant diplomat but not that good of a (modern) politician. However, at the same time, he knew his role in the historical drama in which he partook and had a clear idea about what the end of the Cold War must mean. In his—as it turned out last—State of the Union cited above, he said:

> There are those who say that now we can turn away from
> the world, that we have no special role, no special place. But
> we are the United States of America, the leader of the West
> that has become the leader of the world. And as long as I
> am President, I will continue to lead in support of freedom
> everywhere, not out of arrogance, not out of altruism, but
> for the safety and security of our children. This is a fact:
> *Strength in the pursuit of peace is no vice; isolationism in the*
> *pursuit of security is no virtue.*[299]

Two things can here be noted. First, by paraphrasing his famous quote from 1964, Bush offered Barry Goldwater, who since his huge loss in 1964 had remained a political punchbag and symbol of extremism, a badge of honor for far-sightedness and highlighted the GOP's at large role in opposing communism at times when Democrats wanted to appease the Soviets. Second, by vowing to keep the U.S. involved in world affairs as a promoter of democracy and capitalism, Bush laid down a course that America would follow for three decades. However, it had taken him four years and a full-scale war to get to this point. So, to get the complete picture, we must take a quick step back here.

---

299. Ibid. Emphasis added.

THE GULF WAR

In 1990, Americans viewed the end of the Cold War in the same way as their grandparents had seen World War I—as a historic opportunity to reform the world. And George Bush was one of them. His worldview was firmly rooted in Americanism, and he saw the fall of communism as the onset of what he, as president, would nearly one hundred times call a New World Order with the U.S. as the dominant force. And, here, note *the* and not *a* dominant force. Because the U.S. was from now on to work with other countries and international organizations fully on its terms only. Indeed, this truth was seldom uttered openly, but the change in tone from the Cold War was hard to miss. For example, after assuming office in 1989, Bush began to flash out a new U.S. foreign policy in a series of speeches. And in the first, he said:

> What is it that we want to see? It is a growing community
> of democracies anchoring international peace and stability,
> and a dynamic free-market system generating prosperity
> and progress on a global scale. The economic foundation
> of this new era is the proven success of the free market, and
> nurturing that foundation are the values rooted in freedom
> and democracy.[300]

Hence, even if Bush until December 1991 would avoid provoking Moscow, he, from the start, saw it as his job not to roll back but to extend America's role from being the West's shield against communism to acting as a worldwide patron of democracy and capitalism. So, if Bush, on his way to give this speech, had passed a White House portrait of Woodrow Wilson, it probably blinked.

Still, it was not the breakdown of communism that ultimately deter-

---

300. George Bush, "Remarks at the Texas A&M University Commencement Ceremony in College Station," (May 12, 1989) *APP*, accessed July 30, 2019, https://www.presidency.ucsb.edu/node/263519.

mined Bush's—and so also America's—new foreign policy. It was Iraq's invasion of Kuwait in August 1990. After the assault, its dictator, Saddam Hussein, promised that any international response would trigger "the mother of all wars." However, like Truman after North Korea's attack in 1950, Bush immediately let the world know that he was not to allow himself to be intimidated and later told Congress that "recent events have surely proven that there is no substitute for American leadership. In the face of tyranny, let no one doubt American credibility and reliability."[301] And a few months later, in his 1991 State of the Union on January 29, he explained the by-then rolling war in ideological language:

> Halfway around the world, we are engaged in a great
> struggle in the skies and on the seas and sands. We know
> why we're there: We are Americans, part of something larger
> than ourselves. For two centuries, we've done the hard work
> of freedom. And tonight, we lead the world in facing down
> a threat to decency and humanity.

He also made clear the historical meaning of what was taking place:

> For two centuries, America has served the world as an
> inspiring example of freedom and democracy. For genera-
> tions, America has led the struggle to preserve and extend
> the blessings of liberty. And today, in a rapidly changing
> world, American leadership is indispensable. Americans
> know that leadership brings burdens and sacrifices. But we
> also know why the hopes of humanity turn to us. We are
> Americans; we have a unique responsibility to do the hard
> work of freedom. And when we do, freedom works.[302]

---

301. George Bush, "Address Before a Joint Session of the Congress on the Persian Gulf Crisis and the Federal Budget," (September 11, 1990) *APP*, accessed July 1, 2019, https://www.presidency.ucsb.edu/node/264415.

302. George Bush, "Address Before a Joint Session of the Congress on the State of the Union," (January 29, 1991) *APP*, accessed July 1, 2019, https://www.presidency.ucsb.edu/node/265956.

Thus, it was Bush's reactions to this event more than to the looming collapse of the Soviet soufflé that galvanized a new U.S. foreign policy doctrine.

Moreover, a detail often ignored is that Bush in 1990 threatened to go to war against Iraq without Congressional approval. I.e., he threatened to ignore the Constitution. Technically, he also did so on August 5th when ordering U.S. troops to Saudi Arabia as part of Operation Desert Shield (even if he later did seek and get approval for using military force against Iraq). Hence, the liberal's stepmotherly attitude towards this document had rubbed off. However, Bush's view of how Iraq should be dealt with was so widely shared in Washington D.C. that no one, spare a few left-wingers, libertarians, and paleoconservatives, called him on it. Suggestively, the year before, political theorist Francis Fukuyama had, in the article *The End of History,* expressed the view underlying Bush's action. In short, it was based on the assumption that the fall of communism meant "the end point of mankind's ideological evolution and the universalization of Western liberal democracy as the final form of human government."[303] Hence, the text offered an academic theory clean from exceptionalist wordings but practically identical with the notion of an American mission. And since many liked the ring of what Fukuyama had to say, and even more sought to avoid ending up on the wrong side of history, politicians, pundits, and experts of nearly all stripes crammed themselves in front of TV cameras to explain that it was not President Bush's and America's choice but her *obligation* to oust the Iraqis from Kuwait.

Obviously, this is a historic moment of bipartisanship worth noticing. It signifies a sudden—but at the same time, since the sensations leading forward to it were latent in various exceptionalist notions, long in

303. Francis Fukuyama, "The end of history," *National Interest*, No. 16 (Summer 1989): 3-18, accessed July 1, 2018, https://www.jstor.org/stable/24027184.

the making—transformation of the wrangling between doves and hawks about the Cold War into a principal unity between liberal internationalists and neoconservatives about America's (new) role in the world. With the Gulf War won and the Soviet Union gone, it became safe and chic to give champagne toasts for the world being America's oyster. Henceforth, the game in Washington, D.C., became to offer the most grandiose plans and demands of what America could do in and for the world; a livid contest arguably won by neoconservative Charles Krauthammer, saying that the U.S. should shoulder the role of a New Rome and become a "super-sovereign" declaring a global *Pax Americana*.

But, despite this, Bush only got one more year on the throne behind the Resolute Desk in the White House. In his Farewell Address, he would say that he wished the end of the Cold War would have made U.S. interventionism "a thing of the past" but that if Americans were now to be "passive and aloof," the world risked becoming a place "characterized by chaos, one in which dictators and tyrants threaten their neighbors, build arsenals brimming with weapons of mass destruction, and ignore the welfare of their own men, women, and children."[304] He then also stated that a world "more attuned to the enduring principles that have made this country a beacon of hope for so many for so long, will not just emerge on its own. It's got to be built," before filing away George Washington's "great rule" of foreign policy as obsolete:

> Two hundred years ago, another departing President warned
> of the dangers of what he described as "entangling alliances."
> His was the right course for a new nation at that point in
> history. But what was "entangling" in Washington's day
> is now essential. [. . .] We must engage ourselves if a new
> world order, one more compatible with our values and

---

304. George Bush, "Remarks at the United States Military Academy in West Point, New York," (January 5, 1993) *APP*, accessed July 1, 2019, https://www.presidency.ucsb.edu/node/266384.

congenial to our interest, is to emerge. But even more, we
must lead.[305]

This was also a recommendation that his successor would eagerly follow.

THE NEXT GENERATION ELECTION

When George Bush declared he would run for reelection, pundits yawned
that the Gulf War and the fall of communism ensured him a second term.
There was even talk about a "Republican grip" over the White House that
guaranteed no more Democratic presidents. Shortly, though, Bush began
to lag in the polls. The main reason for this was a short but stinging recession. However, U.S. politics had also changed dramatically in a few years.
In short, after the Cold War—and even more so after the collapse of the
Soviet Union—Bush's foreign policy expertise was no longer needed. And
since he could not offer (as he called it) "the vision thing" people wanted,
he looked old and tired, and his ideas outdated. Moreover, the end of the
Cold War spurred a broad debate about America's future. On one side
were people who viewed the outcome of the Cold War as proof of the
strength of the U.S. system and the 1990/91 recession as only a regular
economic slump, and on the other were those who said that the Cold War
had exhausted the U.S. economy and that the country needed sweeping
change. Thus, this debate was only another high in the old argument
about how to best preserve America's exceptionalist nature: by sticking to
the country's heritage or changing? And for the first time since the 1960s,
disciples of reform found the most compelling advocates.

To Bush's right, Ross Perot, a Texas businessman, argued that America
must scale back its international engagements, renegotiate unfavorable
trade deals, and take drastic actions to close the deficit. He ultimately
won 19 percent of the vote; the most successful independent run for the

305. Ibid.

White House since Theodore Roosevelt in 1912. However, Bush's nemesis became Bill Clinton. He was an intelligent, rhetorically vivid, opportunistic, and unscrupulous policy wonk from Arkansas who became a star in 1978 when he was elected the nation's youngest governor at age thirty-two. In the 1980s, he also became a member of the Democratic Leadership Council (DLC); a group of centrists opposing the party's social democracy by arguing for "expanding opportunity, not the government" and saying that the U.S. should be about "equal opportunity, not equal outcomes."[306] Too, like Carter, Clinton described himself as beyond left and right, hailed traditional American values, and whether his stances were liberal, conservative, or something in between is still hard to judge. For example, in his 1992 DNC Acceptance Speech, he proposed a new form of student loans based on semi-compulsory communitarianism: "You must pay it back, from your paychecks or, better yet, by going back home and serving your communities"[307] through community work.

Thus, Clinton's views on America and various exceptionalist traits are hard to judge. Because, even if he believed in a particular role for the U.S., he was above all "an unabashed enthusiast for globalization, like the eighteenth-century *philosophes* viewing commerce as the essential instrument to promote free markets, democracy, and eventually peace and prosperity."[308] Thus, at this point, because modern Americanism and globalism are both "imperial" philosophies and not contradictory in all respects, the difference between the two needs to be clarified. Since most prominent exceptionalists and globalists in the American context

---

306. Steve Kornacki, *Red and the Blue: The 1990s and the Birth of Political Tribalism* (New York: HarperCollins, 2018), 85.

307. William J. Clinton, "Address Accepting the Presidential Nomination at the Democratic National Convention in New York," (July 16, 1992) *APP*, accessed July 12, 2019, https://www.presidency.ucsb.edu/node/220260.

308. George C. Herring, *From Colony to Superpower: U.S. Foreign Relations since 1776* (New York: Oxford University Press, 2011) 926.

demand, e.g., free trade, low taxes, and an active foreign policy, they tend to sound alike and often collaborate politically. However, exceptionalists aim to make other countries more like America and see a unique role for the U.S. in world affairs. Contrariwise, globalists want the world's cultures to converge, state governments to subject themselves to supranational bodies like the World Trade Organization and the International Court of Justice, create a borderless world, and, ultimately, form some kind of world government.

These differences become even clearer if comparing developments across the Atlantic. After two world wars and four decades of political division, Europeans intuitively perceived all forms of unity as a blessed want, plus a desirable counterweight to what one French philosopher scorned as American "hyperpower." What's more, the fall of communism stimulated the age-old meme of universal empire ingrained in German and French philosophy and both Catholic and Kantian (Protestant) traditions. After the Cold War, all this made globalization popular, at least among European elites, and its high-hats soon began to view the world as destined for "super states" that one day would merge into one planetary community. European countries, therefore, wrote and began to ratify the 1992 Maastricht Treaty, turning the European Economic Community (EEC) into today's E.U., some against popular will. Specifically, France joined after only a very narrow margin in a referendum; in Denmark, a second referendum was held when the first produced the "wrong" result; and the U.K. joined despite solid arguments for that a referendum was required. Since then, the E.U. has also progressively become a centralized union including nearly all European countries west of Russia, Belarus, and Ukraine.

In the U.S., on the other hand, with independence being the core of Americanism, stiff opposition to globalism formed both to the far left, where people didn't like its capitalist stink, and to the right, where binding forms of international cooperation are deemed unconstitutional. Still, for many Boomers who grew up in the "Make Peace—Not War" era, globalism appeared to be a force of nature that could create a peaceful and equal world. And because many of these since the 1960s didn't care about the Constitution, especially if it stood in the way of grand goals, globalization became a catchphrase in big cities, businesses, and other corners prospering from the dot-com economy. Those who could also eagerly join the worldwide cast of politicians, businessmen, and others—"the Davos people"—who feel a little-to-no bond to their home countries, their culture, and supposedly narrow-minded masses. Also, since globalization became seen as a positive force, opposition to it became heretical. Thus, few protested except for some paleoconservatives, libertarians, left-wing radicals, and conspiracy nuts (the latter shaming opposition further by gibbering about secret plans to hand over the policing of the U.S. to the U.N., etc.).

Still, since most Americans were not impressed, to win back Reagan Democrats, in 1992, Clinton subdued his globalism as FDR 1932 had muted his internationalism. Which was easy since he ran as a D.C. outsider and thus seldom needed to dwell deep upon the intricacies of foreign policy. Seemingly, only on one occasion did Clinton reveal the true scale of his globalism. It happened at Georgetown University in late 1991 in a talk that, in hindsight, compared to FDR's 1932 Commonwealth address. He said, "Make no mistake: foreign and domestic policy are inseparable in today's world. If we are not strong at home, we cannot lead the world we have done so much to make. If we withdraw from the world, it will hurt us economically at home."[309] Thus, this was a glassy blend of the old progressive mantra about the necessity of change at home and the

---

309. Bill Clinton, "A New Covenant for American Security," (12 December 1991) *Helvidius*, 14-17, accessed August 3, 2019, http://archive.helvidius.org/1992/1992_Clinton.pdf.

globalist gospel. And since it was given before Clinton became the apparent candidate, it didn't draw much attention. During the campaign, he could therefore continue undisturbed to deliver vague but media-savvy one-liners that often made him sound more traditionally exceptionalist-minded than Bush. Like when he criticized the president for taking . . .

> . . . a lot of credit for Communism's downfall, but fail[ing] to recognize that the global democratic revolution actually gave freedom its birth. He simply does not seem at home in the mainstream pro-democracy tradition of American foreign policy. He shows little regard for the idea that we must have a principled and coherent American purpose in international affairs, something he calls "the vision thing."[310]

Furthermore, because Ross Perot got 19 percent, Clinton won, but only with a meager 43 percent of the popular vote. Nonetheless, after twelve years, Democrats were thrilled, and Clinton, in his Inaugural Address, sounded a tone on foreign affairs that would become a hallmark of his presidency. And even if after 40+ years of Cold War dreariness it by many was seen—and by media eagerly described—as excitingly new and bold, it was, at its core, the same old progressive refrain about that the world had entered an era where old truths no longer applied and the U.S. had to change accordingly. However, Clinton had to admit that since the pressure for change nowadays not mainly came from economic, social, or other developments at home but from international and technological processes, things could no longer be worked from Washington, D.C.:

> When George Washington first took the oath I have just sworn to uphold, news traveled slowly across the land by horseback and across the ocean by boat. Now, the sights and sounds of this ceremony are broadcast instantaneously to

310. William J. Clinton, "Excerpts of Remarks in Milwaukee," (October 2, 1992) *APP*, accessed July 16, 2019, https://www.presidency.ucsb.edu/node/285621.

billions around the world. Communications and commerce are global. Investment is mobile. Technology is almost magical. And ambition for a better life is now universal. We earn our livelihood in America today in peaceful competition with people all across the Earth.[311]

Indeed, for a U.S. president to concede so patently that not even America, the only superpower left, could resist globalism was definitively un-American.

However, aware of this and Americans' general animosity vis-à-vis globalist developments, after this moment of honest clarity, Clinton wrapped his remaining message in paddings of familiar exceptionalist language like, "Our greatest strength is the power of our ideas, which are still new in many lands. Across the world we see them embraced, and we rejoice. Our hopes, our hearts, our hands are with those on every continent who are building democracy and freedom. Their cause is America's cause." In addition, Clinton made it clear that he had no intention of giving up America's military and other roles as a superpower: "While America rebuilds at home, we will not shrink from the challenges nor fail to seize the opportunities of this new world. Together with our friends and allies, we will work to shape change, lest it engulf us." And despite this formal support for multilateralism, there was no question which he, ultimately, saw as being in charge: "When our vital interests are challenged or the will and conscience of the international community are defied, we will act, with peaceful diplomacy whenever possible, with force when necessary."[312]

Clinton stuck to this hybrid exceptionalist-globalist rhetoric for eight years, even when America was the driving force. As in 1994, when he called a U.S. military action to achieve regime change in Haiti an "international

311. William J. Clinton, "Inaugural Address," (January 20, 1993) *APP*, accessed July 21, 2019, https://www.presidency.ucsb.edu/node/219347.
312. Ibid.

effort to restore [that country's] democratic government."[313] However, it was not always practical. For instance, when signing the North American Free Trade Agreement (NAFTA), like Reagan, he could not link free trade with the Founders. The only typical language he used was that the deal offered the U.S. an "opportunity to remake the world" and "We must face the challenges, embrace them with confidence, deal with the problems honestly and openly, and make this world work for all of us. America is where it should be, in the lead, setting the pace, showing the confidence that all of us need to face tomorrow."[314] He even felt forced to repeat that Americans no longer had a choice: "We cannot repeal the international economic competition that is everywhere. We can only harness the energy to our benefit." This emotionally weak argument for NAFTA made the deal divisive until it was replaced with the more favorable (for America) USMCA deal in 2020.

Another problem with Clinton's foreign policy was that he, at first, like Carter, made the spread of human rights a goal for his presidency—and it ended in the same way. While it for Carter had been the tension between human rights and the need for a realist policy toward the Soviet Union that led to trouble, for Clinton, it was his belief in the civilizing force of trade. Precisely, pressure to open the U.S. to imports of cheap clothing, electronics, and other consumer goods led him to meet human rights violations in China and other places with . . . lower tariffs. And this looked so bad that Clinton, already in mid-1993, had to change course, adopting instead "a strategy of enlargement," which meant, instead of spreading human rights, securing high economic growth at home through continuous globalization, strategic democratization, and U.S. military hegemony

---

313. "William J. Clinton, Address to the Nation on Haiti," (September 15, 1994) *APP*, accessed July 21, 2019, https://www.presidency.ucsb.edu/node/218885.

314. William J. Clinton, "Remarks on Signing the North American Free Trade Agreement Implementation Act," (December 8, 1993) *APP*, accessed July 11, 2019, https://www.presidency.ucsb.edu/node/219946.

abroad. To make this policy sound less crass, the silver lining was said to be that the U.S. would no longer be forced to deal with thugs. But this was just talk because to keep the U.S. economy going, he had to deal with countries like China, which never acts on external criticisms anyway.

Furthermore, never expressing a belief that the U.S. was ordained to govern world affairs by God or History, Clinton and members of his administration followed suit with the old Wilsonian view that they, as phrased by Secretary of State Madeleine Albright, had a "duty to be the authors of history."[315] And as one scholar writes, "America was no longer asking; it was telling."[316] Like in 1993, when Clinton told the U.N. to scale back on its interventions because "if the American people are to say yes to U.N. peacekeeping, the United Nations must know when to say no."[317] This statement marks the point where the "liberal faith in international institutions [. . .] collided with post-Cold War liberal faith in human rights,"[318] and Democrats—as most Republicans had done decades ago—gave up on the U.N. and began to rely on U.S.-dominated bodies like NATO instead. This demise of the U.N. became obvious when Clinton, in 1995, stepped in and ended the civil war in Bosnia:

> From our birth, America has always been more than just
> a place. America has embodied an idea that has become
> the ideal for billions of people throughout the world. Our
> Founders said it best: America is about life, liberty, and the
> pursuit of happiness. In this century especially, America
> has done more than simply stand for these ideals. We have
> acted on them and sacrificed for them. Our people fought

---

315. Andrew J. Bacevich, *American Empire: The Realities & Consequences of U.S. Diplomacy* (Cambridge, MA: Harvard University Press, 2002), 33.

316. Ibid, 282.

317. Clinton, "Remarks to the 48th Session of the United Nations" (September 27, 1993).

318. Peter Beinart, *The Icarus Syndrome: A History of American Hubris* (New York: HarperCollins, 2010), 279.

two World Wars so that freedom could triumph over tyranny. [. . .] Today, because of our dedication, America's ideals—liberty, democracy, and peace—are more and more the aspirations of people everywhere in the world. It is the power of our ideas, even more than our size, our wealth, and our military might, that makes America a uniquely trusted nation.[319]

At this moment, Clinton spoke as the *pontifex maximus* of U.S. civil religion and elevated his nation above other countries by stating that it has a unique role in human history. And this speech had historical effects. Because even if Americans' opinions regarding overseas actions stayed cool, Bosnia became a symbol of American might and a warning sign of what could happen worldwide if globalization wasn't allowed to continue. The self-esteem created by this successful imposing of peace also cemented the bipartisan hubris in Washington, D.C., about America's role in the world. For example, Secretary of State Albright said, "If we have to use force, it is because we are America; we are the indispensable nation,"[320] and neoconservative pundit Charles Krauthammer crowed that "the alternative to unipolarity is chaos."[321] Also, Clinton so frequently declared that people not agreeing with him were on the "wrong side of history," trying to figure out how to be politically correct enough to end up on its right side for many turned into a full-time job.

Given all this, it is symptomatic that Clinton in his Farewell Address chose to second Bush's shelving of George Washington's "great rule" from eight years earlier. Recalling that Thomas Jefferson in his Inaugural

319. William J. Clinton, "Address to the Nation on Implementation of the Peace Agreement in Bosnia-Herzegovina," (November 27, 1995) *APP*, accessed August 7, 2019, https://www.presidency.ucsb.edu/node/220919.
320. Micah Zenko, "The Myth of the Indispensable Nation," (November 6, 2014) *Foreign Policy*, accessed December 6, 2019, https://foreignpolicy.com/2014/11/06/the-myth-of-the-indispensable-nation/.
321. Beinart, *Icarus Syndrome*, 300.

Address 1801 too had warned about entangling alliances, Clinton said that "in our times, America cannot and must not disentangle itself from the world."[322] In this speech, he also, one last time, put his globalist spin on the progressive-liberal theme that the U.S. must work well at home to function as a model abroad. And this term had now taken on a much broader meaning than before. No longer emphasizing a robust U.S. economy or fixing social ills, he said:

> We must remember that America cannot lead in the world
> unless here at home we weave the threads of our coat of
> many colors into the fabric of one America. As we become
> ever more diverse, we must work harder to unite around
> our common values and our common humanity. We must
> work harder to overcome our differences, in our hearts and
> in our laws. We must treat all our people with fairness and
> dignity, regardless of their race, religion, gender, or sexual
> orientation, and regardless of when they arrived in our
> country—always moving toward the more perfect Union of
> our Founders' dreams.[323]

Hence, in his last speech, Clinton chose to stress America's standing as a model not as a political and economic free republic but as a multicultural society in a world where racial heritage, cultural differences, and national boundaries played lesser and lesser roles. This underscores his role as a "bridge president" between different eras. Especially since applying memes and merging rhetoric pictures from different paradigms was also one of his domestic specialties.

---

322. William J. Clinton, "Farewell Address to the Nation," (January 18, 2001) *APP*, accessed July 21, 2019, https://www.presidency.ucsb.edu/node/227701.

323. Ibid.

CULTURE WARS: PART II

While American culture in the 1990s consumed the world to such an extent that a French cultural minister called the opening of a Disneyland outside Paris a "cultural Chernobyl," cultural fragmentation at home accelerated. Next to the long-term trends discussed earlier, several new circumstances contributed to this decay. One was that the fall of communism made it possible for Americans, for the first time since the 1920s, to focus more on what divided them than unified them. Another was that the advent of the Internet, new TV channels, and cheaper airfare spurred an information and travel explosion daring traditional habits and worldviews through a steady influx of foreign ideas and tastes. Also, globalism meant that domestic and international trends often clashed *and* reinforced each other. One example here is that at the same time as the groups Evangelical and progressive Christians continued to grow, not only Latin American Catholics but African and Asian Muslims, Hindus, Buddhists, and others immigrated to the U.S. in record numbers, creating new tensions.

Still, the most prominent reason for the cultural fragmentation of America became that Baby Boomers started being elected to high political posts and promoted to tenured professors, editors-in-chief, and CEOs. This meant that the New Class gained complete control of the Democratic Party and near-absolute domination of postmodernist and "deconstructivist" views in the public realm. And as always when ideological zealots gain power, their respect for opposing viewpoints on issues like "abortion, affirmative action, art, censorship, evolution, family values, feminism, homosexuality, intelligence testing, media, multiculturalism, national history standards, pornography, school prayer, [and] sex education"[324] vanished. Since this provoked many conservatives (not least the Christian Right, which was equally eager to push its viewpoints upon people from

---

324. Hartman, *War for the Soul*, 1.

Washington, D.C.) to answer in kind, a record nationalization of politics took place. In other words, leaving things to the states went the same way as the dodo, turning U.S. politics into a king-size statist replica of those in countries like France, Denmark, and Sweden. Also, as "multiculturalists" began not only to oppose policies like English being the official language and controlled immigration but to fight things like public Christmas decorations and label the American flag as a racist symbol, many started considering if "limousine liberals" were not only silly and wrong but mad, mean, and treacherous.

Thus, the Culture Wars between those who wanted to turn the U.S. into a "normal" Western country and people seeing America turning into a "Vulgaria, a land with no limits where nothing was sacred"[325] took a new leap forward. And besides increased tensions, this time, it shaped two political lingos in the process. On the left, political correctness became the norm. This had started as a speech code in the 1970s intended only to evade language that could insult people because of sex, race, etc. But, already in 1976, former Vice President Humphrey called any critique of welfare systems "a disguised new form of racism, a disguised new form of conservatism,"[326] in the 1980s, "PC" began to be used as a tool for censoring rivals, and by the early 1990s, this became so common that President Bush protested that, "What began as a crusade for civility has soured into a cause of conflict and even censorship."[327] And from the mid-90s, it became extreme. For example, pro-choice advocates scourged President Clinton for wanting abortions to be "safe, legal, and rare," and theories like Leonard Jefferies' view that white "Ice Peoples" are evil because they lack coloreds' "Sun Peoples" melatonin levels and Martin Bernal's denial

325. Troy, *Age of Clinton*, 17.

326. Frum, *How We Got Here*, 346.

327. George Bush, "Remarks at the University of Michigan Commencement Ceremony in Ann Arbor," (May 4, 1991) *APP*, accessed July 30, 2019, https://www.presidency.ucsb.edu/node/265030.

of Ancient Greece being an Indo-European civilization, started to gain academic traction.

With this barrage from political rostrums, media megaphones, and academic ivory towers, Republicans felt the country's soul was at stake and fought back. Part of this brawl became a not new but sharpened form of "patriotic correctness" including exceptionalist words and phrases at the same time shaming opponents and stirring grassroots. Republicans also started questioning Democrats' patriotism and declaring political "wars" publicly. Like Pat Buchanan, in a rank-closing speech at the 1992 GOP convention after losing a primary challenge to Bush:

> My friends, this election is about more than who gets what.
> It is about who we are. It is about what we believe, and what
> we stand for as Americans. There is a religious war going on
> in this country. It is a cultural war, as critical to the kind of
> nation we shall be as was the Cold War itself, for this war
> is for the soul of America. And in that struggle for the soul
> of America, Clinton & Clinton are on the other side, and
> George Bush is on our side.[328]

In the early-to-mid 1990s, language like this was still rare, but since shouting matches tend to snowball, spreading fast. For example, to counter right-wing talk radio hosts such as Rush Limbaugh's accusations of liberals betraying American values, these cheerfully labeled opponents things like "right-wing zealots," "extremists," and "homophobes."

Adding to this hubbub was a growing politicization of media. As Boomers took over the newsrooms, TV began to offer evermore poorly disguised support for liberal viewpoints. For example, by airing negative pieces on the U.S. healthcare system, they threw their support behind

---

328. Patrick Joseph Buchanan, "Cultural War Speech: Address to the Republican National Convention" (August 17, 1992), *The Voices of Democracy: University of Maryland*, accessed July 8, 2019, https://voicesof democracy.umd.edu/buchanan-culture-war-speech-speech-text/.

President Clinton's (failed) attempt to introduce universal healthcare. And an alternative "media universe" was forming. Since the 1980s, Republicans had been able to count on support from think tanks, magazines, and talk radio hosts like Rush Limbaugh. Added to this were now Internet outlets such as Drudge Report and Townhall, and, most significantly, the Fox News Channel. It launched in October 1996 and became an instant hit with prime-time hosts like Bill O'Reilly and Sean Hannity arguing for conservative and libertarian viewpoints in studios draped in American imagery. For the non-liberal part of the population, it was a pure relief—and from a democratic-freedom of speech point of view, a badly needed squaring of the liberal media circle. However, the cost of breaking the age-old ABC, CBS, and NBC (plus CNN) news oligopoly was the coming of "media bubbles" wherein people on both sides became shielded from opposing views—and got their prejudices confirmed. Hence, polarization was added to bias.

Moreover, this steady increase in various forms of polarity was a joint venture, but the pilots in command across politics, academia, and media were predominantly on the left. The driving mechanism was thus the modern left's obstinate combo of ideological self-rightfulness—"history is on our side"—and aristocratic, elitist instinct to "protect" the public from malicious views and policies. Or, in a more traditional language, self-censorship (often crossover into indoctrination) was imposed by "responsible" journalists, academics, teachers, and others with liberal views. In addition, by branding facts, views, and opinions on issues like race and immigration that were objectively moderate and true—and that many of them had held themselves a few years or even just months earlier—as "extreme," "racist" and "fascist," left-wingers began to deprive many key political and other terms of true meaning. And the damage done went beyond linguistics. By ditching values and opinions reflecting exceptionalist notions, traditional mores, and religious concepts, radical talking heads not only detached themselves and the Democratic Party further from the mainstream and accelerated the ongoing polarization. They also perilously weakened Americanism's role as a glue keeping the country together. Because as left and right, as a result, now became separated not only by policy but also by lack of a common language, fundamental values, and mental pictures, people started to misjudge—and politicians and pundits misunderstand—each other to such degrees that U.S. politics, in the 1990s, for the first time ever, became more contentious than the European counterpart.

This souring political milieu began to show in 1994. To explain the GOP's historic capture of Congress that year with Republicans' language would be a bridge too far, but the rhetoric both sides used naturally played a role. On the left, Democrats, after decades as the "in-party," cocky about their invulnerability and invigorated by having Clinton in the White House, as usual argued hard for policies lacking majority support. And on the right, Republicans "nationalized" the election by making it a referendum on Clinton and his policies, primarily by talking about the proper size of government, lower taxes, fewer regulations, and more in exceptionalist language. Speaker-to-be Newt Gingrich's *Contract with America* that year also hit a nerve:

> This year's election offers the chance, after four decades of
> one-party control, to bring to the House a new majority
> that will transform the way Congress works. That historic
> change would be the end of government that is too big, too
> intrusive, and too easy with the public's money. It can be the
> beginning of a Congress that respects the values and shares
> the faith of the American family. Like Lincoln, our first

Republican president, we intend to act "with firmness in the right, as God gives us to see the right."[329]

Partly due to its language, Democrats dismissed the *Contract* as reactionary, and Clinton mused about it as a "contract on America."[330] However, it created enough enthusiasm among grassroots to give the GOP its most significant midterm victory since 1946 by gaining fifty-four seats in the House and eight seats in the Senate, thus flipping both chambers for the first time since 1954.

However, because the *Contract* was written to appeal to midterm voters, who are older, whiter, and more conservative, it was ill-fit for presidential politics, where candidates typically move to the center to attract moderates. This became apparent two years later when Clinton, after "reinventing" himself as a moderate, took on Republican Senate leader Bob Dole, who had also rebranded himself by adapting to Gingrich's combative style. But, as a moderate by heart and bland speaker nearing his mid-seventies, this did not work well. Dole was coming forward as an outmoded bitter voice of Reaganites, traditionalists, and others seeing "their country" dissolving in the decade's maelstrom of social and cultural changes. Symbolically, while Clinton hit the campaign trail talking ferociously about the Internet and making his second term "a bridge to the twenty-first century," Dole resentfully looked backward:

> Age has its advantages. Let me be the bridge to an America
> than only the unknowing call myth. Let me be the bridge
> to a time of tranquility, faith and confidence in action.
> And to those who say it was never so, that America's not
> been better, I say you're wrong. And I know because I was
> there. And I have seen it. And I remember. [. . .] I am here

329. "Republican Contract With America," *McClatchy Washington Bureau*, accessed July 8, 2019, http://media.mcclatchydc.com/static/pdf/1994-contract-with-america.pdf.
330. Kornacki, *Red and the Blue*, 275.

to say to America, do not abandon the great traditions that stretch to the dawn of our history. Do not topple the pillars of those beliefs—God, family, honor, duty, country—that have brought us through time, and time, and time, and time again.[331]

Besides, Clinton yet again skillfully used exceptionalist, traditionalist, and religious language to sell his ideas. When he described the global economy as "the new frontier" and talked about pushing back "the frontiers of knowledge,"[332] he sounded like JFK. But this time, his globalism was more open and less excusing. Feeling that the U.S.'s booming economy allowed him to be more open about his true beliefs, and in the worldly, individualistic-hedonistic atmosphere of the 1990s, he, in his DNC Acceptance Speech, even flat-out discounted the need for anchorage: ". . . we do not need to build a bridge to the past; we need to build a bridge to the future."[333]

Still, Clinton easily got reelected, mainly because of the strong economy. But the GOP held on to their majorities in Congress, and he again did not win a majority of the vote, earning 49.2 percent against 40.7 percent for Dole (and 8.4 percent for Ross Perot, whose gloomy view of the U.S. economy's future this time did not go over as well). Hence, the rift between left and right showed no sign of diminishing like it had done in the past during good times. This indicates that America had moved into a situation where elections were decided not primarily by economic factors. Indeed, such elections had occurred earlier, but typically during war and other national emergencies. Today, we also know it was a new, permanent

331. "Text of Robert Dole's Speech To The Republican National Convention" (August 15, 1996), *CNN.com*, accessed September 27, 2019.

332. Siobhán McEvoy-Levy, *American Exceptionalism and US Foreign Policy: Public Diplomacy at the End of the Cold War* (New York: Palgrave, 2001), 161.

333. William J. Clinton, "Remarks Accepting the Presidential Nomination at the Democratic National Convention in Chicago," (August 29, 1996) *APP*, accessed July 24, 2019, https://www.presidency.ucsb.edu/node/222870.

situation, not just a temporary trend. Thus, at this point, U.S. politics was transforming under the pressure of multiple social and cultural changes. And the situation was soon, for carnal reasons, to move from bad to worse.

While running for reelection, Clinton involved himself with a White House intern, Monica Lewinsky. And when the details about their relationship began to leak in January 1998, whatever was left of the media's "don't tell" culture surrounding such aspects of the presidency collapsed. Temporarily shelving their liberal bias, journalists, sniffing a resignation-sized scandal and blockbuster public distaste for a middle-aged man's abuse of a young female, media took the lead into a year-long wacky mix of highbrow moral-religious outbursts and public recitals of sexual act testimonies. And the Republicans opportunely followed the media down the drain on this one by staging the country's second impeachment procedure. Now, since Clinton did commit perjury, this was undoubtedly formally correct. However, after the House put Clinton on trial, but the Senate could not muster enough votes to remove him from office, the only lasting result became that millions of Americans became more than ever convinced that "DC" was corrupt. Thus, the levels of mistrust of politicians and resentment about politics in general hit new lows. Moreover, this was only the beginning. Because while Clinton spent his last two years in the White House as—the joke went—a fixed duck, Milo, the Greek muse of history, was preparing her next dramatical move.

"As President of the United States, I will always put America first, just like you, as the leaders of your countries, will always, and should always, put your countries first."

Donald J. Trump | 2017

CHAPTER 9

From Hubris to Discord

O n New Year's Eve 1999, the future looked bright, and Americans prepared to celebrate the new millennium with optimism. Thanks to the Internet explosion, the U.S. economy was steaming so hot that even the federal budget deficit had closed. And the country's military hegemony appeared to guarantee a prolonged period of world peace. Undeniably, there were dark spots on the map, such as growing income equalities at home and Islamism abroad. Also, that morning, Russian President Boris Yeltsin, without prior notice, resigned and handed over power to his Prime Minister, Vladimir Putin. However, according to nearly all politicians, media personalities, and experts, nothing of this was really to worry about because due to democratization, market reforms, and free trade, all issues were in the process of resolving themselves, as they had done in Central Europe after the Cold War. Even in still troubled states like Russia, autocratic countries such as Belorussia, communist holdouts akin to China and Cuba, and theocratic infernos such as Iran and Afghanistan, developments were said to—due to the Midas touch of globalization—slowly but steadily dancing toward the End of History. Thus, when people that evening dressed to celebrate with friends, most worried only about whether their hard drives were safe or would crash at midnight because of the Y2K Millennium bug. Maybe many also hummed "When You Believe," the song by Whitney Houston and Mariah Carey in Disney's movie *The Prince of Egypt* in the scene where people departed from slavery in Egypt to move to the Promised Land. But the reality was soon to catch up.

THE 2000 ELECTION

Few expected the 2000 election to become a thriller. Certainly, politicians were fighting their usual skirmishes about everything from abortions to taxes to overseas engagement, but outside the Beltway, few cared. Adding to the tediousness were the candidates. On the right, Republican Governor of Texas George W. Bush sailed through the primaries. After taking early life a bit easy, he had sobered up and his goal was now to rectify his father's 1992 loss by replacing Bill Clinton in the White House. And he had several strong sides. Besides money and a thick portfolio of inherent political contacts, he was, despite being verbally challenged, an effective, Truman-like speaker with a good amount of humor. A born-again Christian, he also had not an extreme but sharp ideological profile. It was a mix of religious views and Bush 41's republicanism, and he often spoke about "soft" themes like education and the environment. On his side, Vice President Al Gore, son of a former Democratic Senator from Tennessee, had entered politics early and as Clinton's VP profiled himself as a steward of the Internet and a friend of the environment. He had, therefore, also with ease defeated a single left-wing challenger and been crowned Clinton's heir.

But, even if it looked like a draw, media and left-leaning pundits explained that Gore would win handily. They said that since Americans now had seen that the new, middle-of-the-road Democratic Party's economic policies worked, the people would never vote for truly conservative candidates again. But since they ignored that America was economically, ideologically, and culturally split down the middle, reality would fly in their face. Two things can be pointed out. First, Gore's theatrical style and globalism compared poorly with Bush's folksy persona and patriotism. Second, Bush's sincere religiosity spoke not only to the Religious Right but to Middle America at large since people, after the 1990s' supernova-like explosion of secular hedonism, were looking for a (moderate) redeemer. In addition, even if both candidates were internationalist-minded free traders, Bush set himself apart by accusing the Clinton administration's foreign policy of being over-ambitious and carelessly conducted. And to experts' disbelief, this was enough to put him on par with Gore in opinion polls.

And in the end, Bush's style worked best. Halfway through Election Night, while losing the popular vote, he won a super-slim 271 majority in the Electoral College by winning Florida. And since the GOP held on to its majorities in Congress, things for a couple of hours seemed to settle for an unforeseen but calm presidency. However, Bush's margin was so slight that Gore canceled his concession speech and dragged Florida and the nation down into a month-long recount. This became a flashpoint for both Democrats, who came to see Bush as an illegitimate president, and Republicans, who thought Gore tried to steal the election (which he, by demanding recounts only in Democratic-leaning counties, effectively was). Cultural views further enflamed the bad mood. After eight years of Clinton's worldly manners, silky rhetoric, and moderate policies, liberals supposed America had moved into an era where power would forever stay with the erudite, bipartisan D.C. elite and the New Class. Also, since Clinton and Gore had talked in materialistic, multicultural terms, liberals could not stomach Bush's cavalier style and Texas twang, nor his policies, which they "knew" would be reactionary and neo-isolationist. Thus, the partisan vitriol was magnified. But, within a year, all seemed to change.

THE WAR ON TERRORISM

When the World Trade Center in New York on September 11, 2001, vanished in a dust cloud so big that it could be spotted from the International Space Station, America was transformed. As suicidal fanatics suddenly seemed to lurk everywhere, panic set in, and millions of Americans' worldviews changed as what was left of America's "splendid isolation" from the world collapsed also. As the land overnight draped itself in Stars and Stripes, nearly all social, cultural, and political divisions ostensibly vanished. For more than a year, surveys would show that over 90 percent suddenly felt very proud to be Americans, giving Bush up to 91 percent public support. The reason was that the attacks had taken place at home, rallying people around the flag far beyond the usual after more "natural" catastrophes. Bush also found his true voice. Only hours after the attacks, he said, "Freedom, itself, was attacked this morning by a faceless coward, and freedom will be defended."[334] And that evening, now addressing the nation from the Oval Office, he added:

> A great people has been moved to defend a great nation.
> Terrorist attacks can shake the foundations of our biggest
> buildings, but they cannot touch the foundation of America.
> These acts shattered steel, but they cannot dent the steel of
> American resolve. America was targeted for attack because
> we're the brightest beacon for freedom and opportunity in
> the world. And no one will keep that light from shining.[335]

334. George W. Bush, "Remarks at Barksdale Air Force Base, Louisiana, on the Terrorist Attacks," (September 11, 2001) *APP*, accessed October 9, 2019, https://www.presidency.ucsb.edu/node/216402.
335. George W. Bush, "Address to the Nation on the Terrorist Attacks," (September 11, 2001) *APP*, accessed August 14, 2019, https://www.presidency.ucsb.edu/node/216451.

Thus, from the outset, Bush framed 9/11 not as an assault on symbols of America's military might and economic wealth but as an attack on the country's prime ideal, freedom. He would also stick to this message for seven years, usually following his instincts and talking in a combined deeply human and exceptionalist style. For example, when he toured the demolished parts of the Pentagon the day after the attacks, he said: "Coming here makes me sad, on the one hand; it also makes me angry. Our country will, however, not be cowed by terrorists, by people who don't share the same values we share, by people who are willing to destroy people's lives because we embrace freedom."[336] And a few days later, when asked if he wanted to see Al-Qaeda's leader Osama bin Laden dead, he touched the soul of the nation when saying, "I want him held—I want justice. There's an old poster out West, as I recall, that said, 'Wanted: Dead or Alive.' "[337]

Bush's real masterstroke, though, was to assure the public that the U.S. would prevail because "Americans are generous and kind, resourceful and brave."[338] He used this argument frequently and often resounded Nixon's viewpoint about tough times stirring America's real spirit: "We're living through a unique moment in American history. This is a time of rediscovery, of heroism and sacrifice and duty and patriotism. These are core values of our country, and they're being renewed. We found them waiting for us just when we needed them."[339] Moreover, Bush made 9/11 comprehensible by describing what had happened as a struggle between

---

336. George W. Bush, "Remarks While Touring Damage at the Pentagon in Arlington, Virginia," (September 12, 2001) *APP*, accessed October 9, 2019, https://www.presidency.ucsb.edu/node/216547.

337. George W. Bush, "Remarks to Employees in the Pentagon and an Exchange With Reporters in Arlington, Virginia," (September 17, 2001) *APP*, accessed October 6, 2019, https://www.presidency.ucsb.edu/node/211537.

338. George W. Bush, "Remarks at the National Day of Prayer and Remembrance Service," (September 14, 2001) *APP*, accessed October 6, 2019, https://www.presidency.ucsb.edu/node/213374.

339. George W. Bush, "Remarks at the California Business Association Breakfast in Sacramento, California," (October 17, 2001) *APP*, accessed August 14, 2019, https://www.presidency.ucsb.edu/node/211731.

Good and Evil. Three days after the attacks, he said, "Our responsibility to history is already clear: To answer these attacks and rid the world of evil."[340] And in his 2002 State of the Union, he stressed the planetary scale of the War on Terrorism by calling Iraq, Iran, and North Korea "an axis of evil."[341] Hence, he chose the same basic rhetoric for his fight against Islamism as FDR and Reagan had used in their battles with fascism and communism. He also speedily hammered out a foreign policy for dealing with this menace.

However, we need to examine Bush's worldview in detail before going into this. To start, as an intensely religious man, Bush holds a traditional view of humans as creatures capable of great goodness as well as indefinable evil. He also often seemingly accepts the ramifications of this view in the form of what societal progress can be accomplished top-down. At least his lowering of taxes, deregulations, a proposal to partly privatize Social Security, and faith-based welfare initiatives indicate this. However, at the same time, his acceptance of deficit spending, expansion of Medicare, the "No Child Left Behind" education reform, and more indicates a "big government conservatism" attitude. And, since he on international issues would be much closer to Woodrow Wilson than any previous Republican president, he must be deemed a neoconservative. Proof positive, when in June 2002 presenting his Bush Doctrine, after repeating McKinley's pledge from 1898 that the U.S. could not be imperialistic because "the American flag will stand not only for our power but for freedom," he said that the American world hegemony it required was proper because:

> The 20th century ended with a single surviving model of
> human progress, based on nonnegotiable demands of human
> dignity, the rule of law, limits on the power of the state,

---

340. Bush, "Remarks at the National Day," (September 14, 2001).

341. George W. Bush, "Address Before a Joint Session of the Congress on the State of the Union," (January 29, 2002) *APP*, accessed October 8, 2019, https://www.presidency.ucsb.edu/node/211864.

respect for women, and private property and free speech and equal justice and religious tolerance. America cannot impose this vision, yet we can support and reward governments that make the right choices for their own people.[342]

So, if an active-inclusive form of Americanism can ever be said to define a moment in U.S. history, this is it. Even before presenting his doctrine, Bush's confidence in the primacy of freedom had bullied a decision to, after ousting its Taliban regime for harboring Usama bin Laden, deploy U.S. forces long-term to build a democracy in Afghanistan. And it was affecting his looming decision to invade Iraq. Because, even if Bush would make weapons of mass destruction (WMD) his chief argument for that war, his motives were nervier. Since the Gulf War, neoconservatives had convinced themselves that leaving Saddam Hussein in power had been a mistake. A group had in 1998 even managed to sway Congress to approve—and Clinton to sign—an Iraq Liberation Act declaring "that it should be the policy of the United States to seek to remove the Saddam Hussein regime from power in Iraq and to replace it with a democratic government."[343] Their view had now also become that regime change in Baghdad would trigger revolts throughout the Middle East akin to those in Eastern Europe in 1989. And a few days before the invasion started, Bush hinted that this was his view too:

As we enforce the just demands of the world, we will also honor the deepest commitments of our country. Unlike Saddam Hussein, we believe the Iraqi people are deserving and capable of human liberty. And when the dictator has

---

342. Ibid. Emphasis added.
343. H.R.4655 - Iraq Liberation Act of 1998105th Congress (1997-1998), accessed October 7, 2019, https://www.congress.gov/bill/105th-congress/house-bill/4655.

departed, they can set an example to all the Middle East of a vital and peaceful and self-governing nation.[344]

Thus, the idea that democracy was the way of the future was so controlling that Bush ignored that Iraq was the direct heir of Mesopotamia's Game of Thrones political culture. And this was not his only blind spot. After 9/11, he disregarded signs that the world was moving away from the neoconservative shadow theater, including that Russia under Putin plunged back into despotism and that China hadn't changed a tad. He even described the former as a "partner in the war against terror" and predicted that the latter would soon accept that "social and political freedom is the only true source of national greatness."[345] And he was not alone. In retrospect, the level of groupthink within politics (and media) leading to the subsequent fiasco is staggering. To put it simply: after U.S. tanks rolled into Bagdad, because of the exceptionalist conviction that America could do everything and nothing wrong, an overly optimistic, ill-planned, and rushed nation-building project was executed—and ended in disaster. Because, as during the Vietnam War, when the U.S. body counts began to creep up, things got worse as Bush—like LBJ—dug in his heels. In fact, he drove down to the very end of Folly Lane by, in his second Inaugural, declaring worldwide democratization the lodestar for his foreign policy. And despite no Founding Father ever believing in spreading the U.S. model by force, he made them tokens for this mirage: "Advancing these ideals is the mission that created our Nation. It is the honorable achievement of our fathers."[346]

To finish this part, it is possible that had Bush not been so convinced

---

344. George W. Bush, "Address to the Nation on Iraq," (March 17, 2003) *APP*, accessed October 7, 2019, https://www.presidency.ucsb.edu/node/212791.

345. Bush, "Commencement Address," (June 1, 2002).

346. George W. Bush, "Inaugural Address," (January 20, 2005) *APP*, accessed October 6, 2019, https://www.presidency.ucsb.edu/node/214048.

about the primacy of freedom, the Iraqi War may have been avoided, or at least its follow-up could have been adjusted and the costs in blood and dollars been lowered. But we will never know, and the historical effect of what did happen is clear. The creeping reduction of belief in Americanism going on since the 1970s suddenly took a new, great leap forward, and exceptionalist arguments not only in defense of the War on Terrorism but most things truly began to lose their sway. Still, it was not until a few years later when neocon icon and Reagan's former U.N. ambassador Jeane Kirkpatrick published a posthumous warning about an unelected "deep state" of foreign policy hawks and declared the vision of global democracy humbug that a blame game about Iraq started. Today, we know that this foreshadowed a much broader response to the whole post-World War II paradigm—and that Bush's reelection unleashed political demons that were already testing the Union in ways not seen since the Civil War.

ODIUM POLITICS

In contrast to his father after the Gulf War, Bush for a long time succeeded in employing the patriotic energy created by 9/11 for domestic gains. A month and a half after the attacks, he started ramming through the Patriot Act. Like the Alien and Sedition Act of 1798 and the Espionage Act of 1917, it contained perilous edicts for civil liberties that would not have been accepted under normal circumstances. People like Democratic Wisconsin Senator Russ Feingold, the only member of that chamber to vote nay, said things like, "The Founders [. . .] wrote a Constitution of limited powers and an explicit Bill of Rights to protect liberty in times of war, as well as in times of peace."[347] But all Bush needed to do was to say that it was simply an upgrade of laws "written in the era of rotary tele-

---

347. "Statement Of U.S. Senator Russ Feingold On The Anti-Terrorism Bill: From The Senate Floor," (October 25, 2001), Electronic Privacy Information Center, accessed November 27, 2019, https://epic.org/privacy/terrorism/usapatriot/feingold.html.

phones" guided by "a firm resolve to uphold and respect the civil liberties guaranteed by the Constitution while dealing swiftly and severely with terrorists."[348] Panic, groupthink, and media fever took care of the rest.

The following year, Bush could also use 9/11 and the surge in patriotism it created to mobilize Republicans in front of the 2002 midterms. He began in January by asking for support for his conservative policies: "In America's ideal of freedom, citizens find the dignity and security of economic independence instead of laboring on the edge of subsistence."[349] And during the campaign, he continued to frame his talking points with patriotic-exceptionalist oratory:

> I'm traveling this country, and I can tell you, the American spirit is alive and well, the spirit of people understanding that to be an American means you've got to serve something greater than yourself. The spirit of America says that we're willing to sacrifice for our freedoms. And the spirit of America says that you take nothing in democracy for granted. You see, if you're eligible to vote, you have an obligation to vote. That's what the spirit of America calls for.[350]

And it worked. For the first time since 1934, the White House party picked up seats in both the House and the Senate. How much Bush's patriotic language contributed to this victory is impossible to say, but his use of it to score partisan points was already seen as contentious. And as political life after that began to return to normal, U.S. politics became tetchier than ever.

348. George W. Bush, "The President's Radio Address," (October 27, 2001) *APP*, accessed November 26, 2019, https://www.presidency.ucsb.edu/node/216385.

349. George W. Bush, "Address Before a Joint Session of the Congress on the State of the Union," (January 29, 2002) *APP*, accessed October 8, 2019, https://www.presidency.ucsb.edu/node/211864.

350. George W. Bush, "Remarks in South Bend, Indiana," (October 31, 2002) *APP*, accessed October 19, 2019, https://www.presidency.ucsb.edu/node/212452.

Because, as soon as the polling stations closed that night, the 2004 race for the White House started. And as the pride of the victory in Iraq first gave way to confusion over not finding WMDs, then angst over growing U.S. casualties, and finally anger over feeling deceived by the president, two things happened. On the left, people experienced flashbacks of Vietnam and spotted the specters of big oil and the military-industrial complex behind the war. And on the right, people viewed criticism of the war and attacks on the president during wartime as a betrayal. In other words, the basic outline of U.S. politics from before 9/11 came roaring back, revealing that the discord was not ultimately so much about the war as longstanding political grievances. And it quickly got worse than ever because while liberals anew began to see Bush as an agent of the old nationalistic, racist, and backward U.S. they hoped had vanished with Clinton, conservatives' view of the Democrats as weak, indecisive, and un-American was confirmed.

However, nearly all Democratic leaders had supported the war, so what differed at the top was mainly only rhetoric. Democrat candidate Massachusetts Senator John Kerry—a politician that was said to have a personality making a 2x4 to look cheery and relaxed—thus found himself forced to engage in semantic isometrics like, "I voted for the war before I voted against it." And his attempt to turn the election into a referendum about Bush did succeed only because the president did the same thing. And in this constrained choice between Bush's unapologetic form of Americanism and Kerry's timider variant truncated by globalism and European-like (read: weak) patriotism, most Americans still supported the first. Moreover, in the first presidential debate, when asked about his view on preemptive wars, Kerry also made things worse for themselves by saying that American actions needed to pass a "global test [before] you can prove to the world that you did it for legitimate reasons."[351] Hence,

---

351. Ibid.

he gave the impression that he would be prepared to limit national sovereignty. As a result, Bush attracted enough votes to make him the first president since 1988 to win a majority of the popular vote and expand the GOP's congressional majorities. Still, the country remained deeply divided. Bush earned only 15 more votes in the Electoral College than he had four years earlier—of which fourteen depended on allocated gains for red states after the 2000 census.

To summarize, the mixture of victories and losses between 2000 and 2006 brought long-term consequences for both parties—and mayhem for the country. At first, directly after 9/11, as after Reagan's 1984 landslide, the Democrats seemed to turn into a party of minorities and big cities parked far away from the White House. However, Bush's victories and the GOP's successes in the 2002 and 2004 elections rested upon a few million voters in a handful of swing states whose ideological beliefs and faithfulness at the polls were flimsy. Case in point, they already 2006 handed Congress and two years later the White House back to the Democrats. Moreover, the GOP establishment had become so ossified by moral rightfulness and ideological discipline that grassroots opposition to free trade and wars was long to be ignored. On their side, Gore's and Kerry's defeats and the Iraq War radicalized the Democratic Party to such an extent that it got two dangerous consequences. First, it fed a budding paramilitary left spearheaded by Antifa. Second, their losses caused liberals to pass on their aversion for Bush, Republicans, and traditionalists to the country, or at least its "red" parts. One sign of both these developments is that Democrats describing themselves as "extremely proud" of being Americans began to decrease from 62 percent in 2003 to a so-far nadir of 22 percent in 2019.

Furthermore, as Bush's tenure drew to a close and 9/11 began to fade into history, the political focus shifted toward the Great Recession.

It started with the burst of a thirty-year-old housing bubble created by relaxed loan regulations adopted by the Carter administration. And as the crisis, through a mix of regulations, market interrelations, and psychology spread quickly to other sectors of the U.S. economy, it turned into a political crisis as well. Because as people felt that their American Dream—a good-paying job, a nice car, a big house—was suddenly threatened, the *malaise* of the 1970s about the U.S. being in irreversible decline returned. This fear was also boosted by Democrats' wish to finally "get" Bush and his administration, a worse-than-ever media bias in front of the 2008 election, and a pent-up ideological desire to abolish the Reagan-era's "market fundamentalism." And as this drew attention to the eternal question of whether the U.S. to fix its problems needed to return to its roots or change, strongly ideologically "primary brigades" went to the polls and selected presidential candidates reflecting both parties' extremes.

To the right, Republicans turned to John McCain; a neoconservative war hawk who based both his foreign and domestic policies upon the same worldview and aggressive form of exceptionalist thinking as Bush. If elected, he promised to be perpetually aggressive toward terrorists and stick with an economic policy that principally did not deviate from Reagan, Bush 43, and the GOP's establishment wing. Which pleased neoconservatives but not so many others. Still, as a Vietnam veteran, former POW, and a long-term member of the Senate, McCain technically had a good vita for the White House and was, though halfheartedly, endorsed by the party elite. What poured oil on GOP mandarin's enthusiasm was his reputation as an outspoken maverick, known for attacking pork spending, earmarks, and waste in Congress—which was also the sign of what kind of candidate rank-and-file Republicans had begun to look for but couldn't find. To the left, on the other hand, radicals at long last found what appeared to be not only a new JFK but a true Messiah.

"THE ONE"

Barack Obama owned an unforeseen background for the White House. The son of a white, atheistic, and liberal mother from Kansas and a black, Muslim, and socialist father from Kenya, he grew up in Hawaii, spent part of his youth in Indonesia, attended both Columbia and Harvard and worked as a community organizer in Chicago ghettoes before turning to politics. He was also the first presidential candidate to have grown up in the 1960s and 1970s, when the Civil Rights Movement, the Vietnam War, Watergate, stagflation, and *malaise* marked the U.S. But, instead of becoming a regular left-wing activist-politician, Obama continued upon an uncommon track. The reason was his academic mindset, which made him more of an observer than a participant in society. This attribute had served him well as a student and lecturer of law and history but created problems as a politician. For instance, during the primaries, a typical elitist *von oben* remark about that working-class people losing their jobs "cling to guns or religion or antipathy toward people who aren't like them" created a storm of protests that could have cost him the nomination—if not for the circumstance that his opponent, Hillary Clinton, outdid him in aristocratic style and arrogance.

Furthermore, Obama's mindset is a Byzantine mix of James Madison's republicanism, Auguste Comte's positivism, John Dewey's pragmatism, Reinhold Niebuhr's Christian realism, and Saul Alinsky's bent for social action, topped with a cup of Marxism. This makes his worldview relativistic and ideologically oxymoronic. For example, Obama seems to hold a traditional view of human nature—"we are fallible; we make mistakes and fall victim to the temptations of pride and power and, sometimes, evil"[352]—that prunes his view of the primacy of politics. For example, the

---

352. Barack Obama, "Remarks on Accepting the Nobel Peace Prize in Oslo," (December 10, 2009) *APP*, accessed January 8, 2020, https://www.presidency.ucsb.edu/node/287562.

mix allows him to admit that societal improvements cannot be reached mainly through government fixes but long-term cultural changes. Still, as a member of the Senate, he managed to accumulate the most liberal voting record in that chamber, and he would later often sound like the most radical U.S. president ever. Likewise, Obama's spiritual views are complex. He is a Christian and—relative to being a liberal—surprisingly often expresses positive opinions of religion's role in society. However, his father's heritage also makes him attentive to Islam to such an extent that many Americans question his Christian faith, and some even see him as a Manchurian candidate.

Moreover, Obama's view of America is also complex. On one side, he reflects the ever-harsher academic view of the U.S. symbolized, since the 1970s, by anti-Americanists such as Noam Chomsky. As a candidate, he also talked incessantly about the need to transform the country by reforming its economy, education, and more. On the other side, Obama's background persuades him to call the U.S. a unique place with unparalleled advantages. In a keynote address for John Kerry in 2004, he said: "I stand here knowing that my story is part of the larger American story, that I owe a debt to all of those who came before me, and that, in no other country on earth, is my story even possible."[353] Though, Obama's patriotism is best described as broad but thin, and four things should be noted. First, he often speaks in the tradition of JFK, stressing the collective story of U.S. history. Second, he holds that since the U.S.'s founding documents are "stained and imperfect" because they permitted slavery, it is a political task "to purify and perfect their core ideas and purposes."[354] Third, he talks more about America's negative sides (racism, prejudices, economic

---

353. Barack Obama, "Keynote Address at the 2004 Democratic National Convention," (July 27, 2004) *APP*, accessed December 12, 2019, https://www.presidency.ucsb.edu/node/277378.

354. Philip S. Gorski & William McMillian, "Barack Obama and American Exceptionalism," in Dennis R. Hoover (ed.), *Religion and American Exceptionalism* (London: Routledge), 2014.

inequalities, etc.) than her virtues. Fourth, his readiness to let "our values [. . .] be tested against fact and experience" is so impatient that it must be deemed radical, not conservative.

Also, Obama's views allow him an inimitable speaking style. His primary strength is that he for people on the left who usually dislike exceptionalist talk for ideological reasons, sounds like a redeemer, and for people on the right, who demand a sizable amount of patriotism in their presidents, sounds okay. Attractive is also his ability to, like Reagan, sound optimistic even in defeat. As when he, after losing the New Hampshire primary, gave his iconic "Yes, we can!" speech. Still, it shall not be forgotten that Obama in 2008 appeared worrying for nearly as many, implying that his message truly touched American's imaginations for both good and bad. Still, he sounded moderate enough to appear as a "conciliator, a post-partisan, sensible centrist whose appealing manner, lack of ideological passion, and absence from the red-hot political fights of the last two decades would allow him to bridge the political divide in Washington."[355] And his 53 percent of the vote, 365 electors, and his party adding to its majorities in Congress was the closest thing to a landslide in America since 1988. But, given the economic crisis, it was a decent result at best.

Nevertheless, compared to the previous two decades of political anger, economic bedlam, and military setbacks, the first days of Obama's presidency appeared to confirm forecasts about him ushering in a new era. For a moment, the nation came together, his ratings went high into the 60s, and enthusiasm about what he could accomplish was boundless. However, these predictions were political, not analytical. In his first State of the Union, he admitted that he had nothing to offer but blood, sweat, and tears in the form of taxes, regulation, and more debt. This was not the

---

355. Scott Rasmussen & Douglas Schoen, *Mad as Hell: How the Tea Party Movement is Fundamentally Remaking Our Two-Party System* (New York: HarperCollins, 2010), 263.

change most expected, and Obama's honeymoon ended only a few days later when a reporter accused him of being un-American by propping up the housing market with subsidies:

> This is America! How many of you people want to pay
> for your neighbor's mortgage that has an extra bathroom
> and can't pay their bills? [. . .] We're thinking of having a
> Chicago Tea Party in July," and "I'll tell you what, if you
> read our founding fathers, people like Benjamin Franklin
> and Jefferson . . . What we're doing in this country now is
> making them roll over in their graves.[356]

As this spark went viral, a political wildfire spread across the nation. A week later, Tea Party rallies, where people protested government spending, stimulus bills, and bank bailouts and demanded a return to free-market policies, budget discipline, and other principles they understood once had made America great, took place in over forty cities. Larger meetings also soon followed, e.g., on Tax Day, April 15. And the lot from the movement's name, via participants' penchant to dress up in colonial uniforms, to waving of "Don't Tread on Me" flags indicated its members' belief in Americanism. Indeed, had the Tea Party's demands been limited to more *laissez-faire*, lower taxes, and curbed spending, it could—as was done by liberals and media—have been written off as an astroturf event staged by traditional right-wing forces. But, even if such groups eventually overtook the movement, it was born as a spontaneous protest attracting broad support not only from Republicans but Independents and even Democrats. Many Tea Party activists also advocated for protectionist and isolationist ideas that had existed only as grapevine chatter within the GOP for decades. A sign of an atmospheric change was also that talking heads like TV anchor Lou Dobbs and New York billionaire Donald Trump com-

---

356. "Rick Santelli: Tea Party," (February 19, 2009) *Freedom Eden*, accessed December 16, 2019, http://freedomeden.blogspot.com/2009/02/rick-santelli-tea-party.html.

plained more vehemently than ever not only about governmental waste, fraud, and abuse but also the need for "fair" rather than free trade.

However, the Democrats, now in control of all three government branches, arrogantly dismissed the Tea Party and moved to fix what they saw as the last big "unfinished business from the New Deal era."[357] A bill centered on mandating Americans to buy health insurance, the Affordable Care Act (ACA), was introduced and became extremely popular on the left. However, most Americans came to view "Obamacare" as a threat to their private health care plans, a breach of privacy, and a break with the U.S. political tradition. House Speaker Nancy Pelosi also showed modern liberals' true face when asked about the constitutionality of the bill by mockingly laughing "Are you serious?"[358] Thus, the bill only fueled the Tea Party fire. In Florida, a U.S. District Court justice dismissed the bill as unconstitutional: "If Congress penalizes a passive individual for failing to [buy health insurance, the country] would have a Constitution in name only. Surely this is not what the Founding Fathers could have intended."[359] And in January 2010, Republican Scott Brown shook liberal America to its core by winning a special election to fill Ted Kennedy's Senate seat in deep-blue Massachusetts. This deprived the Democrats of their filibuster-safe super-majority in that chamber and set the scene for the GOP to following November also recapture the House by winning sixty-three new seats, six more Senators, and some seven hundred state legislators.

The Tea Party was also only one of Obama's problems. In the fall of 2011, it got an ideological mirror image on the left in Occupy Wall Street; a similarly spontaneous movement protesting that Obama did not change the country fast enough. It was "standing up for the 99 percent" against

---

357. Michael Tomasky, *Bill Clinton* (New York: Times Books, 2017), 47.

358. Watson, *Progressivism*, 188.

359. Stephen Brooks, *American Exceptionalism in the Age of Obama* (New York: Routledge, 2013), 28f.

crony capitalists and demanded higher taxes, more regulations, and higher minimum wages. I.e., standard left-wing driftwood. What gave the OWS a special flair was that its members were camping out in tents in big-city parks. Flushed with memories of the good old days, Boomers throughout politics, academia, and media thus saw it as a "new 1968." In December, Obama also added to the fever by, like Theodore Roosevelt, going to Osawatomie, Kansas, and describing the U.S. economic system in class-warfare language. He, e.g., criticized "trickle-down theory" as a system that "fits well on a bumper sticker [but] doesn't work."[360] However, the OWS was certainly an overall humiliation for him. And even if the movement disintegrated shortly after (when cynics noted it started to get too cold to live in tents), next to Antifa, it was a precursor of what was to become present-day U.S. left-wing radicalism—a street mob under the spell of brattish, internationalist, and cell-based elitists nested in academic, media, and other influential circles viewing establishment Democrats as sell-outs.

LEADING FROM BEHIND

While partly refurbished worldviews were bull-horned from both sides of the political aisle at home, Obama had to deal with world events. Given the Great Recession, foreign policy should have played a minor role in the 2008 campaign, but terrorism, the Iraq War, and McCain's candidacy made it necessary for him to address the subject at length. And as a man of the academic left, Obama had not much praise for Bush's overreach or McCain's exceptionalist bravado. But as seen, he was not a usual Ivy League America-basher either, and he based his foreign policy upon the same "soft" and neutered form of Americanism as his domestic views. Among other things, he pledged to leave Iraq, close Guantanamo Bay, and

360. Barack Obama, "Remarks at Osawatomie High School in Osawatomie, Kansas," (December 6, 2011) *APP*, accessed January 21, 2020, https://www.presidency.ucsb.edu/node/297773.

argued that with him, America's lost power, prestige, and standing would return: "We are going to be the America that has made us that bright and shining light all around the world."[361] As president, Obama would also sometimes act if not overly smart so stoic. For example, directly after committing thirty thousand more U.S. troops to Afghanistan, he went to Oslo, Norway, to accept the 2009 Nobel Peace Prize and said:

> War, in one form or another, appeared with the first man
> [. . .] A non-violent movement could not have halted
> Hitler's armies. Negotiations cannot convince al Qaeda's
> leaders to lay down their arms. To say that force is some-
> times necessary is not a call to cynicism—it is a recognition
> of history; the imperfections of man and the limits of
> reason.[362]

However, despite defending an active international role for the U.S. and the just war principle in this speech, Obama had already squandered his chance to earn bipartisan support for his foreign policy. He had done so by going on an "Apology Tour," giving speeches abroad that many deemed supportive of "the concept that the U.S. is a flawed nation that must seek redemption by apologizing for its past 'sins.' "[363] And his biggest mistake had been to say, "I believe in American exceptionalism, just as I suspect that the Brits believe in British exceptionalism and the Greeks believe in Greek exceptionalism."[364] For this, one pundit hooted that he . . .

> . . . suggests a belief that the United States doesn't stand
> alone with a particular greatness but that every nation is great

---

361. Barack Obama, "Press Release – Obama Files to Appear on New Hampshire Ballot," (October 22, 2007) *APP*, accessed December 19, 2019, https://www.presidency.ucsb.edu/node/293079.

362. Obama, "Remarks on . . .," (December 10, 2009).

363. Nile Gardiner & Morgan Lorraine Roach, "Barack Obama's Top 10 Apologies: How the President Has Humiliated a Superpower," (June 2, 2009) *The Heritage Foundation*, accessed January 15, 2020, https://www. heritage.org/node/14384/print-display.

364. Barack Obama, "The President's News Conference in Strasbourg," (April 4, 2009) *APP*, accessed December 19, 2019, https://www.presidency.ucsb.edu/node/286249.

in its own way and America is simply one of many nations with something cool to offer. This kind of multicultural, politically correct, "we're all unique in unique ways, every kid must win at dodgeball" thinking is the basis for his economic and foreign policies, from his schemes to nationalize the auto, banking, and health care industries to his lollygagging on behalf of those fighting for greater freedom in Iran. It is the rationale for his Vesuvian explosion of big government and the much higher taxes required to finance it.[365]

And on this issue, Obama was swimming against public opinion. The following year, 80 percent still believed that "the U.S. has a unique character that makes it the greatest country in the world."[366] Yet, beneath this generic opinion, Americans had begun to shift stances. For instance, the number accepting military cuts had risen, over half now saw foreign trade more as a threat than an opportunity, and opposition to new overseas involvement stood at 46 percent. So, when Obama took a step back toward Bush 43's foreign policy, things got messy.

In January 2011, when popular revolts spread across the Middle East and North Africa against the region's autocratic regimes, Obama was torn between idealist and realist views. While he personally leaned toward supporting the status quo, Secretary of State Hillary Clinton—who in the 1990s as First Lady had sided with the activist wing of her husband's administration—saw the event as "a new 1989" that must be supported. As a result, Obama turned from backing Egypt's moderate autocrat (and long-term U.S. ally) Hosni Mubarak in January to "leading from behind" air attacks to unseat Libya's dictator Muammar Gaddafi in March. But

---

365. Monica Crowley, "American exceptionalism . . .," (July 1, 2009) *Washington Times*, accessed January 15, 2020, https://www.washingtontimes.com/news/2009/jul/1/american-exceptionalism/.

366. Byron York, "Poll: Americans believe in American exceptionalism, not as sure about Obama" (December 22, 2010) *Washington Examiner*, accessed January 16, 2020, https://www.washingtonexaminer.com/poll-americansbelieve-in-american-exceptionalism-not-as-sure-about-obama.

despite saying this was to protect "the democratic values that we stand for," public support for the action became weak. A new attitude also showed in Washington, D.C., where the GOP-controlled House criticized him for failing "to provide Congress with a compelling rationale based upon United States national security interests for current activities regarding Libya."[367] But Obama had by now got "the D.C. bug" and answered with another aggressive move—to funnel U.S. support to what he believed were friends of freedom in Syria. Which would lead to another disaster. But we will have to return to this. As 2012 opened, Obama tried to put the Middle East on the back burner to get reelected.

SECOND-TERM BLUES

Because of the mediocrity of Obama's first term, in 2012, a row of Republicans lined up to take him down. And as the GOP had managed to absorb the Tea Party without changing its core policies, right-wing pundits thought the odds for someone to succeed looked good. And even if primary voters were grunting more loudly about foreign policy and trade than before, the party's established ideological structures held as the nomination went to Country Club Republican, businessman, and neoconservative gospeler Mitt Romney. To foster his run, he had declared support for the U.S.' role in the world after World War II—"The United States is unique. American strength does not threaten world peace. American strength helps preserve world peace"[368]—and after joining the race, on a question about his view of America, he said:

> This election is about the soul of America. The question is, what is America going to be? And we have in Washington

---

367. Kyle Adams, "Libya Vote Highlights House GOP Shift on Use of Military," (June 6, 2011) *Real Clear Politics*, accessed January 16, 2020, https://www.realclearpolitics.com/articles/2011/06/06/libya_vote_highlights_house_gop_shift_on_use_of_military.html.

368. Mitt Romney, *No Apology: The Case for American Greatness* (New York: St. Martin's Press, 2010), 11.

> today a president who has put America on a road to decline, militarily, internationally, and, domestically, he's making us into something we wouldn't recognize. We're increasingly becoming like Europe. Europe isn't working in Europe. It will never work here.[369]

However, Romney had been most people's second, third, or even fourth choice, and his most noticeable feature—besides being a Mormon—was his difficulty to excite the party's base. His nomination was therefore received with equal amounts of pantomime yawns, sighs, and hisses.

On his side, Obama struggled with recreating the passion for himself from four years earlier. In his DNC Acceptance Speech, besides standard left-wing gestures, he used plenty of his "thin" exceptionalism but to no avail. And of the few moments marked by patriotic themes and overtones during the campaign, all went against him. Like on July 13, when Obama stressed the collective side of U.S. history by saying, "You didn't build that," referring to successful entrepreneurs, and Romney described the comment as a "slap in the face to the American Dream."[370] Another shame came when four Americans, including an ambassador, were killed by terrorists in Benghazi, Libya, and Romney blamed the attack on Obama's "apologizing for America's values."[371] However, patriotic and exceptionalist language played a much less significant role in 2012 than in 2008. Instead, polarization was back with a vengeance. One poll showed that voters' ideological views this time were more important than gender, age, race, and class, and over 60 percent self-identified as "strong partisans."

---

369. Felicia Sonmez, "2012 ABC/Yahoo!/WMUR New Hampshire GOP primary debate (Transcript)," (January 7, 2012) *Washington Post*, accessed January 17, 2020, https://www.washingtonpost.com/blogs/election-2012/post/2012-abcyahoowmur-new-hampshire-gop-primary-debate-transcript/2012/01/07/gIQAk2AAiP_blog.html.

370. John Sides, & Lynn Vavreck, *The Gamble: Choice and Chance in the 2012 Presidential Election* (Princeton: Princeton University Press, 2013), 116.

371. Dan Balz, *Collision 2012: The Future of Election Politics In a Divided America* (New York: Penguin Books, 2013), 296.

Consequently, the campaign turned nasty already during the summer with, for example, one TV ad depicting Romney as personally liable for a woman's death from cancer.

Toward the end, after holding a steady lead throughout the year, Obama seemingly lost momentum after stumbling in the first presidential debate. But it was just Republicans that, after deciding that they, after all, disliked Obama more than Romney, returned home. The latter thus not only lost but did so nearly as decisively as McCain, winning 47 percent and 206 electoral votes to Obama's 51 percent and 332. The foremost reason for this was that even if the U.S. economy had improved painfully slowly, most voters continued to blame Bush for the Great Recession, not Obama. However, another factor is that Romney's musty establishment praise of free trade and an active foreign policy, plus being a Mormon, caused millions of Republicans to stay home. This is shown by the fact that he won independents but lost the party base. Which was an omen. The ongoing long-term shift among Republicans about, e.g., trade and wars would only four years later lead scores of them to vote for a man with policies the opposite of Romney's. But we are not there yet, and the 2012 election turned out to be more of a Romney loss than an Obama win.

The morning after the election, Americans woke up more divided than ever. The day before, only seven percent of Republicans and seventeen GOP House districts had voted for Obama and just eight percent of Democrats and nine Democratic districts for Romney. This was a political and ideological line separating red from blue America almost as concretely as the Berlin Wall had divided East and West Germany during the Cold War. Obama, therefore, tried to unite the nation by making his second Inaugural Address an exercise in exceptionalist lyrics. He talked in soaring ways about both domestic affairs—"Today we continue a never-ending journey to bridge the meaning of those words with the realities of our time"—and international matters:

> We will support democracy from Asia to Africa, from the Americas to the Middle East, because our interests and our conscience compel us to act on behalf of those who long for freedom. And we must be a source of hope to the poor, the sick, the marginalized, the victims of prejudice—not out of mere charity, but because peace in our time requires the constant advance of those principles that our common creed describes: tolerance and opportunity, human dignity and justice.[372]

But the magic was gone. His second term was mostly to offer new and worsening troubles at home and abroad. And poison the political atmosphere even more.

Which takes us back to Syria. As the country descended into civil war, Obama tried to balance demands from liberal interventionists and neoconservatives to stop the regime's human rights violations with public opposition to the U.S. being dragged into another "endless war" in the Middle East. He first chose to do nothing except declare the use of chemical weapons a "red line" that would not go unpunished. And when poison gas was used anyway, he settled for a deal with Russia to destroy the regimes' stockpiles instead of attacking. However, after the Assad regime the following year used gas anew, and Obama could not again afford not to live up to his word, he started the military engagement that continues until today. In a message to the nation, he said: "This is American leadership at its best: We stand with people who fight for their own freedom, and we rally other nations on behalf of our common security and com-

---

372. Barack Obama, "Inaugural Address," (January 21, 2013) *APP*, accessed January 12, 2020, https://www.presidency.ucsb.edu/node/303425.

mon humanity."[373] But, naïveté, flawed intelligence, or both made him arm forces that would turn out to be extremists and assist in creating ISIS, or the Islamic State; a bunch of thugs so ruthless that Saddam Hussein and even Usama bin Laden looked almost benign in comparison.

Furthermore, the Syria debacle and the floundering economy undermined Obama's popularity at home and fed the growing fatalism creeping up on the nation after the Iraq War and the Great Recession. In 2014, over 80 percent of Americans agreed that "the last several years had seen the United States take a step back,"[374] 35 percent thought that the U.S. should be globally active, and during his last year in office, the number who were "extremely proud to be Americans" for the first time ever dropped below 50 percent.[375] Since this development had started under Bush, to what extent Obama is to blame for it can never be fully judged. But only a partisan blockhead can deny that his "critical exceptionalism" must have added to the decline. And, of course, so did eight years of weak recovery, high unemployment, over 40 million on food stamps, an uptick in violent crime, and throngs of illegal immigrants bringing drugs and raising welfare costs. Moreover, Obama's rhetoric about class and—especially—race greased groupings like Antifa and its more politically acceptable extra Black Lives Matter (BLM) that originated in 2013.

To conclude, Obama's presidency fitted a broader Western trend. Just as Reagan had matched ideologically and personally with U.K. Prime Minister Margaret Thatcher, West German Chancellor Helmut Kohl, and

373. Barack Obama, "Address to the Nation on United States Strategy To Combat the Islamic State of Iraq and the Levant Terrorist Organization (ISIL), (September 10, 2014) *APP*, accessed July 27, 2020, https://www.presidency.ucsb.edu/node/307345.

374. Marc Dunkelman, "The Crisis of American Exceptionalism," (August 13, 2014) *Real Clear Politics*, accessed January 25, 2020, https://www.realclearpolitics.com/articles/2014/08/13/the_crisis_of_american_exceptionalism_123644.html.

375. Jeffrey M. Jones, "In U.S., Record-Low 47% Extremely Proud to Be Americans," (July 2, 2018) *Gallup.com*, accessed January 25, 2020, https://news.gallup.com/poll/236420/record-low-extremely-proud-americans.aspx.

Pope Johannes Paulus II in the 1980s, Obama lined up with contemporary figures like Swedish Prime Minister Fredrik Reinfeldt, French President François Hollande, and Canadian Prime Minister Justin Trudeau. They were all media-savvy pseudointellectuals hooked on scientifically dubious (at best) but politically attractive subjects like "structural discrimination," global warming, and open borders; the latter a dogma born at the juncture of left-wing humanism and right-wing free trade theory that considers massive immigration a cure for the lot from Third World poverty to low Western birthrates (and, as it happened, also was giving left-wing parties like the Democrats boosts at the polls). Moreover, that Obama described present woes as a "new normal" created by globalization and other changes beyond anybody's control did not help. Just as in the 1970s, this made people feel that their opinions didn't count and that the world didn't make sense. Plus, even if most understood that this did not fit Americans' minds any better than Carter's *malaise* had done forty years prior, no politician dared to say so. Which, after three decades of center-left-neoconservative radical elitism, finally opened the political bullring for a potent alternative.

The Great Disruptor

The son of a real-estate developer who made a fortune by ripening the outskirts of New York City during the Great Depression, Donald Trump was raised to work hard, think big, be optimistic, and win by always being on the offensive. He set out to defy the gloom of the 1970s by building his own real-estate empire in Manhattan, which mixture of political corruption, Mafia-ridden construction businesses, and celebrity settings made him a tough negotiator, a straight talker, and a public relations aficionado. In the 1980s, Trump also expanded his enterprise to casinos, golf courses, airlines, and other ventures. And even if some of these undertakings failed, he turned TRUMP into a world brand long before landing the TV show *The Apprentice* in 2004; a gig that truthfully made him a household luminary. In addition, Trump became known as bombastic and extravagant but also a supportive father, philanthropist, and a person who helps friends and strangers in need without thinking about personal gain.

Consequently, when the Great Recession hit, Trump had been seen as a symbol of the American Dream for decades. And as the crisis deepened, he increasingly began to speak his political mind. But, when discussing issues like immigration, free trade, and other matters, he didn't sound like a Democrat *or* a Republican. On top of that, his habit of testing different viewpoints in public before making up his mind and his off-the-cuff speaking style make it difficult to pinpoint some of his core philosophical and political views. Nevertheless, speeches and writings indicate that Trump holds a classic view of human nature, believes in good and evil, views history as a worldly, materialistic, and non-deterministic process, and measures success in finite units like money, media clips, and victories. At the same time, he's not an untainted materialist, politically or privately. For instance, he has written that he has "learned that wealth and happiness are two completely different things,"[376] equated love for country with love of neighbor, and favorably quoted Adam Smith's maxim, "The man who barely abstains from violating either the person, or the estate, or the reputation of his neighbors, has surely very little merit."[377]

These outlooks make Trump's view of Americanism complex. To start, he views politicians' prime duty to always put their country first, leaving little-to-no room for mystic destinies and missions stretching over generations. In 2015, just a week ahead of announcing his candidacy, he also downright said that he dislikes American Exceptionalism, or at least

---

376. Roderick P. Hart, *Trump and Us: What He Says and Why People Listen* (Cambridge, MA: Cambridge University Press, 2020), 127.

377. Donald J. Trump, *Time To Get Tough: Make America Great Again* (New York: Regnery Publishing, 2011; updated reprint 2015), 40.

what that specific phrase has come to denote: "I don't think it's a very nice term."[378] On the other hand, Trump does see the U.S. as a special place with many unique qualities. In 2016, he stated, "America is the leader of the free world [. . .] willing to do whatever is necessary to defend this country as well as liberty anywhere in the world."[379] Still, given the trouble Obama and others have gotten into for voicing less serious doubt about Americanism, it may seem puzzling that remarks like these didn't hurt Trump's candidacy. However, he also clarified that he believes the U.S. can be great when diligent people are in charge. And if we posit that voters by 2016 had begun to associate the term exceptionalism—which is an academic term that only became more commonly used after 9/11—with Iraq, Benghazi, Syria, and other failures, both his view of the concept and voters' discounting of his negative comments do make sense.

Furthermore, Trump used the weakening of exceptionalist rhetoric to break free from the foreign policy language dominant since World War II and to bring political "holy cows" like nation-building free trade to slaughter. For example, when announcing his run, he said, "I'm a free trader. But the problem with free trade is you need really talented people to negotiate for you [. . .] if you don't have people that know business [. . .] free trade [is] terrible."[380] Thus, by signing trade deals more profitable for countries like China than the U.S., American politicians had failed in their duty to protect national interests. Also, in April 2016, Trump in a speech on foreign policy said he wanted to replace "randomness with purpose, ideology with strategy, and that, "instead of trying to spread universal values that

---

378. David Corn, "Donald Trump Says He Doesn't Believe in American Exceptionalism," (June 7, 2016) *Mother Jones*, accessed January 31, 2020, https://www.motherjones.com/politics/2016/06/donald-trump-american-exceptionalism/.

379. Donald J. Trump, *Crippled America: How to Make America Great Again* (New York: Threshold Editions, 2015), 136.

380. Donald J. Trump, "Remarks Announcing Candidacy for President in New York City," (June 16, 2015) *APP*, accessed February 4, 2020, https://www.presidency.ucsb.edu/node/310310.

not everybody shares or wants, we should understand that strengthening and promoting Western civilization and its accomplishments will do more to inspire positive reforms around the world than military interventions." In the same speech, he also took a strong stand against globalism: "We will no longer surrender this country or its people to the false song of globalism. The nation-state remains the true foundation for happiness and harmony."[381]

In total, Trump's views on foreign policy and free trade can both be called unorthodox in that his positions are more in line with the Founding Fathers' than the GOP's support for the country's superpower role and trade since World War II. But it is vital to note that they do deviate from both. Because even if Trump often talked about getting the U.S. "out of the nation-building business" by promising things like routing the Islamic terrorist group ISIS, he bound himself to keep America involved internationally. Also, by promising to deal seriously with decades-old problems like North Korea and stop Iran from acquiring nuclear weapons, he committed himself to be, if necessary, more aggressive than earlier presidents.

To move on, since Trump had flirted with entering politics since the 1980s, had lived a personal life unfit for an office-seeker, and had a long history of advanced publicity stunts, many did not take his bid for the 2016 GOP nomination seriously. For several months, therefore, he escaped tougher scrutiny. Indeed, CNN would, next to Fox News, often cover his rallies live; the former certainly for the double reason to boost its rating and believing that what he said would frighten people. But it had the opposite effect. Also, Trump's mastery of public relations and knowledge of the inner workings of media gave him an almost unfair advantage vis-à-vis his opponents. He would for years be so far ahead not only of other politicians but the media itself that many refused to admit that he regularly outwitted them all. In his Announcement Speech, one example is that he seemingly destroyed himself by talking about immigration in ways that got journalists, pundits, and political opponents to declare him a dead horse from the get-go: "When Mexico sends its people, they're not sending their best. [. . .] They're bringing drugs. They're bringing crime. They're rapists. And some, I assume, are good people."[382] However, by opening his campaign this way, knowing that this line would be endlessly quoted, he broke through the media chatter, set his candidacy apart, and tapped into "normal folks" discontent with illegal immigration. And it worked. Within two months, he took the lead in the strongest field of GOP candidates in a generation.

Moreover, picking *Make America Great Again* as his campaign theme made it possible for Trump to evade the depressed "new normal" discourse and project a victory for him as "a return to better times—economically and culturally—[like] in America's past."[383] This had been Reagan's strategy in 1980, and Trump linked himself to him politically, even if some of their policies did not pair. On the stump, he also turned out to be a juggernaut worthy of comparison not only with Reagan but William Jennings Bryan, Theodore Roosevelt, FDR, and Harry Truman. During the fall of 2015, Trump's meetings thus began to dwarf Obama's eight years earlier. They exploded into "MAGA rallies" where his high-energy persona, uncooked populism, and media dexterity played out in front of tens of thousands where he, besides policy points like building a wall and letting Mexico pay for it, stressed his outsider status. When formally accepting his candidacy, he stepped forward as a combined Andrew Jackson and Theodore

382. Donald J. Trump, "Remarks Announcing Candidacy for President in New York City," (June 16, 2015) *APP*, accessed January 30, 2020, https://www.presidency.ucsb.edu/node/310310.
383. Michael Kranish & Marc Fisher, *Trump Revealed: The Definitive Biography of the 45th President* (New York; Scribner, 2016), 318.

Roosevelt figure. About his opponent, Hillary Clinton, he said:

> Big business, elite media and major donors are lining up
> behind the campaign of my opponent because they know
> she will keep our rigged system in place. They are throwing
> money at her because they have total control over every
> single thing she does. She is their puppet, and they pull
> the strings. [. . .] I have joined the political arena so that
> the powerful can no longer beat up on people that cannot
> defend themselves.[384]

At times, Trump too turned to the Founding Fathers and Lincoln for
support, e.g., for his trade policy: "One of the first major bills signed
by George Washington called for 'the encouragement and protection of
manufactur[ing]' in America. Our first Republican President, Abraham
Lincoln, warned us by saying: 'The abandonment of the protective policy
by the American government will produce want and ruin among our people.' "[385] However, such nods were few and contributing more to Trump's
victory was his patriotism, optimism, use of everyday American words like
"huge," "beautiful," and "wonderful," his aura of being a man "always in a
hurry and constantly ready for a fight," and promise that America under
him would "start winning again."[386] This appealed to people disgruntled
with lost jobs, low incomes, crime, political correctness, and "the D.C.
mess" in general.

It was also Trump's argument that America had lost its way that tipped
the scale in his favor. The composition of his vote tells this story. Of the 62
percent who thought the country was on the wrong track, almost seven in

---

384. Donald J. Trump, "Address Accepting the Presidential Nomination at the Republican National
Convention in Cleveland, Ohio," (July 21, 2016) *APP*, accessed February 10, 2020, https://www.presidency.
ucsb.edu/node/318521.

385. Donald J. Trump, "Remarks at Trump SoHo in New York City," (June 22, 2016) *APP*, accessed
February 3, 2020, https://www.presidency.ucsb.edu/node/317885.

386. Hart, *Trump and Us*, 11.

ten voted for him. He also won traditionalist- and exceptionalist-minded groups like conservatives (81 percent), evangelicals (80 percent), rural voters (61 percent), veterans (60 percent), whites (57 percent), men and people over 65 (both 52 percent), people with little or no college education (51 percent), and Catholics (50 percent). In addition, he increased Romney's share of African Americans (8 percent), Latinos (28 percent), and Asian Americans (27 percent). Trump also won in the right places. Besides the South and the Rockies, he swept most of the Midwest and—for the first time for a Republican since 1988—the Rustbelt. This gave him an easy victory in the Electoral College of 306 to 232 for Clinton. However, he lost the popular vote, showing the country was more divided than ever.

Actually, only one group united that evening. The establishment. TV studios filled up with stuttering commentators, blaming Trump's victory on everything from "a total fucking war" to "a whitewash." And the next day, academics went to work to explain (away) his win. Ignoring that the political situation for decades had been moving toward an exceptionalist-globalist clash, they pointed to his stance on immigration and claimed that his rhetoric had attracted poor and undereducated whites with racist views. However, the "levels of anger and anxiety were no greater in 2016 than in recent years,"[387] and white voting patterns were still behind the levels of "racialization" among African Americans, Latinos, and Asian Americans. Also, they blamed whites for crediting the socioeconomic inequality of blacks to lack of effort and their view that immigrants are "stealing their place in line" as racist, disregarding that these views only reflect traditional opinions of equal opportunity and fair play. In short, because "experts" wanted Clinton to win (and were confident that the U.S. electorate would forever continue moving left), nearly all missed what really happened.

387. Sides, Tesler & Vavreck, *Identity Crisis*, 25-31, 87ff.

And it was only to get worse. Not only would the chock turn into an absolutistic distaste—and in many cases pure hatred—for Trump personally. And as the hope that he would smooth things over after the election turned out to be wrong (since he swiftly learned how to walk the D.C. walk but also proved that to talk the talk was not in his DNA), the panic was institutionalized. Already his Inauguration spoke volumes. With good parts of the U.S. establishment, including several Bushes and Clintons, sitting stone-faced behind him in front of the Capitol Building, he said:

> Today we are not merely transferring power from one
> administration to another or from one party to another, but
> we are transferring power from Washington, DC, and giving
> it back to you, the people. For too long, a small group in
> our Nation's Capital has reaped the rewards of Government
> while the people have borne the cost.

And even if he did use some standard language—"We stand at the birth of a new millennium, ready to unlock the mysteries of space, to free the Earth from the miseries of disease, and to harness the energies, industries, and technologies of tomorrow"—he ended with the crescendo from his MAGA rallies: "Together, we will make America strong again. We will make America wealthy again. We will make America proud again. We will make America safe again. And, yes, together, we will make America great again. Thank you. God bless you, and God bless America."[388]

This was the most daring Inauguration Address given by a president since Andrew Jackson. Throughout his presidency, Trump would also seldom disappoint those who wanted to have "new blood" transfused into Uncle Sam's arteries. For instance, since his ability to predict pub-

---

388. Donald J. Trump, "Inaugural Address," (January 20, 2017) *APP*, accessed January 29, 2020, https://www.presidency.ucsb.edu/node/320188.

lic moods remained extraordinary after stepping into the White House "bubble," he took controversial stances on social and cultural issues. Like when football player Colin Kaepernick began to "take a knee" during the national anthem to protest racism. Trump complained about this—and polls showed that he was in tune with more than seven of ten Americans. Moreover, when it came to domestic politics in general, he could, besides protests for breaking the tone of political correctness, count on near-unanimous Republican support for tax reductions, deregulations, and . . . deficit spending. Indeed, the first two policies created such a vibrant economy that unemployment plummeted simultaneously as growth for the first time in decades rose to such healthy levels that some argued it might even be enough to close the deficit. But that was not to be.

Regarding world affairs, Trump contrary had to fight every step of the way as he threw himself into a historic clash with the bipartisan "War Party" in Washington, D.C., and large parts of the "international community" that, since 1945, had grown used to two things. Grand talk about democracy as the end-station for History, the self-evidence of social equality and cultural relativism, and the good of ever-closer political, economic, and other kinds of interdependency. And leaders prepared to pay endless amounts of American blood and dollars to back it up. In practical terms, this meant that Trump began to wind down military involvements around the globe and ignored protests, e.g., against the U.S. walking away from the Paris Agreement on climate change. To the aghast of don't-rock-the-boat-elites, he also threatened to leave NATO (if European members did not increase their military spending) and the WTO (if countries like China did not start to follow agreements on, e.g., intellectual property rights); promised to sign a bilateral trade deal with the U.K. after its exit from the E.U.; and explained bluntly why the U.S. would never join the International Criminal Court: "We will never surrender America's sovereignty to an unelected, unaccountable, global bureaucracy. America is governed by Americans."[389]

Hence, Trump's foreign policy did not sit well anywhere except with the American people. Aligning himself with state theorists going back to John Selden, who in the seventeenth century had portrayed the nation-state as the only alternative to an anarchic world of clans and tribes on one side and despotic empires on the other, he could also make good cases for his actions. For example, in 2017, when abandoning the Trans-Pacific Partnership negotiated by Obama as a NAFTA-like deal for the Pacific region, "everyone" protested, but Trump said: "I will [instead] make bilateral trade agreements with any Indo-Pacific nation [. . .] What we will no longer do is enter into large agreements that tie our hands, surrender our sovereignty, and make meaningful enforcement practically impossible." He also defined this as a return to a state of normalcy: "In America, like every nation that has won and defended its sovereignty, we understand that we have nothing so precious as our birthright, our treasured independence, and our freedom. That knowledge has guided us throughout American history. It has inspired us to sacrifice and innovate."[390]

Moreover, Trump's goals were more ambitious than just disentangling the U.S. from costly overseas engagements and unfavorable international trade deals. Like all other post-World War II presidents, he used the power and prestige of his office to reshape the world order. He began his presidency by giving several speeches on world politics and culture. In July 2017, in Warsaw, Poland, he defined Western civilization and its freedom ethos as unique in human history:

389. Donald J. Trump, "Remarks to the United Nations General Assembly in New York City," (September 25, 2018) *APP*, accessed February 21, 2020, https://www.presidency.ucsb.edu/node/332698.

390. Donald J. Trump, "Remarks at the Asia-Pacific Economic Cooperation CEO Summit in Danang, Vietnam," (November 10, 2017) *APP*, accessed February 25, 2020, https://www.presidency.ucsb.edu/node/331585.

The world has never known anything like our community of nations. We write symphonies. We pursue innovation. We celebrate our ancient heroes, embrace our timeless traditions and customs, and always seek to explore and discover brand new frontiers. We reward brilliance. We strive for excellence and cherish inspiring works of art that honor God. We treasure the rule of law and protect the right to free speech and free expression. We empower women as pillars of our society and of our success. We put faith and family, not government and bureaucracy, at the center of our lives. And we debate everything. We challenge everything. We seek to know everything so that we can better know ourselves. And above all, we value the dignity of every human life, protect the rights of every person, and share the hope of every soul to live in freedom. That is who we are.[391]

A U.S. president had not been heard delivering such a battle cry for Western ideals since World War II. Two months later, in his first address to the U.N. General Assembly, he also formulated a "Trump Doctrine" encompassing both a general view of world affairs . . .

We do not expect diverse countries to share the same cultures, traditions, or even systems of government. But we do expect all nations to uphold these two core sovereign duties: to respect the interests of their own people and the rights of every other sovereign nation. [. . .] Strong, sovereign nations let diverse countries with different values, different cultures, and different dreams not just coexist, but work side by side on the basis of mutual respect.

. . . a comprehensive stance on America's place, role, and actions in the world . . .

---

391. Donald J. Trump, "Remarks in Warsaw, Poland," (July 6, 2017) *APP*, accessed February 18, 2020, https://www.presidency.ucsb.edu/node/329413.

The United States will forever be a great friend to the world and especially to its allies. But we can no longer be taken advantage of or enter into a one-sided deal where the United States gets nothing in return. As long as I hold this office, I will defend America's interests above all else. We want harmony and friendship, not conflict and strife. We are guided by outcomes, not ideology.

. . . and aligned himself with those opposing globalism and multiculturalism everywhere:

As president of the United States, I will always put America first, just like you, as the leaders of your countries, will always, and should always, put your countries first. All responsible leaders have an obligation to serve their own citizens, and the nation-state remains the best vehicle for elevating the human condition. But making a better life for our people also requires us to work together in close harmony and unity to create a more safe and peaceful future for all people.[392]

Thus, Trump's views of America, freedom, and Western civilization are traditionally conservative. Specifically, it stands opposite of classic liberals and neoconservatives, who consider freedom a natural state of human affairs that may need political help to emerge but then will be self-subsisting. Instead, Trump reckons freedom to be an achieved state, specific for the West, that must be continuously cultivated and protected from internal and external enemies. In his Warsaw speech, he compared the modern threat of Islamism with communism and criticized "the steady creep of government bureaucracy that drains the vitality and wealth of the people." However, Trump never promised active financial or military

392. Trump, "Remarks to the United Nations General Assembly in New York City," (September 19, 2017) *APP*, accessed February 20, 2020, https://www.presidency.ucsb.edu/documents/remarks-the-united-nations-general-assembly-new-york-city-13.

support for "neo-nationalists" or any other schemes seeking to roll back globalism and multiculturalism in other countries—and he left the exact definition of freedom to every people to decide. That is to say, he placed himself in line with the Founding Father's view of the U.S. as a model and an always benevolent but aloof custodian of freedom.

NEW ERA OR PARENTHESIZE?

In February 2020, Trump launched his campaign for a second term in his State of the Union. He opened with boasting about economic and other successes and a rhetorical exercise in his by-then signature passive-exclusive form of Americanism, using words Washington, Lincoln, or Reagan could well have spoken:

> The American nation was carved out of the vast frontier
> by the toughest, strongest, fiercest, and most determined
> men and women ever to walk on the face of the Earth.
> Our ancestors braved the unknown; tamed the wilderness;
> settled the Wild West; lifted millions from poverty, disease,
> and hunger; vanquished tyranny and fascism; ushered the
> world to new heights of science and medicine; laid down the
> railroads, dug out the canals, raised up the skyscrapers. And,
> ladies and gentlemen, our ancestors built the most excep-
> tional republic ever to exist in all human history, and we are
> making it greater than ever before. This is our glorious and
> magnificent inheritance. We are Americans. We are pioneers.
> We are the pathfinders.[393]

At that moment, most analysts, however grudgingly, agreed that Trump would probably win a second term. But, as he spoke, the COVID-19 virus was finding its way into the U.S., and a couple of months later, the politi-

---

393. Trump, "Address Before a Joint Session of the Congress on the State of the Union," (February 4, 2020) *APP*, accessed February 4, 2020, https://www.presidency.ucsb.edu/documents/address-before-joint-session-the-congress-the-state-the-union-27.

cal scene—including Trump's path to reelection—had been upended.

The pandemic and its consequences—lockdowns, stock shortages, price gouging, political overreach, bureaucratic power grabs—created a war-like state of mind. Trump was therefore forced to conduct his campaign parallel with organizing a national effort to handle the virus. Under a more "normal" emergency, this would probably have worked in his favor by rallying people around the flag and the president. The Democrats, however, decided to sabotage Trump's COVID-19 response and use it against him. This unprecedented maneuver would never have worked if it hadn't been for the media, gory-minded after failing to take Trump down for four years, and local and state politicians, federal bureaucrats, and groups such as unionized teachers and nurses playing along. In a word, by reporting Trump's actions as insufficient or mistaken, often both—amidst daily news featuring death numbers and interviews with fearful citizens, health care professionals, and others all wearing masks—journalists did everything they could to add confusion to fear. Also, by classifying criticism of draconian measures to stop the virus taken by mayors, governors, and federal bureaucracies as almost terrorism, they contributed to the most extensive breach not only of the American people's right to free speech but also of religion, press, assembly, and petition in history.

Moreover, as lockdowns intended "to flatten the curve" turned into what can only be described as an indefinite state of emergency, people began to protest. And while roughly one-half protested that politicians didn't take drastic actions enough, the other half protested measures going too far. Which is a pretty standard distribution curve regarding any political issue. However, the line between those who trusted authorities and accepted restrictions and those who refused followed, almost perfectly, the red-blue political divide. For example, while New Yorkers and Californians continued to accept wearing masks, sneezing in responsible ways, and placing themselves under curfew, Texans and Floridians returned to work and life in general after a few months. In other words, while people in blue parts of the country panicked, trusted "experts" blindly, and so fell back on positivist, technocratic methods, folks in red states leaned toward traditional self-reliance and defiance against elites. Thus, mass psychology not only blended with political worldviews but was arguably formed by them in ways never seen before except, maybe, during the Civil War.

Also, COVID-19 didn't become media and the left's only way to dethrone Trump. Spotting an opportunity fitting their "social justice" and standard racist narrative, after a police officer killed a black criminal in Minneapolis, media and Democrats whipped up a frenzy by expressing sympathy (read: support) and protesting what they described as an established pattern of police violence. Which in the heads and hands of BLM led to a string of violent demonstrations from coast to coast, costing at least twenty-five lives and roughly two billion dollars in property damage. These protests also led to demands for "Defund the police"—a drive to cut funds to the police and (in a classic behaviorist manner) reallocate them to social services, housing, education, etc. And in places where this was done, crime rates immediately went sky-high. What's more, since the BLM and Defund protests came on top of other disturbances by groups demanding the removal of Civil War statues, etc., in his Fourth of July speech at Mount Rushmore, Trump felt forced to ask both for calm and for the people to protect the country's heritage:

> I am here as your President to proclaim before the country
> and before the world: This monument will never be
> desecrated, these heroes will never be defaced, their legacy
> will never, ever be destroyed, their achievements will never

be forgotten, and Mount Rushmore will stand forever as an eternal tribute to our forefathers and to our freedom. [394]

But the ideological polarization and extreme partisanship that had been growing for decades, the personal hatred of Trump, and extreme media bias made reconciliation impossible. In the end, he, therefore, lost (if straight or because of illegal ballot harvesting and other irregularities is a question that will not be explored here).

Still, the ideas, hopes, and worries that led Trump to the White House are far from dead. If anything, since 2020, they have continued to develop and gained even more support. Also, the exceedingly radical Biden administration has turned into such a political, economic, and cultural tragedy that he, at the moment this is written, seems to be moving toward a possible comeback in 2024. And if he wins—or someone with policies like his runs and wins in 2028—this will probably open a new era marked by foreign and other policies more in tune with the Founding Fathers than the string of elitist liberals, RINOs, and neoconservatives that almost uninterruptedly has occupied the White House since 1933. On the other hand, America today is more divided than ever, so whoever wins will have a hard time holding the Union together. If that is even possible anymore. Because the demise of Americanism as national "glue" brought on by failed liberal and neoconservative policies is certainly not helping. Case in point, in 2021, according to the Center for Politics at the University of Virginia, the support for breaking up America into one blue and one red part stood at 41 and 52 percent among Democrats and Republicans respectively.

394. Donald J. Trump, "Remarks at an Independence Day Celebration at the Mount Rushmore National Memorial in Keystone, South Dakota," (July 4, 2020) *APP*, accessed July 7, 2021, https://www.presidency. ucsb.edu/documents/remarks-independence-day-celebration-the-mount-rushmore-national-memorial-keystone-south.

"We Athenians alone do good to our neighbors not upon a calculation of interest, but in the confidence of freedom and in a frank and fearless spirit."

Thucydides | 431 BC

Concluding Reflections

The significance of Americanism in the great flow of U.S. history cannot be overstated. Since the Revolutionary War, it has offered a collective identity, a civic sense, and a political loadstar for citizens and immigrants, Republicans and Democrats, blacks and whites, rich and poor alike. Thus, Americanism has overall been an awesome, positive force. At the same time, there can be no denying that some exceptionalist views and sentiments have occasionally been abused. Manifest Destiny, leading to the ethnic cleansing of American Indians; the fusion of exceptionalist notions with Social Darwinism, deepening many whites' antipathy toward African-Americans; and the post-1898 foreign policy pulling the country into a string of wars are three examples. But this makes Americanism no different from European-style nationalism. Like these, as well as other collective ideas and ideologies, including liberalism, socialism, communism, and fascism, Americanism is a double-edged sword, able to cut in different directions, and a hammer, that can be used to build orphanages as well as to crush skulls. So, if Americanism is to be deemed good, bad, or something in between is continuously determined but never settled by its employers' actions.

Furthermore, Americanism did not begin to affect day-to-day U.S. politics until the late nineteenth century seriously. Before that, it was a nebulous concept construed in support of the republican constitutionalism fashioned by the Founding Fathers, which proclaimed only that the U.S. was destined to stretch from coast to coast and to play a role as a model of freedom. As such, it was not controversial for the simple reason that it threatened no one (except, of course, loyalists, American Indians, and a few others when standing in America's way). Consequently, Americanism maintained the Founder's socioeconomic order and remained a source of political strength and national pride. In fact, the Founders' core political principles—small government, states' rights, low taxes, and few regulations—turned into a "super ideology" adhered to by nearly all. This became especially true after the Civil War, when accepting exceptionalist notions, plus learning English, became a highway to assimilation for millions of former slaves and massive bodies of ethnically, religiously, and culturally diverse immigrants. Together with the 1898 Spanish-American War, this transformed Americanism into a full-blown nationalist ideology, complete with notions about, e.g., the essence of man and the direction of History.

However, around 1900, by dismissing the Constitution as no more than a time-typical piece of paper and claiming that America had to reform itself indefinitely, progressives broke the historic political consensus. This change depended upon increasing influence from European ideologies and viewpoints, mainly on the elite level of society, and as they spread, the concept of Americanism began to split in two. On one side, it turned into a philosophy centered on three harmonious ideas: a classical view of an essentially fixed, dual human nature with limiting effects on politics; the subsequent need to preserve the U.S. as a decentralized federation with a small government and a free economy; and America's role as a model of freedom. On the other side, radical exceptionalism similarly focused on three themes: a modern "plastic" view of human nature, America as a prototype of infinite improvements through reforms, and the U.S. as an active implementor of a new world order based on "human rights." And even if most people's views fall in between these two archetypes, as in the case of orthodox and liberal Christians, nearly all Americans have come to lean closer to one side than the other, with traditionalists tending to be conservatives and radicals becoming liberals (and neoconservatives as a kind of in-between creatures).

Moreover, despite most Americans long remaining social and cultural traditionalists, radicals came to dominate post-1898 U.S. politics. This paradox has several reasons. One is that radical Americanism got a grand rhetor in Theodore Roosevelt and a prime theorist in Woodrow Wilson. They together framed a discourse that defined modern U.S. foreign policy. They also stressed the importance of reforms at home to keep America attractive abroad so intensely that domestic and foreign policies became interlinked. Thus, as America grew into a world power, parallel with other countries also becoming wealthier and better functioning, the pressure for reforms allegedly grew also. Explicitly, this radical view, supported by exceptionalist-sounding arguments, could be used to push for social and other reforms independent of actual needs—and was so at a rate that the U.S., as a low-tax country, couldn't afford. Or, put differently, liberals tied America's destiny at home to keeping up with Europe's welfare state Joneses.

A second reason for radicals' dominance of twentieth-century U.S. politics is that the above turned exceptionalist rhetoric into a staple of both U.S. foreign and domestic politics, presidential oratory in particular, which in turn pushed the parties to adopt increasingly different programs and policies derived from the two basic forms of exceptionalist thinking.

On the right, traditional Americanism became a conservative force that could be used to argue against the elitist urge to turn the U.S. into a "normal" Western top-down welfare state, while on the left, as proven by a string of well-spoken politicians from FDR to JFK to Obama, exceptionalist rhetoric could, at least to some extent, also be used to argue for it. And since many easily get used to and dependent upon entitlements and other perks that effectually weakened America's economic development and social, and cultural cohesion, the rest is, as one saying goes, history.

The third reason for the left's soon-hundred-year-old political predominance is thus that since 1933, the Democratic Party has managed to use deficit spending, pork barrel projects, the New Class, and academic and media biases during an era of overall low turnout to secure strong electoral support from substantial voting blocs such as blacks, women, immigrants, and the youth. Or put differently, since few oppose receiving gifts that according to politicians' guarantee are paid for by "the rich" and described as "rights," the left has been able to impose their policies upon a generally oblivious majority. This, in turn, means that America—as presidential hopeful Vivek Ramaswamy in 2023 so eloquently described it when talking about the disproportionate influence of the by the militant left appropriated "LGBTQ+ community"—has become a minoritarian tyranny, but with drag queens being far from the main problem.

However, the liberal view of what the U.S. should be cannot be explained or defended by exceptionalist-sounding arguments in the long run. Since the 1960s, therefore, Democrats have been forced to abandon exceptionalist rhetoric gradually and so distanced themselves from the mainstream. As a result, even if polarization is frequently blamed on the GOP taking a "hard right-turn" under Goldwater and Reagan, Democrats' radicalization by far succeeds the increase in Republicans' conservative seal. In fact, the latter was only a reaction to the former. Since the 1970s, Americanism has accordingly become a source of political conflict more than a theme for national pride and unity. This is especially true in domestic politics, where ideological differences between liberals and conservatives naturally are most pronounced. That American culture at the same time has passed a tipping point between communitarian and atomistic-individualist cultures also diluted the political importance of Americanism. However, exceptionalist language did keep more of its emotional appeal in foreign policy. In the 1980s, it helped Ronald Reagan to win the Cold War and in the next decade offered support for Bush 41's and Bill Clinton's turning of the U.S. into a world police. But after Bush 43 invaded Iraq in 2003, and the ensuing ghost chase of Saddam Hussein's WMDs, the concept's lure was also wrecked in that realm. We will return to this.

First, let's look at some more specific findings. When listing the exceptionalist views of U.S. presidents according to the four definitions presented in the Introduction—active/passive, inclusive/exclusive—and adding party affiliation and info about whether or not they took the country to war and tried to conduct important domestic reforms (Appendix), several interesting patterns occur. Starting with foreign policy, of the twenty-one presidents between 1898 and 2020, more than half (fourteen) wanted to spread American values abroad actively, and of the seven who did not, all but one (Obama) were Republicans. Also, three of these seven (Harding, Coolidge, Trump) were exclusive-minded, believing spreading American values abroad was not even feasible. Further, of nine war presidents, all but one (Obama) has held an active-inclusive view of Americanism, while no passive or exclusive-minded president except one (Obama) has ever purposely taken the country to war. Also, twice as many war presidents have been Democrats (Wilson, FDR, Truman, LBJ, Clinton, Obama) as Republicans (McKinley, Bush 41, Bush 43). Thus, the only exception to the patterns shown here is Obama. His Americanism is also in many ways unique, and his wars in Libya and Syria were seemingly more dependent upon expectations created by his grand rhetoric than will—and nervousness for appearing weak on terrorism.

Consequently, one critical deduction must be that presidents believing strongly in Americanism per se is *not* an indication of them being ready to go to war, but holding an active-inclusive variant of the concept is. Supporting this assumption is that all presidents' decisions to go to war since 1898 except one (FDR) have been active choices based on what good for the world they thought U.S. participation could bring. It's also worth noting that FDR by the end of 1941 had taken such a strong stand against Germany that history may have unfolded similarly without Pearl Harbor. Indeed, circumstances beyond presidents' control sometimes do play decisive roles. It is, for example, possible that Truman may not have gone to war if North Korea hadn't attacked its southern neighbor. However, since this also goes for Bush 43 after 9/11, the main point—that war presidents *can* act differently but are swayed by exceptionalist convictions—stands. In other words, there's a clear link between presidents' exceptionalist views and their foreign policies.

The impression that exceptionalist views direct presidents' actions is also strong in domestic politics. Most basically, five of seven reform presidents since 1898 have held an active view of Americanism. Of these four (Wilson, FDR, LBJ, Obama) were liberal Democrats and one (Theodore Roosevelt) a progressive Republican, who thought reforms were necessary both for domestic reasons and to keep America attractive as a model—and the fifth (Reagan) a conservative who wanted to roll back liberal policies for the very same reason. Moreover, since three of these five reform presidents (Wilson, FDR, LBJ) were also war presidents and two passive-inclusive reform presidents (Nixon, Obama) were in other ways very internationally active, the impression that presidents believing in vigorous forms of

Americanism are prone to both reforms and war is hard to shake. The fact that Democratic presidents have gone to war twice as often as Republicans also supports this conclusion. As believers in the primacy of politics and social, economic, and cultural engineering, they naturally have an optimistic view of what can be accomplished both at home and abroad. And that Bush 43 can be classified as a big government neoconservative further augments this pattern.

Given the crucial role of exceptionalism in Americans' self-image, none of these findings are surprising (except maybe, for some, that Democrat presidents are more prone to warmongering than Republicans). Even so, to apply them when evaluating presidents' worldviews, policies, and actions is crucial. Let's consider two examples. First, exceptionalist convictions risk blinding people to the fact that cultural and religious traits not only underlie Western-type democracy and capitalism but make these systems work. If this fact is forgotten or disregarded, cost assessments for wars and nation-building projects inevitably become flawed. Iraq, Afghanistan, and Haiti spontaneously pop into one's mind. And this problem worsens if such ignorance is combined with the view that both individual attitudes and cultural traits can be altered by political means. This is what happened in America around 1900 when the Spanish-American War of 1898 let loose an "imperialist bug," and the Progressive Movement's influence upon politics, academia, and other important sectors distorted the view of how hard it is to change both genetically based behaviors and time-tested cultural traits. This double whammy can be seen in Woodrow Wilson's belief that he could change U.S. politics top-down, broker a "scientific peace," and create a New World Order after World War I, as well as in LBJ's Vietnam policy and Bush 43's behavior after 9/11.

A second example of the influence of (corrupted) exceptionalist thinking and ditto rhetoric is FDR's New Deal, his four freedoms, and the elevation of democratism and human rights into dogma during World War II. Together with LBJ's Great Society, they encouraged levels of nanny statism and ideological belligerence that eventually began to wreck not only America's economy but also her culture and international stature. To catalog all the welfare and other kinds of reforms contributing to this rolling catastrophe at home is impossible. But we can list the wars in Korea, Vietnam, Laos, Indonesia, Lebanon (twice), Dominican Republic, Cambodia, Grenada, Libya (twice), Iraq (twice), Somalia (twice), Haiti, Bosnia-Herzegovina, Kosovo, Afghanistan, Yemen, Pakistan, Uganda, Niger, and Syria. And while gracefully honoring the heroism and sacrifice of all those who served in these conflicts, we should remember that their costs in blood and dollars, with a partial exception in Vietnam, for a long time were—often grudgingly but still—accepted by the American people because politicians motivated them with exceptionalist arguments.

But, if we look forward to the 2003 Iraq War, we can take stock in that when it became clear that Saddam Hussein had had no WMDs, something finally broke. After that, even Obama—a grand rhetor with imposing exceptionalist and humanitarian credentials—couldn't arouse public enthusiasm for his wars in Libya and Syria. And he was, in turn, followed by Donald Trump, whose victory in 2016 to some extent depended upon his promise to end America's role as world police. Moreover, Trump's victory depended even more on his stances on foreign trade and globalism. To recall, after the Cold War, Americans grew wary about Daddy and Baby Bush's, Clinton's, and Obama's international agendas. Still, exceptionalist assurances that America could thrive in a globalist world blared, and the costs for both wars and bad trade deals like NAFTA (in the form of, e.g., deindustrialization, lost jobs, and wage reduction) were long ignored, belittled, and even ridiculed by elites. Over time, therefore, qualms morphed into anger, and when the Great Recession hit after the

Iraq War, a public reaction against the post-Cold War *Zeitgeist*—after Obama turned out to be just another elitist globalist—commenced.

However, before dealing with the effects of this historic shift, we need to return to the 1960s and make a couple more comments. Since LBJ's creation of a European-like federal welfare state went opposite both to the general philosophy of traditional Americanism and most policies that sensibly can be drawn from some of its specific exceptionalist notions, around 1970, something, obviously, needed to give: either the U.S. went back to its original politically decentralized, free economic order, or the country's societal contract had to be rewritten. If either of these things had happened, U.S. history could, perhaps, have taken a different, more harmonious track.

However, not only had liberals pushed so quickly and far that a more profound restructuring of people's view of what America should be hadn't had time to come to pass. They also refused to pause and allowed themselves to be even more radicalized. The result of this was the Culture Wars, whereby partisanship, ideological polarization, and popular resentments have ever since pitted growing parts of the U.S. citizenry against each other. And even if the constellations for and against different issues vary, the camps have since the 1970s been so cemented that the parties have moved further and further toward their ideological extremes. This development has also been driven by perfectionist thinking stemming from the fundamentalistic attitude that since God is good and perfect, nothing less than perfection is good enough. And while this works well as a theological topic of conversation, such thinking never leads to good consequences in politics.

Besides ideological extremism, perfectionist thinking has until today in the U.S. continued to nurture the conviction that Americans can do anything, or at least much more than other people. Throughout the twentieth century, this view was apparently proven right by real events such as the U.S. defeating both fascism and communism and Americans walking on the Moon. But it also fed dangerous fantasies such as the U.S. having nothing to learn from foreign experiences and that Americans can get things failing everywhere else to work. Examples abound. While liberals blissfully ignore European countries' problems with high taxes, undue regulations, and national healthcare systems, conservatives argue that lowered taxes can spur economic growth enough to pay for everything. And the result of this is that both sides have been forced to leave the experiment of the U.S. being a joint welfare-warfare state running, creating structural deficits so severe and a national debt so massive that for well over a half-century the country has been speeding down the road toward political sclerosis and state bankruptcy.

Which brings us back to today's situation. A hard-to-miss observation is that Democrats' frantic support for a federal welfare state, forced secularization, and speedy globalization—plus some Republicans' likewise extreme opposition to things like a realistic abortion policy—today creates a societal division so deep that people are being alienated not only politically but socially and culturally as well. In addition, the left's deliberate creation of racial, economic, and other subgroup identities has, since the 1960s, contributed to a schizophrenic confusion about what it means to be an American. One example is that the worldviews of a flag-burning Antifa activist in Portland, Oregon, and a blue-collar Trump voter in Howell, Michigan, today are so far apart that they could not sit down and discuss politics constructively even if they wanted to. The same also goes for those football fans who on Twitter in 2021 sided with the Tampa Bay Buccaneers and Kansas City Chiefs in *Super Bowl LV* based on their view of Florida's Republican Governor Ron DeSantis' COVID-19 policy. Thus, the growing demand for political perfection—meaning no exceptions allowed and one-size-fits-all national solutions from coast to coast—on issues stretching from regulation of cow farts to reduce CO_2 emissions to totally free (or absolutely banned) abortions is deadlocking the political system—and weakening the glue of Americanism.

This sundering of America shows in many ways. Besides vitriolic partisanship, skyrocketing crime rates, and bureaucratic obstructionism, one sign is the erosion of political civility. Like all modern democracies, America must, next to the Constitution and other written laws ensuring free and fair elections, freedom of speech, etc., have a set of informal but commonly held rules. For example, politicians must show a basic level of respect for their opponents, keep a civil tone in public debates, and be prepared to admit defeat. If they don't, the system will go sour. In fact, relying on formal rules alone can make things worse (like when Trump in December 2020 tried to get Vice President Mike Pence to refuse to accept electors from contested states). And it is not an exaggeration to say that the U.S. today is sliding on many such accounts. Among other things, accusations of voter fraud (from the right) and voter intimidation (from the left) are legion; all post-Cold War presidents have had to deal with opponents who have stated publicly that their prime goal is to get rid of them; presidential candidates since 2012 have publicly shown personal contempt for each other; and after the last two elections, the losing candidates have refused to concede; Clinton in 2016 by calling Trump an "illegitimate president" and talking about "joining the resistance" and Trump in 2020 by continuing to dispute the results even after the Electoral College had voted.

To make things worse, lying in public has become all but accepted; at least when elites deem it better for what they consider the greater good. One example is the "Russian collusion" story born before the 2016 election. Similarly, lies and provocations aimed to please hardliners and hurt opponents are now taken without long-term consideration. For instance, after a group of Trump supporters on January 6, 2021, forced themselves into the Capitol building in Washington D.C., the Democrats and the media, only a few months after openly defending the BLM riots, described the chaos as a planned, full-blown coup attempt (without explaining how a bunch of madcaps that were surrounded by thousands of police officers could have taken over the country, or stopped Joe Biden from becoming president two full weeks later). This ploy has since also been backed up by congressional hearings staged to pin what happened on Trump personally. A related example of another form of deplorable behavior is that the Biden administration, like in a classic South American banana republic, is using government institutions—including the FBI and the Department of Justice—to get Trump locked up. Most disturbing of all is that not even political violence is uncommon anymore. It so far comes predominantly from the left, where it is also often hailed as understandable—and sometimes openly welcomed. Like in front of the 2020 election, when many Democrats, President-to-be Joe Biden included, endorsed the BLM protests. So far, the authorities have managed to control the political violence. But who knows how long this will last when the political will to condemn and condone it is so blatantly selective.

As should be clear, besides politicians and the New Class, the main force behind this deteriorating political climate is the professional armies of opinion-driven journalists and pundits driving the 24/7 news cycle. They have become a political cancer, growing by feeding on whatever healthy tissue is left. For example, by staging blame-game spectacles on prime time looking more like kayfabe wrestling matches than debates, they create a political atmosphere where people have begun to "regard each other as a bigger enemy than Russia or North Korea and just as dangerous as China."[395] Because of this, as seen in the case of COVID-19, people can no longer agree on simple facts and even less about scientific results. To what was said earlier about this issue, it can be added that many left-wingers mocking the "Trump vaccine" before the 2020 election demanded mandatory jabs afterward and that "anti-vaxx" did not become a thing for many conservatives until Trump was out and Biden in. And COVID-19 is just one example. While Democrats deny that genes define, among other things, gender roles, violence patterns, and sexual behaviors, Republicans tend to doubt notions like evolution. So, without saying that skepticism isn't healthy or in any way denying that scientific findings often turn out to be half-true or false, it is obvious that many on both sides today often deny facts not because they honestly doubt them but because they do not fit their ideological views. And there's a word for causing such conduct: brainwashing.

Furthermore, because a durable collective self-image is as vital to a multiethnic state like America as it was to the Roman Empire two thousand years ago, continued socio-cultural fragmentation must be avoided. In fact, several findings in this book beg speculation about whether Americanism will stay a sociocultural glue strong enough to hold the U.S. together. At least two things can be mulled over. One, America's worldly powers, or at least its relative strengths, will continue to decrease because of the rise of giant nations like China, India, and Brazil. Two, millions of Americans every year through academia, media, and other means will be continuously exposed to worldviews based on secularization, atomistic individualism, and globalism. And since both these "megatrends" are out of everyone's real control, political focus should instead be turned toward manageable

395. "Voters See Each Other as America's Enemy," (December 1, 2020) *Rasmussen Reports*, accessed December 8, 2020, https://www.rasmussenreports.com/public_content/politics/general_politics/november_2020/voters_see_each_other_as_america_s_enemy?fbclid=IwAR2Zm8HhSz3QD_79osdQBgQlkiAr3IsHEakyr5FKoXn4m9e3eiSG8CKmkIs.

tendencies. For example, college curriculum that includes content such as gender, diversity, and equity can be pushed back on through student loan rules and state regulations, while mass immigration and cultural fragmentation can be counteracted by federal actions like improved border security and increased assimilation (through making English the official language, extending the period as well as tightening the rules for becoming a U.S. citizen, making it easier to deport criminals, and more).

However, as radicals have found out, politics and bureaucracy are blunt tools when it comes to changing culture. Individuals, families, churches, and other small communities must therefore do the heavy lifting. In other words, if *We the People* do not do something, American society will continue to develop along today's trajectory. And this will, without a doubt, end in disaster since elites are unable to offer an identity more concrete than "humankind," larger than tribe, but different from religion.

Moreover, if national and patriotic identities continue to fade, the only unifying force left throughout the West will soon be the visible cold hand and army-booted foot of government. This will be a lesser problem in statist countries like Sweden and France and autocracies like Russia and China. But in America, with our Constitution written to advance, protect, and control a decentralized republican federation, the continued waning of Americanism will lead to power-grabbing and, in the end, national downfall. In fact, this is already happening since every president since Clinton—except Bush 43 for a brief period after 9/11—has for half the country been "Not my president!" So, the U.S. may soon face a hard choice between national dissolution and totalitarian government because, without a solid civil religion, the latter will be the only way to avoid the former. And since a large portion of the population, as in 1776, is bent on not losing their freedoms—and armed to the teeth—this may indeed become a messy dispute.

Additionally, all Western nations today deal with the harmful impact of radical leftists and other antitraditional forces. But in the U.S., the influence of a small but powerful group of radical-minded right-wingers adds a particular snag to this problem. Explicitly, because of neoconservatives, America has not only been dragged into a row of unwanted, pointless, and failed wars, but their "big government conservativism" has ruined some of the nation's most cherished freedoms and needed domestic policies. Most supreme is, of course, their blind reliance on supply-side theory. It has persuaded GOP leaders from Reagan to Trump and many in-betweens that lowering taxes will create such high growth that the cuts will pay for themselves, cover high military and welfare costs, and close the federal deficit. Moreover, since 9/11, many neocons have, like the liberal aristocracy, displayed autocratic tendencies. The Patriot Act and many Republicans' blind trust in the "intelligence community" and the military-industrial complex are but three examples. Therefore, the GOP's current "Trump reformation" must not only mean cleaning house with neoconservatives' foreign policy. It must also restore qualities like budget discipline, respect for individual rights, and a healthy suspicion about *all* special interests.

To end on a more positive note, let us consider some factors that point in politically, socially, and culturally healthy directions. Outside academic and other narrow minded circles, trash-talking America still bothers people almost as much as Carter's *malaise* babble did in the 1970s. Moreover, since the U.S. will remain a politically, economically, and militarily prominent country for generations to come, there is no reason to expect a radically negative revision of Americans' basic self-image. It's also worth pointing out that it's no God-given fate that immigrants—at least in the second or third generation—should not continue to adopt a healthy exceptionalist outlook on America. This is especially true since globalization's Western nature today is waning as powers like China and the other BRIC countries, of which many are dictatorships, wobbly semi-democracies, and culturally everything but progressive, are rising. This will make continued globalization hard to swallow for Americans—even most New Classers. Also, Americanism itself offers a potential cure in the form of optimism, determination, and bravery. All it takes to turn today's development around is thus to provide people with an updated, stern but less hyperbolic form of Americanism that helps them realize that what they have learned in school and through the media about liberalism not being a bad choice but a great destiny is a lie. And most importantly, since political culture and language have changed so dramatically since 1787, a new Constitutional Convention needs to be called in order to polish the Constitution's language, clarify what the Founding Fathers intended, and fix the weaknesses progressives and liberals have been so ingenious to find and exploit. The rest should, as the physicists say, be chemistry.

Appendix

Name	Classification	Party	WP	RP
WILLIAM MCKINLEY (1897-1901)	ACTIVE-INCLUSIVE	R	√	
THEODORE ROOSEVELT (1901-1909)	ACTIVE-INCLUSIVE	R		√
WILLIAM H. TAFT (1909-1913)	ACTIVE-INCLUSIVE	R		
WOODROW WILSON (1913-1921)	ACTIVE-INCLUSIVE	D	√	√
WARREN HARDING (1921-1923)	PASSIVE-EXCLUSIVE	R		
CALVIN COOLIDGE (1923-1929)	PASSIVE-EXCLUSIVE	R		
HERBERT HOOVER (1929-1933)	PASSIVE-INCLUSIVE	R		
FRANKLIN D. ROOSEVELT (1933-1945)	ACTIVE-INCLUSIVE	D	√	√
HARRY S. TRUMAN (1945-1953)	ACTIVE-INCLUSIVE	D	√	
DWIGHT EISENHOWER (1953-1961)	ACTIVE-INCLUSIVE	R		
JOHN F. KENNEDY (1961-1963)	ACTIVE-INCLUSIVE	D		
LYNDON B. JOHNSON (1963-1969)	ACTIVE-INCLUSIVE	D	√	√
RICHARD NIXON (1969-1974)	PASSIVE-INCLUSIVE	R		√
GERALD FORD (1974-1977)	PASSIVE-INCLUSIVE	R		
JIMMY CARTER (1977-1981)	ACTIVE-INCLUSIVE	D		
RONALD REAGAN (1981-1989)	ACTIVE-INCLUSIVE	R		√
GEORGE BUSH (1989-1993)	ACTIVE-INCLUSIVE	R	√	
BILL CLINTON (1993-2001)	ACTIVE-INCLUSIVE	D	√	
GEORGE W. BUSH (2001-2009)	ACTIVE-INCLUSIVE	R	√	
BARACK OBAMA (2009-2017)	PASSIVE-INCLUSIVE	D	√	√
DONALD TRUMP (2017-2020)	PASSIVE-EXCLUSIVE	R		

■ "War President" (WP) is defined as presidents' engaging the U.S. in at least one major conflict, like Wilson in 1917; escalating low-intensive operations into full-scale war, like LBJ in Vietnam; or engaging the country in large-scale international operations, like Bush in 2003. Minor incidents with fewer than 100 U.S. military deaths such as the Banana Wars 1898-1934 and inherited operations like Nixon's in Vietnam and Trump's in Syria are neglected. ■ "Reform President" (RP) are presidents who not only want to adjust or expand existing welfare systems but expresses ambitions to change the scale and scope of the U.S. government's social, cultural, and other obligations, like FDR and LBJ through the New Deal and the Great Society, and Nixon and Reagan, who wanted to return federal commitments to state and local authorities.

Bibliography

Books

Abramson, Paul R., John H. Aldrich & David W. Rohde. *Change and Continuity in the 1984 Elections: Revised Edition*. Washington, D.C.: CQ Press, 1987.

Ambrose, Stephen E. *Eisenhower: Soldier and President*. New York: Simon & Shuster, 1991.

Anderson, Benedict. *Imagined Communities: Reflections on the Origin and Spread of Nationalism*. London: Verso, 1983; revised edition 1991.

Andrew III, John A. *Lyndon Johnson and the Great Society*. Chicago: American Ways Series, 1999.

Arnn, Larry P. *The Founders' Key: The Divine and Natural Connection Between the Declaration and the Constitution and What We Risk by Losing It*. Nashville: Thomas Nelson 2012.

Axelrod, Alan. *Selling the Great War: The Making of American Propaganda*. New York: Palgrave MacMillan, 2009.

Babbitt, Irving. *Democracy and Leadership*. Boston: Houghton Mifflin, 1924; reprint, with a foreword by Russel Kirk, Indianapolis: Liberty Fund, 1979.

Bacevich, Andrew J. *American Empire: The Realities & Consequences of U.S. Diplomacy*. Cambridge, MA: Harvard University Press, 2002.

Bailey, Thomas A. *Presidential Greatness: The Image and the Man from George Washington to the Present*. New York: Appleton Century Crofts, 1966.

Bailey, Jeremy D. *The Idea of Presidential Representation: An Intellectual and Political History*. Lawrence, KS: University Press of Kansas, 2019.

Ball, Howard. *The USA Patriot Act; Balancing Civil Liberties and National Security*. Santa Barbara, CA: ABC-Clio, 2004.

Balmer, Randall. *God In the White House A History: How Faith Shaped the Presidency from John F. Kennedy to George W. Bush*. New York: HarperOne, 2008.

Balz, Dan & Haynes Johnson. *The Battle For America. The Story of an Extraordinary Election*. New York: Viking Penguin, 2009.

Balz, Dan. *Collision 2012: The Future of Election Politics In a Divided America*. New York: Penguin Books, 2013.

Bannister, Robert C. *Social Darwinism: Science and Myth in Anglo-American Social Thought*. Philadelphia: Temple University Press, 1979.

Barber, James David. *The Presidential Character: Predicting Performance in the White House*. New York, Pearson Longman, 2009, 4th edition.

Beard, Mary. *SPQR: A History of Ancient Rome*. New York: Liveright Publishing Corporation, 2015.

Beasley, Vanessa B. *You, the People: American National Identity in Presidential Rhetoric*. College Station: Texas A&M University Press, 2004.

Beinart, Peter. *The Icarus Syndrome: A History of American Hubris*. New York: HarperCollins, 2010.

Belmonte, Laura A. *Selling the American Way: U.S. Propaganda and the Cold War*. Philadelphia: University of Pennsylvania Press, 2008.

Beisner, Robert L. *From the Old Diplomacy to the New 1865-1900*. Wheeling, IL: Harlan Davidson, Inc., 1986.

Bender, Thomas. *A Nation Among Nations: America's Place in World History*. New York: Hill & Wang, 2006.

Berman, Sheri. *The Primacy of Politics: Social Democracy and the Making of Europe's Twentieth Century*. Cambridge, MA: Cambridge University Press, 2006.

Berggren, Henrik & Lars Trägårdh. *Är Svensken Människa? Gemenskap och Oberoende i det Moderna Sverige*. Stockholm: Norstedts, 2006.

Blaisdell, Bob (ed.). *Infamous Speeches: From Robespierre to Osama bin Laden*. Mineola, NY: Dover Publications, 2011.

Black, Edwin. *War Against the Weak: Eugenics and America's Campaign to Create a Master Race*. New York: Four Walls Eight Windows, 2003.

Boaz, David (ed.). *Toward Liberty: The Idea That is Changing the World*. Washington, D.C., 2002.

Borgwardt, Elizabeth. *A New Deal for the World: America's Vision for Human Rights*. Cambridge, MA: Belknap Harvard, 2005.

Bourg, Julian (ed.). *After the Deluge: New Perspectives on the Intellectual and Cultural History of Postwar France*. Lanham, MD: Lexington Books, 2004.

Brands, H.W. *Traitor to His Class: The Privileged Life and Radical Presidency of Franklin Delano Roosevelt*. New York: Doubleday, 2008.

American Colossus: The Triumph of Capitalism, 1865-1900. New York: Anchor Books, 2011.

Breitman, George (ed.). *Malcolm X Speaks: Selected Speeches and Statements*. New York: First Grove Press Edition 1966; reprint New York: First Grove Weidenfeld Evergreen, 1990.

Brinkley, Douglas. *Gerald R. Ford*. New York: Times Books, 2007.

Brody, David & Scott Lamb. *The Faith of Donald J. Trump*. New York: HarperCollins Publishers, 2017.

Brooks, Stephen. *American Exceptionalism in the Age of Obama*. New York: Routledge, 2013.

Brownlee, W. Elliot & Graham Huge Davis (ed.). *The Reagan Presidency: Pragmatic Conservatism & Its Legacies*. Lawrence, KS: University Press of Kansas, 2003.

Brownson, Orestes A. *The American Republic*. New York: P. O'Shea, 1865; reprint Wilmington, DE: ISI Books, 2003, with an Introduction by Peter Augustine Lawler.

Bruce-Briggs (ed.), B. *The New Class?* New Brunswick, NJ: Transaction Book 1979.

Buchanan, Patrick J. *A Republic, Not an Empire: Reclaiming America's Destiny*. Washington, DC: Regnery Publishing, 2002.

Buckley Jr., William F. *Up From Liberalism*. Toronto: Bantam Books, reprint 1968.

Busch, Andrew E. *Reagan's Victory: The Presidential Election of 1980 and the Rise of the Right*. Lawrence, KS: Kansas University Press, 2005.

Byrne, David T. *Ronald Reagan: An Intellectual Biography*. Lincoln, NE: Potomac Book, 2018.

Campbell, Karlyn Kohnrs & Kathleen Hall Jamieson. *Presidents Creating the Presidency: Deeds Done in Words*. Chicago: The University of Chicago Press, 2008.

Cannon, Lou. *President Reagan: The Role of a Lifetime*. New York: Public Affairs, 2000.

Cappozzola, Christopher. *Uncle Sam Wants You: World War I and the Making of the Modern American Citizen*. Oxford: Oxford University Press, 2008.

Carson. Rachel. *Silent Spring*. New York: Houghton Mifflin Company 1962; reprint 2002.

Ceaser, James & Busch, Andrew. *Upside Down and Inside Out: The 1992 Elections And American Politics*. Lanham, MD: Littlefield Adams Quality Paperbacks, 1993.

Cheney, Lynne V. *Telling the Truth: Why Our Culture and Our Country Have Stopped Making Sense—and What We Can Do About It*. New York: Touchstone, 1995.

Churchwell, Sarah. *Behold America: A History of America First and the American Dream*. London: Bloomsbury Publishing, 2018.

Clausing, Kimberly. *Open: The Progressive Case for Free Trade, Immigration, and Global Capital*. Cambridge, MA: Harvard University Press, 2019.

Coffman, Tom. *Nation Within: The History of the American Occupation of Hawaii*. Kihei, HI: Koa Books, 1998.

Combs, Jerald A. *The History of American Foreign Policy From 1895*. Armonk, NY: M.E. Sharp, Inc., 2012.

Conant, Charles A. *The United States in the Orient: The Nature of the Economic Problem*. Cambridge: The Riverside Press, 1900; reprint Victoria, Australia: Leopold Classic Library, 2017.

Cooper Jr., John Milton. *Breaking the Heart of the World: Woodrow Wilson and the Fight for the League of Nations*. Cambridge: Cambridge University Press, 2001.

Costigliola, Frank. *Awkward Dominion: American Political, Economic and Cultural Relations with Europe, 1919-1933*. Ithaca: Cornell University Press, 1984.

Coyne, Christopher J. *After War: The Political Economy of Exporting Democracy*. Stanford, CA: Stanford Economics and Finance, 2008.

Crapol, Edward P. *John Tyler: The Accidental President*. Chapel Hill, NC: The University of North Carolina Press, 2006.

Crèvecoeur, J. Hector St. John De. *Letters from an American Farmer and Sketches of Eighteenth-Century America*. New York: Penguin Book, 1981.

Cull, Nicholas J. *The Cold War and the United States Information Agency: American Propaganda and Public Diplomacy, 1945-1989*. New York: Cambridge University Press, 2008.

Cullen, Jim. *The American Dream: A Short History of an Idea That Shaped a Nation*. Oxford, UK: Oxford University Press, 2003.

Cunningham, Jr., Noble E. *In Pursuit of Reason: The Life Of Thomas Jefferson*. New York: Ballantine Books, 1987.

D'Antonio, William V. Steven A. Tuch & Josiah R. Baker. *Religion, Politics, and Polarization: How Religiopolitical Conflict Is Changing Congress and American Democracy*. Lanham, MD: Rowman & Littlefield Publishers, Inc., 2013.

Daalder & Ivo H. James M. Lindsay. *America Unbound: The Bush Revolution in Foreign Policy*. Hoboken, NJ: John Wiley & Sons, Inc., 2003.

Dallek, Robert. *Franklin D. Roosevelt: A Political Life*. New York: Viking, 2017.

   – An Unfinished Life: John F. Kennedy 1917-1963. New York: Back Bay Books, 2003.

Daniels, Roger. *Coming To America: A History of Immigration and Ethnicity in American Life*. New York: Perennial, 2002.

Davies, Norman. *The Isles: A History*. London: Macmillan, 1999.

Deale, Howard K. *Theodore Roosevelt and the Rise of America to World Power*. New York: Collier Books, 1965.

Dean, John W. *Warren G. Harding*. Times Book, 2004.

Dearborn, John A. *Exceptionalist-in-Chief: Presidents, American Exceptionalism, and U.S. Foreign Policy Since 1897.* University of Connecticut: Honors Scholar Thesis, 2013.

Dinan, Desmond. *Europe Recast: A History of European Union.* London: Lynne Rienner Publishers, 2014.

Dionne Jr., E.J. & Joy-Ann Reid (ed.). *We Are the Change We Seek: The Speeches of Barack Obama.* New York: Bloomsbury, 2017.

Domke, David & Kevin Coe. *The God Strategy: How Religion Became a Political Weapon in America.* Oxford: Oxford University Press, 2008.

Donald, David Herbert. *Lincoln.* New York: Simon & Schuster, 1995.

Donaldson, Gary A. *Liberalism's Last Hurrah: The Presidential Campaign of 1964.* New York: Skyhorse Publishing, 2002.

Dorrien, Gary. *The Neoconservative Mind. Politics, Culture and the War of Ideology.* Philadelphia: Temple University Press, 1993.

Douglass, Fredrick. *Great Speeches by Fredrick Douglass.* Edited by James Daley. Mineola, NY: Dover Publications, 2013.

Doyle, Michael V. (ed.). *Gerald R. Ford: Selected Speeches.* Arlington, VA: R.W. Beatty, Ltd, 1973.

Drew, Elizabeth. *Richard M. Nixon.* New York: Times Books, 2007.

Duke Steven B. & Gross, Albert C. *America's Longest War: Rethinking Our Tragic Crusade Against Drugs.* New York: Jeremy P. Tarcher/Putnam Book, 1993.

Dulles, John Foster. *War or Peace.* New York: The MacMillan Company, 1950.

Edwards, Jason A. & David Weiss (ed.). *The Rhetoric of American Exceptionalism: Critical Essays.* Jefferson, NC: McFarland & Company, Inc. Publishers, 2011.

Edwards, Jason A. & Joseph M Valenzano III (ed.). *The Rhetoric of American Civil Religion: Symbols, Sinners, and Saints.* Lanham, MD: Lexington Books, 2016.

Edwards, Lee. *The Conservative Revolution: The Movement that Remade America.* New York: The Free Press, 1999.

Ellis, Richard J. *American Political Cultures*. New York: Oxford University Press, 1993.

Ertman, Thomas. *Birth of the Leviathan: Building States and Regimes in Medieval and Early Modern Europe*. Cambridge: Cambridge University Press, 1997.

Farber, David. *The Age of Great Dreams: America in the 1960s*. New York: Hill & Wang, 1994.

Fea, John. *Was America Founded as a Christian Nation? A Historical Introduction*. Louisville, KY: Westminster John Knox Press, 2011.

Federici, Michael P. *The Political Philosophy of Alexander Hamilton*. Baltimore: The John Hopkins University Press, 2012.

Ferguson, Niall. *Colossus: The Rise and Fall of the American Empire*. New York: Penguin Books, 2005.

Fischer, David Hackett. *Albion's Seed: Four British Folkways in America*. New York: Oxford University Press, 1989.

Flamm, Michael W. & David Steigerwald. *Debating the 1960s: Liberal, Conservative, and Radical Perspectives*. Lanham, MD: Rowman & Littlefield Publishers, 2007.

Fluck, Winfried, Donald E. Pease & John Carlos Rowe (ed.). *Re-framing the Transnational Turn in American Studies*. Hanover, NH: University Press of New England, 2011.

Foner, Eric. *The Story of American Freedom*. New York: W. W. Norton & Company, 1998.

Foucault, Michel. *The Archaeology of Knowledge: And the Discourse on Language*. New York: Vintage Books, 1982.

Fowler, Robert Booth, et al. *Religion and Politics in America: Faith, Culture, and Strategic Choices*. Philadelphia, PA: Westview Press, 2010.

Friedman, Milton. *Capitalism and Freedom*. Chicago: The University of Chicago, 1962; reprint 2002.

Friedman, Murray. *The Neoconservative Revolution. Jewish Intellectuals and the Shaping of Public Policy*. New York: Cambridge University Press, 2005.

Frum, David. *How We Got Here: The 70's The Decade That Brought You Modern Life (For Better or Worse).* New York: Basic Books, 2000.

Frum, David & Richard Perle. *An End to Evil: How to Win the War on Terror.* New York: Random House, 2003/04.

Frymer, Paul. *Building An American Empire: The Era of Territorial and Political Expansion.* Princeton: Princeton University Press, 2007.

Fulbright, J. William. *The Arrogance of Power.* New York: Random House, 1966.

Galbraith, John Kenneth. *The Affluent Society.* Cambridge, MA: The Riverside Press, 1958.

Gamble, Richard M. *In Search of the City On A Hill: The Making and Unmaking of an American Myth.* London: Continuum, 2012.

  – *The War for Righteousness: Progressive Christianity, the Great War, and the Rise of the Messianic Nation.* Wilmington, DE: ISI Books, 2003.

Gardella, Peter. *American Civil Religion: What Americans Hold Sacred.* New York: Oxford University Press, 2014.

Garrison, Justin. *"An Empire of Ideals:" The Chimeric Imagination of Ronald Reagan.* New York: Routledge, 2013.

Gaustad, Edwin & Leigh Schmidt. *The Religious History of America: The Heart of the American Story from Colonial Times to Today.* New York: Harper San Francisco, 2004.

Gelernter, David. *Americanism: The Fourth Great Western Religion.* New York: Doubleday, 2007.

Genovese, Eugene D. *The Southern Tradition: The Achievement and Limitations of an American Conservatism.* Cambridge: Harvard University Press, 1994.

Gerring, John. *Party Ideologies in America, 1828-1996.* Cambridge, MA: Cambridge University Press, 1998.

Gitlin, Todd. *Occupy Nation: The Roots, the Spirit, and the Promise of Occupy Wall Street.* New York: Itbooks, 2012.

Glendon, Mary Ann. *Rights Talk: The Impoverishment of Political Discourse.* New York: The Free Press, 1991.

Goldman, Eric F. *Rendezvous with Destiny*. New York: Vintage, 1952.

Goldwater, Barry. *Where I Stand*. New York: McGraw-Hill, 1964.

Gottfried, Paul. *The Conservative Movement*. New York: Twayne Publishers, rev. ed. 1993.

Gould, Lewis L. *The Presidency of William McKinley*. Lawrence, KS: University Press of Kansas, 1980.

– *America in the Progressive Era 1890-1914*. Harlow, UK: Longman, 2001.
– *Grand Old Party: A History of the Republicans*. New York: Random House, 2003.

Grant, Michael. *The Ancient Mediterranean*. New York: Charles Scribner's Sons, 1969.

Green, John C., Mark J. Rozell & Clyde Wilcox (ed.). *The Values Campaign: The Christian Right and the 2004 Elections*. Washington, D.C.: Georgetown University Press, 2006.

Green, Nathanial C. *The Man of the People: Political Dissent and the Making of the American Presidency*. Lawrence, KS: University Press of Kansas, 2020.

Greene, Jack P. *The Intellectual Construction of America: Exceptionalism and Identity From 1492 to 1800*. Chapel Hill: The University of North Carolina Press, 1997.

Groseclose, Tim. *Left Turn: How Liberal Media Bias Distorts the American Mind*. New York: St. Martin's Griffin, 2011.

Hahn, Peter L. *Crisis and Crossfire: The United States and the Middle East Since 1945*. Washington, D.C.: Potomac Books, 2005.

– "Securing the Middle East: The Eisenhower Doctrine of 1957." *Presidential Studies Quarterly* 36.1 (2006): 38-47.

Haidt, Jonathan. *The Righteous Mind: Why Good People Are Divided by Politics and Religion*. New York: Pantheon Books, 2012.

Hamby, Alonzo L. (ed.). *Harry S. Truman and the Fair Deal*. Lexington, MA: D. C. Heath and Company, 1974.

Harding, Warren G. *Our Common Country: Mutual Good Will in America*. Indianapolis: Bobbs-Merrill Co., 1921; reprint Whitefish, MT: Kessinger Publishing LLC, 2017.

Hart, Roderick P. *Trump and Us: What He Says and Why People Listen*. Cambridge, MA: Cambridge University Press, 2020.

Hartman, Andrew. *A War for the Soul of America: A History of the Culture Wars*. Chicago: The University of Chicago Press, 2015.

Hartz, Louis. *The Liberal Tradition in America*. San Diego: Mariner Books, 1991.

Hayek, Friedrich von. *The Road to Selfdom*. New York: George Routledge & Sons, 1944; reprint London: Routledge Classics 2006.

Hayward, Steven F. *The Age of Reagan: The Fall of the Old Liberal Order 1964-1980*. Roseville, CA: Prima Publishing, 2001.

 – *The Age of Reagan: The Conservative Counterrevolution 1980-1989*. New York: Crown Forum, 2009.

Hazony, Yoram. *The Virtue of Nationalism*. New York: Basic Books, 2018.

Healy, David. *US Expansionism: The Imperialist Urge in the 1890s*. Madison, WI: The University of Wisconsin Press, 1970.

Herman, Arthur. *Joseph McCarthy: Reexamining the Life and Legacy of America's Most Hated Senator*. New York: The Free Press, 2000.

Herring, George C. *From Colony to Superpower: U.S. Foreign Relations since 1776*. New York: Oxford University Press, 2011.

Hicks, Stephen R. C. *Explaining Postmodernism: Skepticism and Socialism from Rousseau to Foucault*. Loves Park, IL: Ockham's Razor Publishing, 2011; expanded edition.

Hietala, Thomas R. *Manifest Design: American Exceptionalism and Empire*. Ithaca: Cornell University Press, 2002.

Himmelfarb, Gertrude. *The Roads To Modernity: The British French And American Enlightenments*. New York, Vintage Books, 2005.

Hodgson, Godfrey. *The Myth of American Exceptionalism*. New Haven, CT: Yale University Press, 2009.

Hofstadter, Richard. *The Age of Reform*. New York: Vintage Book, 1955.

Hofstede, Geert & Hofstede, Gert Jan. *Cultures and Organizations; Software of the Mind*. New York: McGraw-Hill, 2005.

Hogan, Michael J. *A Cross of Iron: Harry S. Truman and the Origin of the National Security State 1945-1954*. Cambridge, MA: Cambridge University Press, 1998.

Hollander, Paul (ed.). *Understanding Anti-Americanism: Its Origins and Impact at Home and Abroad*. Chicago: Ivan R. Dee, 2004.

Horsman, Reginald, *Race and Manifest Destiny*. Cambridge, MA: Harvard University Press, 1981.

Hoover, Dennis R. (ed.). *Religion and American Exceptionalism*. London: Routledge, 2014.

Hoover, Herbert. *American Individualism*. New York: Doubleday, Page & Co., 1922; reprint with an Introduction of George H. Nash, Stanford, CA: Hoover Institution Press, 2016.

   – *The Challenge to Liberty*. New York: Charles Scribner's Sons, 1934; reprint Rockford, IL: The Herbert Hoover Foundation, 1971.

Hunter, James Davison. *Culture Wars: The Struggle to Define America*. New York: Baric Books, 1991.

Huntington, Samuel P. *The Clash of Civilization and the Remaking of World Order*. New York: Simon & Schuster Paperbacks, 1996/2011.

   Who Are We?: The Challenges to American National Identity. New York: Simon & Schuster, 2004.

Ikenberry, G. John. *Liberal Leviathan: The Origins, Crisis, and Transformation of the American World Order*. Princeton: Princeton University Press, 2011.

Indick, William. *The Psychology of the Western: How the American Psyche Plays Out on Screen*. Jefferson, NC: McFarland, 2008.

Irons, Peter. *War Powers: How the Imperial Presidency Hijacked the Constitution*. New York: Metropolitan Books, 2005.

Irwin, Douglas A. *Trade Policy Disaster: Lessons from the 1930s*. Cambridge, MA: The MIT Press, 2011.

Jacobs, Joseph J. *The Compassionate Conservative: Assuming Responsibility and Respecting Human Dignity*. Oakland, CA: ICS Press, 2000.

Jasanoff, Maya. *Liberty's Exiles: American Loyalists in the Revolutionary World*. New York: Alfred A. Knopf, 2011.

Jefferson, Thomas. *The Jeffersonian Cyclopedia*. London: Forgotten Books, 2017.

Johnson, Donald Bruce & Kirk H. Porter. *National Party Platforms 1840-1972*. Chicago: University of Illinois, 1973.

Johnson, Lyndon B. *The Speeches of President Lyndon B. Johnson*. Filibust Publishing, 2015.

Johnson, Paul. *A History of the American People*. New York: HarperCollins Publishers, 1997.

Kabaservice, Geoffrey. *Rule and Ruin: The Downfall Of Moderation And The Destruction Of The Republican Party, From Eisenhower To The Tea Party*. Oxford: Oxford University Press, 2012.

Kagan, Robert. *Of Paradise and Power: America and Europe in the New World Order*. New York: Alfred A. Knopf, 2003.

Kalb, James. *The Tyranny of Liberalism: Understanding and Overcoming Administered Freedom, Inquisitorial Tolerance, and Equality by Command*. Wilmington, DE: ISI Books, 2008.

Kant, Immanuel. *Toward Perpetual Pease and Other Writings on Politics, Peace, and History*. New Haven: Yale University Press 2006.

Kantorowicz, Ernst H. *The Kings Two Bodies: A Study In Medieval Political Theology*. Princeton, NJ: Princeton University Press, 1957; reprint 2016.

Kaplan, Fred. *John Quincy Adams: American Visionary*. New York: Harper Collins, 2014.

Karabell, Zachary. *The Last Campaign: How Harry Truman Won the 1948 Election*. New York: Vintage Books, 2000.

Kazin, Michael. *The Populist Persuasion: An American History*. Ithaca: NY: Cornell University Press, 1995; reprint with a new preface 2017.

    – *A Godly Hero: The Life of William Jennings Bryan*. New
       York: Alfred A. Knopf, 2006.

Kedourie, Elie. *Nationalismen: En studie av nationalismen som ideologi*.
Stockholm: SNS Förlag, 1995.

Kendall, Willmoore & George W. Carey. *The Basic Symbols of the American Political Tradition*. Washington, D.C.: The Catholic University of America Press, 1970; reprint 1995.

Kengor, Paul. *God and Ronald Reagan: A Spiritual Life*. HarperCollins: New York, 2004.

    – *God and George W. Bush: A Spiritual Life*. HarperCollins:
       New York, 2004.

Kennedy, Paul M. *The Rise and Fall of the Great Powers: Economic Change and Military Conflict from 1500 to 2000*. New York: Random House, 1987.

Kennedy, Ross A. *The Will to Believe: Woodrow Wilson, World War I, and America's Strategy for Peace and Security*. Kent, OH: Kent State University Press, 2009.

Kenski, Kate, Bruce W. Hardy & Kathleen Hall Jamieson. *The Obama Victory: How Media, Money and Message Shaped the 2008 Election*. Oxford, UK: Oxford University Press, 2010.

Kesler, Charles R. *I Am the Change: Barack Obama and the Crisis of Liberalism*. New York: Broadside Books, 2012.

Kiehl, William P. (ed.). *America's Dialogue with the World*. Washington, D.C.: The Public Diplomacy Council, 2006.

Kiernan, V.G. *America: The New Imperialism. From White Settlement To World Hegemony*. London: Verso, 2005.

King, David. *Finding Atlantis: A True Story of Genius, Madness, and an Extraordinary Quest for a Lost World*. New York: Harmony Books, 2005.

King Jr., Martin Luther. *A Testament of Hope: The Essential Writings and Speeches of Martin Luther King Jr.* Edited by James M. Washington. New York: Harper One, 1986.

King, Richard H. *Civil Rights and the Idea of Freedom*. Athens, GA: The University of Georgia Press, 1996.

Kinzer, Stephen. *Overthrow: America's Century of Regime Change From Hawaii to Iraq*. New York: Times Books, 2006.

– *The True Flag: Theodore Roosevelt, Mark Twain, and the Birth of American Empire*. New York: Henry Holt and Company, 2017.

Kirk, Russel. *The Conservative Mind: From Burke to Eliot*. Washington, D.C.: Regnery Publishing, Inc., 1953; reprint 2001.

– *The Roots of American Order*. Washington, DC: Regnery Gateway, 1991.

Kline, Benjamin. *First Along the River: A Brief History of the U.S. Environmental Movement*. New York: Rowman & Littlefield Publishers; 4th edition, 2011.

Kloppenberg, James T. *Reading Obama: Dreams, Hope, and the American Political Tradition*. Princeton, NJ: Princeton University Press, 2011.

Knock, Thomas J. *To End All Wars: Woodrow Wilson and the Quest for a New World Order*. Princeton, NJ: Princeton University Press, 1992.

Koffler, Keith. *Bannon: Always the Rebel*. Washington, D.C.; Regnery Publishing, 2017.

Kornacki, Steve. *The Red and the Blue: The 1990s and the Birth of Political Tribalism*. New York: HarperCollins, 2018.

Kranish Michael & Marc Fisher. *Trump Revealed: The Definitive Biography of the 45th President*. New York; Scribner, 2016.

Kristol, Irving. *The Neoconservative Persuasion. Selected Essays, 1942-2009*. New York: Basic Books, 2011.

Kutler, Stanley I. *The American Inquisition: Justice and Injustice in the Cold War*. New York: Hill and Wang, 1982.

Kuypers, Jim A. *Partisan Journalism: A History of Media Bias in the United States*. Lanham, MD: Rowman & Littlefield, 2014.

Lacey, Michael J (ed.). *The Truman Presidency*. New York: Woodrow Wilson International Center for Scholars & Cambridge University Press, 1989.

LaFeber, Walter. *The American Age: United States Foreign Policy at Home and Abroad since 1750*. New York: W.W. Norton & Company, 1989.

Langley, Lester D. *The Banana Wars: United States Intervention in the Caribbean, 1898-1934*. Lanham, MD: Rowman & Littlefield Publishers, 2001.

Larson, Sven R. *The Rise of Big Government: How Egalitarianism Conquered America*. London: Routledge, 2018.

Launius, Roger D. *NASA: A History of the U.S. Civilian Space Program*. Malabar, FL: Krieger Publishing Company, 1994.

Lawrence, John A. *The Class of '74: Congress After Watergate and the Roots of Partisanship*. Baltimore, MD: Johns Hopkins University Press, 2018.

Lawrence, Mark Atwood. *The Vietnam War: A Concise International History*. New York: Oxford University Press, 2008.

Leffler, Melvyn P. *A Preponderance of Power: National Security, the Truman Administration, and the Cold War*. Stanford, CA: Stanford University Press, 1992.

    – *For the Soul of Mankind*. New York: Hill & Wang, 2007.

Lehman, Christopher P. *Power, Politics, and the Decline of the Civil Rights Movement: A Fragile Coalition, 1967-1973*. Westport, CT: Praeger, 2014.

Lerner, Max. *America as a Civilization: Life and Thought in the United States Today*. New York: Simon & Schuster, 1957.

Leuchtenburg, William E. *In the Shadow of FDR: From Harry Truman to Ronald Reagan*. Ithaca, NY: Cornell University Press, 1983.

    – *The Lodge-Lowell Debate of the Proposed League of Nations*. Boston: Old Trust Company, 1919.

Lincoln, Abraham, *Great Speeches*. New York: Dover Publications, Inc., 1991.

Linenthal, Edward Tabor. *Symbolic Defense: The Cultural Significance of the Strategic Defense Initiative.* Chicago: University of Illinois Press, 1989.

Linfield, Michael. *Freedom Under Fire: U.S. Civil Liberties in Times of War.* Boston, MA: South End Press, 1990.

Lippmann, Walter. *Drift and Mastery.* Originally published 1914; reprint Madison, WI: The University of Wisconsin Press, 1985.

Lipset, Seymour Martin. *American Exceptionalism: A Double-Edged Sword.* New York: W. W. Norton & Company, 1996.

– *The First New Nation: The United States in Historical & Comparative Perspective.* New York: W. W. Norton & Company, Inc., 1973.

Litke, Justin. *Twilight of the Republic: Empire and Exceptionalism in the American Political Tradition.* Lexington, KY: University Press of Kentucky, 2013.

Little, Douglas. *American Orientalism: The United States and the Middle East Since 1945.* Chapel Hill: The University of North Carolina Press, 2008.

Lockhart, Charles. *The Roots of American Exceptionalism: Institutions, Culture, and Policies.* New York: Palgrave Macmillan, 2003.

Logan, Rayford W. *The Betrayal Of The Negro: From Rutherford B. Hayes To Woodrow Wilson.* New York: Collier Books, 1965; reprint, New York: Da Capo Press, 1997.

Longley, Clifford. *Chosen People: The big idea that shapes England and America.* London: Hodder & Stoughton, 2002.

Madsen, Deborah L. *American Exceptionalism.* Jackson: University Press of Mississippi, 1998.

Mahan, Alfred T. *The Influence of Seapower upon History 1660–1783.* Boston, MA: Little, Brown & Company, 1890.

Mann, James. *George W. Bush.* New York: Times Books, 2015.

Mann, Jim. *The Rebellion of Ronald Reagan: A History of the End of the Cold War.* New York: Viking, 2009.

May, Ernest R. *Imperial Democracy: The Emergence of America as a Great Power*. Chicago: Imprint Publications, 1991.

McCullough, David. *Mornings on Horseback*. New York: Simon & Schuster, 1981.

– *Truman*. New York: Touchstone, 1992.

McDonald, Forrest. *The American Presidency: An Intellectual History*. Lawrence, KS: University Press of Kansas, 1994.

– *Novus Ordo Seclorum: The Intellectual Origins of the Constitution*. Lawrence, KS: Kansas University Press, 1985.

McDougall, Walter A. *Promised Land, Crusader State: The American Encounter with the World Since 1776*. New York: Houghton Mifflin, 1997.

McEvoy-Levy, Siobhán. *American Exceptionalism and US Foreign Policy: Public Diplomacy at the End of the Cold War*. New York: Palgrave, 2001.

McGirr, Lisa. *The War on Alcohol: Prohibition and the Rise of the American State*. New York: W. W. Norton & Company, 2015.

Meacham, Jon. *Destiny and Power: The American Odyssey of George Herbert Walker Bush*. New York: Random House, 2015.

Meerman Scott, David & Richard Jurek. *Marketing the Moon: The Selling of the Apollo Lunar Program*. Cambridge, MA: The MIT Press, 2014.

Meier, Christian. *A Culture of Freedom: Ancient Greece and the Origins of Europe*. Oxford, UK: Oxford University Press, 2011.

Meyer, Jeffrey F. *Myths in Stone: Religious Dimensions of Washington, D.C.* Berkeley, CA: University of California Press, 2001.

Micklethwait, John & Wooldridge, Adrian. *The Right Nation: Conservative Power In America*. New York: The Penguin Press, 2004.

Milkis, Sidney M. & Mileur. Jerome M. (ed.). *The Great Society and the High Tide of Liberalism*. Amherst, MA: University of Massachusetts Press, 2005.

Miller, Robert J. *Native America, Discovered And Conquered: Thomas Jefferson, Lewis & Clark, And Manifest Destiny*. Westport CN: Praeger Publishers, 2006.

Moffitt, Kimberly R. & Campbell, Duncan A. (ed.). *The 1980s: A Critical and Transitional Decade.* Lanham, MD: Lexington Books, 2011.

Mondak, Jeffery J. & Dona-Gene Mitchell (ed.). *Fault Lines: Why the Republicans Lost Congress.* New York: Routledge, 2009.

Morgan, H. Wayne. *William McKinley and His America.* Syracuse; NY: Syracuse University Press, 1963.

Morone, James A. *Hellfire Nation: The Politics of Sin in American History.* New Haven: Yale University Press, 2003.

Morris, Ian. *War! What It Is Good For: Conflict and Progress of Civilization from Primates to Robots.* New York: Farrar, Straus & Giroux, 2014.

Mueller, John D. *Redeeming Economics: Rediscovering the Missing Element.* Wilmington, DE: ISI Books, 2010.

Murray, Charles. *Coming Apart: The State of White America, 1960-2010.* New York: Crown Forum, 2012.

– *American Exceptionalism: An Experiment in History.* Washington, DC: AEI Press, 2013.

Myrdal, Gunnar. *An American Dilemma: The Negro Problem and Modern Democracy.* New York: Harper & Brothers Publishers, 1944.

Naftali, Timothy. *George H. W. Bush.* New York: Times Book, 2007.

Nash, George H. *The Conservative Intellectual Movement in America: Since 1945.* Wilmington, DE: ISI Books, 1976; reprint 2008.

National Review (ed.), *We Will Prevail: President George W. Bush on War, Terrorism, and Freedom.* New York: Bloomsbury Academic, 2003.

Nelson, Patricia. *The Legacy of Conquest: The Unbroken Past of the American West.* New York: W.W. Norton & Co., 1987.

Nisbet, Robert A. *The Present Age. Progress and Anarchy in Modern America.* Indianapolis, IN: Liberty Press, 1988.

Nixon, Richard. *In the Arena: A Memoir of Victory, Defeat and Renewal.* New York: Simon & Schuster, 1990.

– *Richard Nixon: Speeches, Writings, Documents*. Princeton: Princeton University Press, edited and introduced by Rick Perlstein.

Noel, Hans. *Political Ideologies and Political Parties in America*. New York: Cambridge University Press, 2013.

Novak, Michael. *Choosing Our King*. New York: MacMillan Publishing Co., Inc., 1974.

Norberg, Johan. *Financial Fiasco: How America's Infatuation With Homeownership and Easy Money Created the Financial Crisis*. Washington, D.C.: Cato Institute, 2012.

Oakeshott, Michael. *On Human Conduct*. Oxford: Clarendon Press, 1975.

Obama, Barack. *Dreams from My Father: A Story of Race and Inheritance*. New York: Three Rivers Press, 2004.

O'Brien, David M. *Storm Center: The Supreme Court in American Politics*. New York: W.W. Norton & Company, 2011; 9th edition.

O'Brien, Conor Cruise. *God Land: Reflections on Religion and Nationalism*. Cambridge, MA: Harvard University Press, 1988.

Okrent, Daniel. *Last Call: The Rise and Fall of Prohibition*. New York: Scribner, 2011.

Osgood, Robert Endicott. *Ideals and Self-Interest in American Foreign Policy: The Great Transformation of the Twentieth Century*. Chicago: The University of Chicago Press, 1953.

Pafford, John M. *The Forgotten Conservative: Rediscovering Grover Cleveland*. Washington, DC: Regnery History, 2013.

Paine, Thomas, *Common Sense*. Philadelphia: W. & T. Bradford, 1776; reprint Mineola, NY: Dover Publications, Inc., 1997.

Pariser, Eli. *The Filter Bubble: How the New Personalized Web Is Changing What We Read and How We Think*. New York: Penguin Books 2011; reprint 2012.

Parsons, Timothy H., *The Rule of Empires: Those Who Build Them, Those Who Endured Them, and Why They Always Fall*. Oxford, UK: Oxford University Press, 2010.

Patterson, James T. *America's Struggle Against Poverty 1900-1980*. Cambridge, MA: Harvard University Press, 1981.

Pease, Donald E. *The New American Exceptionalism*. Minneapolis, MN: University of Minnesota Press, 2009.

Pérez Jr., Louis A. *Cuba in the American Imagination: Metaphor and the Imperial Ethos*. Chapel Hill: The University of North Carolina Press, 2008.

Perlstein, Rick. *Before the Storm: Barry Goldwater and the Unmasking of the American Consensus*. New York: Hill & Wang, 2001.

– *Nixonland: The Rise of a President and the Fracturing of America*. New York: Scribner, 2008.

– *Richard Nixon: Speeches, Writings, Documents*. Princeton, NJ: Princeton University Press, 2008.

Pestritto, Ronald J. *Woodrow Wilson and the Roots of Modern Liberalism*. Lanham: Rowman & Littlefield Publishers, Inc., 2005.

– *Woodrow Wilson: The Essential Political Writings*. Lanham, MD: Rowman & Littlefield Publishers, Inc., 2005.

Peterson, Merrill D. (ed.) *The Portable Thomas Jefferson*. New York: Penguin Books, 1975.

Pierard, Richard V. & Robert, D. Linder. *Civil Religion & the Presidency*. Grand Rapids, MI: Academie Books, 1988.

Pierson, Paul. *Politics in Time: History, Institutions, and Social Analysis*. Princeton, NJ: Princeton University Press, 2004.

Pinker, Steven. *The Blank Slate: The Modern Denial of Human Nature*. London: Penguin Allen Lane, 2002.

Pomper, Gerald M. (ed.). *The Election of 1988: Reports and Interpretations*. Chatham, NJ: Chatham House, 1989.

Porter, Bruce D. *War and the Rise of the State: The Military Foundations of Modern Politics*. New York: The Free Press, 1994.

Powell, Anton. *Athens and Sparta: Constructing Greek Political and Social History from 478 B.C.* London: Routledge, 1988.

Powell, Jim. *FDR's Folly: How Roosevelt and His New Deal Prolonged the Great Depression*. New York: Crown Forum, 2003.

Preble, Christopher A. *Peace, War, and Liberty: Understanding U.S. Foreign Policy*. Washington, D.C: Cato Institute, 2019.

Raff, Diether. *A History of Germany: From the Medieval Empire to the Present*. Oxford, UK: Berg Publishers, 1988.

Rasmussen, Scott & Douglas Schoen. *Mad as Hell: How the Tea Party Movement is Fundamentally Remaking Our Two-Party System*. New York: HarperCollins, 2010.

Reed, Lawrence W. *Great Myths of the Great Depression*. Midland, MI: The Mackinac Center for Public Policy, 2016.

Remnick, David. *The Bridge: The Life and Rise of Barack Obama*. New York: Alfred A. Knopf, 2010.

Rich, Norman. *Great Power Diplomacy 1814-1914*. Boston, MA: McGraw Hill, 1992.

Richman, Sheldon. *America's Counter-Revolution: The Constitution Revisited*. Ann Arbor, MI: Griffin & Lash, 2016.

Riley, Jason L. *Let Them In: The Case for Open Borders*. New York: Gotham Books, 2008.

Romney, Mitt. *No Apology: The Case for American Greatness*. New York: St. Martin's Press, 2010.

Roosevelt, Franklin Delano. *Great Speeches*. Mineola, New York: Dover Publications, Inc.

Roosevelt, Theodore. *The Strenuous Life: Essays and Addresses*. Reprint Mineola, NY: Dover Publications, Inc., 2009.

Rostow, W. W. *The Stages of Economic Growth: A Non-Communist Manifesto*. London: Cambridge University Press, 1960.

Rousseau, Jean-Jacques. *On the Social Contract*. Mineola, NY: Dover Thrift Editions, 2003.

Rudalevige, Andrew. *The New Imperial Presidency: Renewing Presidential Powers after Watergate*. Ann Arbor, MI: The University of Michigan Press, 2006.

Ryn, Claes G. *Will, Imagination, and Reason: Babbitt, Croce, and the Problem of Reality.* Washington, D.C.: Regnery Books, 1986.

– *Democracy and the Ethical Life: A Philosophy of Politics and Community.* Washington, D.C.; The Catholic University of America Press, second edition, expanded, 2001.

– *America the Virtuous: The Crisis of Democracy and the Quest for Empire.* New Brunswick, NJ: Transaction Publishers, 2010.

– *The New Jacobinism: America as Revolutionary State.* Bowie, MD: National Humanities Institute, 2011.

Sabato, Larry J. (ed.). *Toward the Millennium: The Elections of 1996.* Needham Heights, MA: Allyn & Bacon, 1997.

– *Midterm Madness: The Elections of 2002.* Lanham, MD: Rowman & Littlefield Publishers, Inc., 2003.

– *Divided States of America: The Slash and Burn of the 2004 Presidential Election.* New York: Person Longman, 2006.

– *The Year of Obama: How Barack Obama Won the White House.* New York: Longman, 2010.

– *Barack Obama and the New America: The 2012 Election and the Changing Face of Politics.* Lanham, MD: Rowman & Littlefield Publishers, 2013.

– *Trumped: The 2016 Election That Broke All the Rules.* Lanham, MD: Rowman & Littlefield, 2017.

Saunders, Frances Stonor. *The Cultural Cold War: The CIA and the World of Arts and Letters.* New York: The New Press, 1999.

Schweizer, Peter. *Reagan's War: The Epic Story of his Forty-Year Struggle and Final Triumph Over Communism.* New York: Doubleday, 2002.

Schulman, Bruce J. *The Seventies: The Great Shift in American Culture, Society, and Politics.* New York: The Free Press, 2001.

Schwartz, Bernard. *A History of the Supreme Court.* New York: Oxford University Press, 1993.

Scott, David Meerman & Richard Jurek. *Marketing the Moon: The Selling of the Apollo Lunar Program*. Cambridge, MA: The MIT Press, 2014.

Shermer, Michael. *The Science of Good & Evil: Why People Cheat, Gossip, Care, Share, and Follow the Golden Rule*. New York: Owl Books, 2004.

Shlaes, Amity. *The Forgotten Man: A New History of the Great Depression*. New York: Harper Perennial, 2008.

Shoemaker Pamela J. & Timothy Vos, *Gatekeeping Theory*. New York: Rutledge, 2009.

Sides, John & Lynn Vavreck. *The Gamble: Choice and Chance in the 2012 Presidential Election*. Princeton: Princeton University Press, 2013.

Sides, John, Michael Tesler & Lynn Vavreck. *Identity Crisis: The 2016 Presidential Campaign and the Battle for the Meaning of America*. Princeton: Princeton University Press, 2018.

Schneider, Gregory L. (ed.). *Conservatism in America Since 1930*. New York: New York University Press, 2003.

Sestanovich, Stephen. *Maximalist: America In the World From Truman to Obama*. New York: Vintage Books, 2014.

Shesol, Jeff. *Supreme Power: Franklin Roosevelt vs. the Supreme Court*. New York: W.W. Norton, 2010.

Skinner, B. F. *The Behavior of Organisms*. New York: D. Appleton & Company, 1938; reprint Acton, MA: Copley Publishing Group, 1991.

Skinner, Kiron K., Annelise Anderson & Martin Anderson (ed.). *Reagan, In his Own Hand*. New York: The Free Press, 2001.

Skocpol, Theda & Vanessa Williamson, *The Tea Party and the Remaking of Republican Conservatism*. New York: Oxford University Press, 2012; updated ed. 2016.

Smaldone, William. *European Socialism: A Concise History With Documents*. Lanham, MD: Rowman & Littlefield Publishers, Inc., 2014.

Smith, Anthony D. *Nationalism: Theory, Ideology, History*. Cambridge, MA: Polity Press, 2001; 2nd ed. 2010.

– *Chosen People*. New York: Oxford University Press, 2003.

Smith, Gary Scott. *Faith & The Presidency: From George Washington to George W. Bush*. Oxford, UK: Oxford University Press, 2006.

Smith, Jean Edward. *Bush*. New York: Simon & Schuster, 2016.

Snow, Nancy. *Propaganda, Inc.: Selling America's Culture to the World*. New York: Seven Story Press, 2010, 3rd edition.

Sorensen, Theodore C. (ed.). *Let the Word Go Forth: The Speeches, Statements, and Writings of John F. Kennedy 1947 to 1963*. New York: Dell Publishing, 1988.

Sowell, Thomas. *A Conflict of Visions: Ideological Origins of Political Struggles*. Cambridge, MA: Basic Books, 1987; revised edition 2007.

Stark, Rodney. *The Victory of Reason: How Christianity Led to Freedom, Capitalism, and Western Success*. New York: Random House, 2005.

Steger, Manfred B. *The Rise of the Global Imaginary: Political Ideologies from the French Revolution to the Global War on Terror*. Oxford: Oxford University Press, 2008.

Steinfels, Peter. *The Neoconservatives: The Men Who are Changing America's Politics*. New York: Touchstone, 1980.

Stern, Alexandra Minna. *Eugenic Nation: Faults and Frontiers of Better Breeding in Modern America*. Berkeley, CA: University of California Press, 2005.

Stuckey, Mary E. *Playing the Game: The Presidential Rhetoric of Ronald Reagan*. New York: Praeger, 1990.

– *Defining Americans: The Presidency and National Identity*. Lawrence, KA: University Press of Kansas, 2004.

Tamir, Yael. *Why Nationalism*. Princeton, NJ: Princeton University Press, 2019.

Thach, Jr., Charles C. *The Creation of the Presidency 1775-1789: A Study In Constitutional History*. Indianapolis, IN: Liberty Fund, 2007.

Thelin, John R. *A History of American Higher Education*. Baltimore & London: The Johns Hopkins University Press, 2004.

Thompson, Robert Ellis. *The Hand Of God In American History: A Study Of National Politics*. New York: T. Y. Crowell & Co., 1902.

Tocqueville, Alexis de. *Democracy in America and Two Essays on America*. London: Penguin Books, 2003.

— *The Treaty of Versailles, American opinion*. Boston: Old Colony Trust Company, 1919.

Tomasky, Michael. *Bill Clinton*. New York: Times Books, 2017.

Troy, Gil. *Morning In America: How Ronald Reagan Invented the 1980s*. Princeton, NJ: Princeton University Press, 2005.

— *The Age of Clinton: America in the 1990s*. New York: Thomas Dunne Books, 2015.

Trump, Donald J. *Time To Get Tough: Make America Great Again*. New York: Regnery Publishing, 2011; updated reprint 2015.

— *Crippled America: How to Make America Great Again*. New York: Threshold Editions, 2015.

Tulis, Jeffrey K. *The Rhetorical Presidency*. Princeton, NJ: Princeton Paperbacks, 1988.

Turner, Frederick Jackson. *The Significance of the Frontier in American History*. New York: Henry Holt & Company, 1920; reprint Mineola, NY: Dover Publications, Inc., 1996.

Tuveson, Ernest Lee. *Redeemer Nation: The Idea of America's Millennial Role*. Chicago: University of Chicago, 1968; Midway reprint 1980.

Taylor, Charles. *Modern Social Imaginaries*. Durham, NC: Duke University Press, 2004.

Van Engen, Abram C. *City on a Hill: A History of American Exceptionalism*. New Haven, CT: Yale University Press, 2020.

Veblen, Thorstein. *The Theory of the Leisure Class: An Economic Study of Institutions*. New York: Penguin Books, 1994; original 1899.

Walker III, William O. *National Security and Core Values In American History*. New York: Cambridge University Press, 2009.

Wall, Wendy L. *Inventing the "American Way": The Politics of Consensus From the New Deal to the Civil Rights Movement*. Oxford: Oxford University Press, 2008.

Watson, Bradley C.S. *Living Constitution, Dying Faith: Progressivism and the New Science of Jurisprudence*. Wilmington, DE: ISI Books, 2009.

— *Progressivism: The Strange History of a Radical Idea*. Notre Dame, IN: University of Notre Dame Press, 2020.

Wayne, Morgan, H. *William McKinley and His America*. Syracuse, NY: Syracuse University Press, 1963.

Weiss, David & Jason A. Edwards (ed.). *The Rhetoric of American Exceptionalism: Critical Essays*. Jefferson, NC & London: McFarland & Company, Inc., 2011.

White, John Kenneth. *The New Politics of Old Values*. Hanover, NH: University Press of New England, 1988; second edition 1990.

— *Still Seeing Red: How the Cold War Shapes the New American Politics*. Boulder, CO: Westview Press, 1997.
— *The Values Divide: American Politics and Culture in Transition*. Washington, D.C.: CQ Press, 2002.
— *Barack Obama's America: How New Conceptions of Race, Family, and Religion Ended the Reagan Era*. Ann Arbor, MI: The University of Michigan Press, 2009.

White John Kenneth & Sandra L. Hanson. *The American Dream in the 21st Century*. Philadelphia, PA: Temple University Press, 2011.

White, Theodore H. *Breach of Faith: The Fall of Richard Nixon*. New York: Atheneum Publishers, 1975.

Wicker, Christine. *The Simple Faith of Franklin Delano Roosevelt: Religion's Role in the FDR Presidency*. Washington, DC: Smithsonian Books, 2017.

Wilentz, Sean. *The Politicians & The Egalitarians: The Hidden History of American Politics*. New York: W. W. Norton & Company, 2016.

Williamson Jr., Chilton. *After Tocqueville: The Promise and Failure of Democracy*. Wilmington, DE: ISI Books, 2012.

Willis, Clint (ed.), *The I Hate George W. Bush Reader: Why Dubya Is Wrong About Absolutely Everything*. New York: Thunder's Mouth Press, 2004.

Wills, Garry. *Reagan's America: Innocents at Home*. New York: Penguin Books, 2000.

Wilsey, John D. *American Exceptionalism and Civil Religion: Reassessing the History of an Idea*. Downers Grove, IL: IVP Academic, 2015.

Wilson, Charles Reagan. *Baptized in Blood: The Religion of the Lost Cause, 1865-1920*. Athens, GA: University of Georgia Press, 1980, reprint 2009.

Wilson, Graham K. *Only in America: The Politics of the United States in Comparative Perspective*. Chatham, NJ: Chatham House Publishers, Inc., 1989.

Wilson, Joan Hoff. *Herbert Hoover: Forgotten Progressive*. Long Grove, IL: Waveland Press, Inc.

Wilson, John K. *Patriotic Correctness: Academic Freedom and Its Enemies*. New York: Routledge, 2008.

Witcover, Jules. *Party of the People: A History of the Democrats*. New York: Random House, 2003.

Willis, Clint (ed.). *The I Hate George W. Bush Reader: Why Dubya Is Wrong About Absolutely Everything*. New York: Thunder's Mouth Press, 2004.

Woods, Randall Bennett. *Fulbright: A Biography*. Cambridge, MA: Cambridge University Press, 1995.

– *LBJ: Architect of American Ambition*. New York: Free Press, 2006.

Worden, Blair. *The English Civil Wars 1640-1660*. London: Orion Books, 2009.

Wrobel, David M. *The End Of American Exceptionalism: Frontier Anxiety From The Old West To The New Deal*. Lawrence, KS: University Press of Kansas, 1996.

Yergin, Daniel & Joseph Stanislaw. *The Commanding Heights: The Battle for the World Economy*. New York; Touchstone, 1998.

Zelizer, Julian E. *Jimmy Carter*. New York: Times Books, 2019.

– *The Fierce Urgency of Now: Lyndon Johnson, Congress, and the Battle for the Great Society*. Penguin Press, 2015.

Zinn, Howard. *A People's History of the United States*. New York: Harper Perennial, 2005.

ARTICLES

Anton, Michael. "The Trump Doctrine: An insider explains the president's foreign policy" (April 20, 2019). *Foreign Policy*. Accessed February 22, 2020. https://foreignpolicy.com/2019/04/20/the-trump-doctrine-big-think-america-first-nationalism/.

Auxier, George W. "Middle Western Newspapers and the Spanish American War, 1895-1898." *The Mississippi Valley Historical Review*, Vol. 26, No. 4 (Mar. 1940): 523-534.

Bellah, Robert. "Civil Religion in America." *Journal of the American Academy of Arts and Sciences*. Winter 1967, Vol. 96, No. 1: 1-21.

Blake, Nelson M. "Background of Cleveland's Venezuelan Policy." *The American Historical Review* 47, no. 2 (1942): 259-77.

Boyle, T. "The Venezuela Crisis and the Liberal Opposition, 1895-96." *The Journal of Modern History* 50, no. 3 (1978): D1185-1212.

Christopher Caldwell, "The Roots of Our Partisan Divide." *Imprimis*, February 2020, Vol. 49, No. 2.

Ceaser, James W. "The Origins and Character of American Exceptionalism." *American Political Thought: A Journal of Ideas, Institutions, and Culture* 1 (Spring 2012): 3-28.

Clinton, Bill. "A New Covenant for American Security" (12 December 1991). *Helvidius*: 14-17. Accessed August 3, 2019. http://archive.helvidius.org/1992/1992_Clinton.pdf.

Crider, Jonathan B. "De Bow's Revolution: The Memory of the American Revolution in the Politics of the Sectional Crisis, 1850-1861." *American Nineteenth Century History*, Volume 10, 2009 - Issue 3.

Cukier, Kenneth & Viktor Mayer-Schönberger. "The Dictatorship of Data: Robert McNamara epitomizes the hyper-rational executive led astray by numbers" (May 31, 2013). *MIT Technology Review*. Accessed January 18, 2018. https://www.technologyreview.com/s/514591/the-dictatorship-of-data/.

Cuomo, Mario Matthew. "1984 Democratic National Convention Keynote Address" (16 July, 1984). *American Rhetoric*. Accessed April 11, 2019. https://www.americanrhetoric.com/speeches/mariocuomo1984dnc.htm.

Edwards, Jason A. "The Fight Over the League of Nations: Rhetorical Tension within America's Exceptionalist Narratives." *Ohio Communication Journal* 47 (October 2009): 265-282.

Feingold, Russ. "Statement Of U.S. Senator Russ Feingold On The Anti-Terrorism Bill: From The Senate Floor" (October 25, 2001). *Electronic Privacy Information Center*. Accessed November 27, 2019. https://epic.org/privacy/terrorism/usapatriot/feingold.html.

Feldmann, Linda. "Left and right, pundits applaud Obama Nobel Peace Prize speech" (December 10, 2009). *Christian Science Monitor*. Accessed January 15, 2020. https://www.csmonitor.com/USA/Politics/2009/1210/left-and-right-pundits-applaud-obama-nobel-peace-prize-speech.

Fukuyama, Francis. "The end of history?" *National Interest*, No. 16 (Summer 1989): 3-18. Accessed July 1, 2019. https://www.jstor.org/stable/24027184.

Friedrich, Otto. "FDR's Disputed Legacy" (February 1, 1982). *Time*. Accessed July 1, 2019. http://content.time.com/time/subscriber/article/0,33009,954983,00.html.

Gamble, Sonya B., et al. "Abortion Surveillance—United States, 2005." *Division of Reproductive Health, National Center for Chronic Disease Prevention and Health Promotion*. Accessed March 20, 2019, https://www.cdc.gov/mmwr/preview/mmwrhtml/ss5713a1.htm.

Gilmore, Jason. "Translating American Exceptionalism: Comparing Presidential Discourses About the United States Home and Abroad." *International Journal of Communication*, no 8 (2014): 2416-2437. Accessed December 17, 2019. https://ijoc.org/index.php/ijoc/article/view/2336/1263.

 – "American Exceptionalism in the American Mind: Presidential Discourse, National Identity, and U.S. Public Opinion." *Communication Studies*. Volume 66, no 3 (April 2015): 1-20.

– "The Glorious Revolution: Factsheet G4 General Series" (August 2010). *House of Commons Information Office*. Accessed September 7, 2016. http://www.parliament.uk/documents/commons-information-office/g04.pdf.

Greve, Joan E. "What Richard Nixon's Impeachment Looked Like" (August 5, 2014). *Time Magazine*. Accessed July 26, 2018. http://time.com/3063704/nixon-impeachment/.

Grossman, Zoltan. "From Wounded Knee to Syria: A Century of U.S. Interventions." *The Evergreen State College*. Accessed on March 2, 2017. http://academic.evergreen.edu/g/grossmaz/interventions.html.

Hahn, Peter L. "Securing the Middle East: The Eisenhower Doctrine of 1957." *Presidential Studies Quarterly* 36.1 (2006): 38-47.

Hamilton, Alexander. "Second Letter from Phocion, (New York, April, 1784). *National Archives*. Accessed February 22, 2020. https://founders.archives.gov/documents/Hamilton/01-03-02-0347#.

Hendrickson, John. "Herbert Hoover's American Exceptionalism." *Library of Law and Liberty* (July 10, 2012). Accessed March 30, 2020. http://www.libertylawsite.org/2012/07/10/herbert-hoovers-american-exceptionalism/. Accessed June 23, 2017.

Higgs, Robert. "The Economics of the Great Society: Theory, Policies, and Consequences" (February 1, 2011). *The Independent Institute*. Accessed January 21, 2018. http://www.independent.org/issues/article.asp?id=3157.

Hofstadter, Richard. "The Paranoid Style in American Politics." *Harper's Magazine*, November 1964: 77-86.

Jacobsen, Gary C. "Terror, Terrain, and Turnout: Explaining the 2002 Midterm Elections." Political Science Quarterly, Vol. 118, No. 1 (Spring 2003), 1-22.

Keller, Jared. "What Makes Americans So Optimistic? Why the U.S. tends to look on the bright side" (March 25, 2015). *Atlantic*. Accessed December 12, 2018. https://www.theatlantic.com/politics/archive/2015/03/the-american-ethic-and-the-spirit-of-optimism/388538/.

Klautke, Egbert. "Anti-Americanism in Twentieth-Century Europe." *Historical Journal* 64 (4), 2011: 1125-1139.

Lawrence B. Finer, "Trends in Premarital Sex in the United States, 1954–2003." *US National Library of Medicine National Institutes of Health*, Public Health Rep. 2007 Jan-Feb; 122(1): 73–78. Accessed March 20, 2019. https://www.ncbi.nlm.nih.gov/pmc/articles/PMC1802108/.

Leetaru, Kalev. "The Game of the Name: Media Bias and Presidents" (October 15, 2018). *Real Clear Politics*. Accessed February 10, 2020. https://www.realclearpolitics.com/articles/2018/10/15/the_game_of_the_name_media_bias_and_presidents_138351.

Leuchtenburg, William E. "Progressivism and Imperialism: The Progressive Movement and American Foreign Policy, 1898-1916." *The Mississippi Valley Historical Review*. Vol. 39, No. 3 (December 1952): 483-504.

Lowi, Theodore J. *The End of Liberalism: The Second Republic of the United States.* New York: W.W. Norton & Company, 1979. 2nd edition.

Luce, Henry R. "The American Century" *Life Magazine* (February 17, 1941). Accessed June 13, 2018, http://www-personal.umich.edu/~mlassite/discussions261/luce.pdf.

McNamara, Adam. "Can we measure memes?" *Frontiers in Evolutionary Neuroscience*. Accessed June 28, 2017. http://journal.frontiersin.org/article/10.3389/fnevo.2011.00001/full.

Mead, Walter Russel. "The Tea Party and American Foreign Policy: What Populism Means for Globalism." *Foreign Affairs*, Vol. 90, No. 2 (March/April 2011): 28-44.

Mondale, Walter F. "American Exceptionalism, Global Security, and Human Dignity: The Great Challenge of the 21st Century." *University of St. Thomas Law Journal*, Volume 3, Issue 2, Fall 2005, accessed July 27, 2020. https://ir.stthomas.edu/cgi/viewcontent.cgi?article=1078&context=ustlj.

Monthly Vital Statistics Report Provisional Data From the National Center for Health Statistics (August 28, 1991), Vol 39, No. 13. Accessed March 20, 2019, https://www.cdc.gov/nchs/data/mvsr/supp/mv39_13.pdf.

Myers, Peter C. "Martin Luther King, Jr., and the American Dream." *Heritage Foundation's First Principles Foundational Concepts to Guide Politics and Policy*, No. 50, March 28, 2014.

Nixon, Richard. "The Meaning Of Communism To Americans" (August 21, 1969). *Watergate.info*. Accessed June 26, 2018. http://watergate. info/1960/08/21/nixon-the-meaning-of-communism-to-americans. html.

Nunberg, Geoffrey. "The Liberal Label: The Substance is Alive and Well, But the Brand is in Trouble." *The American Prospect*, September 2003, volume 14, issue 8: 36-38. Accessed February 13, 2019. http://www. uvm.edu/~dguber/POLS125/articles/nunberg.htm.

O'Gorman, Ned. "Eisenhower and the American Sublime." *Quarterly Journal of Speech*, 94:1 (2008): 44-72.

O'Sullivan, John. "Annexation." *United States Magazine and Democratic Review* 17, no.1 (July-August 1845): 5-10.

Proctor, Redfield. "Cuban Reconcentration Policy and its Effects," (March 17, 1898). *Latin American Studies*. Accessed February 1, 2017, www. latinamericanstudies.org/1895/reconcentration-camps.htm.

   – *Rasmussen Reports*. "67% Disagree With Cuomo About America's 'Greatness' " (August 20, 2018). Accessed August 21, 2018. http://www.rasmussenreports.com/public_content/politics/general_politics/august_2018/67_disagree_with_cuomo_about_america_s_greatness; www.foxnews.com/politics/2018/08/13/trump-dares-ny-gov-cuomo-to-run-against-him-in-2020-says-anybody-that-runs-against-trump-suffers.html.

Ryn, Claes G. "Imaginative Origins of Modernity: Life as Daydream and Nightmare." *Humanitas*, Volume X, No. 2, 1997. Accessed September 18, 2018. http://www.nhinet.org/humsub/ryn10-2.htm.

   – "The Ideology of American Empire." *Orbis* Vol. 47, Issue 3 (Summer 2003): 383-397.

– "Leo Strauss and History: The Philosopher as Conspirator."
Humanitas, Volume XVIII, Nos. 1 and 2, 2005. Accessed
March 31, 2020. http://www.nhinet.org/ryn18-1&2.pdf.

– "Allan Bloom and Straussian Alienation." *Humanitas*,
Volume XXV, Nos. 1 and 2, 2012. Accessed July 5, 2019.
http://www.nhinet.org/ryn25-1.pdf.

Schatz, Robert T., Ervin Staub & Howard Lavine. "On the Varieties of
National Attachment: Blind versus Constructive Patriotism." *Political
Psychology*, Vol. 20, No. 1 (Mars 1999): 151-174. Accessed December
10, 2019. https://www.jstor.org/stable/3792008.

Schneider Susan M. & Edward K. Morris. "A History of the Term Radical
Behaviorism: From Watson to Skinner." *Behavior Analyst* 1987, 10,
No. 1 (Spring): 27-39.

Siegfried, Evan. "Media bias against conservatives is real, and part of
the reason no one trusts the news now" (July 29, 2018). *NBC/Think*.
Accessed February 10, 2020. https://www.nbcnews.com/think/opin-
ion/media-bias-against-conservatives-real-part-reason-no-one-trusts-
ncna895471.

Smith, William S. "Jeane J. Kirkpatrick: 30 Years Unheeded" (June 13,
2020). *The National Interest*. Accessed July 27, 2020. https://nation-
alinterest.org/feature/jeane-j-kirkpatrick-30-years-unheeded-162667.

Stewart, Watt. "George Bancroft Historian of the American Republic."
The Mississippi Valley Historical Review Vol. 19, No. 1 (Jun., 1932):
77-86.

Strong, Josiah. "Our Country: Its Possible Future and Its Present
Crisis." On-line edition at *Questia*. Accessed February 17, 2017.
https://www.questia.com/read/11531354/our-country-its-
possible-future-and-its-present-crisis.

Todd Brenda K. et al. "Sex differences in children's toy preferences: A sys-
tematic review, meta-regression, and meta-analysis." *Infant and Child
Development*, Volume 27, Issue 2, March/April 2018.

Voegelin, Eric. "Liberalism and its History." *The Review of Politics*, Vol. 36,
No. 4, Oct. 1974: 504-520.

Washburn, Anthony N. & Linda J. Skitka. "Science Denial Across the Political Divide: Liberals and Conservatives Are Similarly Motivated to Deny Attitude-Inconsistent Science." *Social Psychological and Personality Science*, September 2017. Accessed January 28, 2020. https://www.researchgate.net/publication/319859531_Science_Denial_Across_the_Political_Divide_Liberals_and_Conservatives_Are_Similarly_Motivated_to_Deny_Attitude-Inconsistent_Science.

Zakheim, Dov S. "The Trump Doctrine, Explained" (February 17, 2020). *National Interest.* Accessed February 19, 2020. https://nationalinterest.org/feature/trump-doctrine-explained-123341.

Zenko, Micah. "The Myth of the Indispensable Nation" (November 6, 2014). *Foreign Policy.* Accessed December 6, 2019. https://foreign-policy.com/2014/11/06/the-myth-of-the-indispensable-nation/.

ONLINE SOURCES

American Merchant Marine at War. "American Merchant Marine at War." Accessed August 14, 2017. http://www.usmm.org/libertyships.html.

Adams, John Quincy. "Celebrating the Declaration of Independence," (July 4, 1821). *Teaching American History.* Accessed September 22, 2018, http://teachingamericanhistory.org/library/document/speech-on-independence-day/.Adams, Kyle.

"Libya Vote Highlights House GOP Shift on Use of Military" (June 6, 2011). *Real Clear Politics.* Accessed January 16, 2020. https://www.realclearpolitics.com/articles/2011/06/06/libya_vote_highlights_house_gop_shift_on_use_of_military.html.

Anderson, Annelise. "Ronald Reagan and American Exceptionalism" (date unknown). *Hoover Institute.* Accessed September 18, 2018. https://www.hoover.org/sites/default/files/research/docs/amerex_ch12.pdf.

Bluey, Rob. "New CNN Poll: 59% Oppose Obamacare" (March 22, 2010). *Daily Signal.* Accessed January 17, 2020. https://www.dailysignal.com/2010/03/22/new-cnn-poll-59-oppose-obamacare/.

Bovard, James. "Killing in the Name of Democracy" (June 1, 2006). *The Future Of Freedom Foundation.* Accessed March 10, 2017. http://www.fff.org/explore-freedom/article/killing-democracy/.

Brenan, Megan. "American Pride Hits New Low; Few Proud of Political System" (July 2, 2019). *Gallup.com*. Accessed December 4, 2019. https://news.gallup.com/poll/259841/american-pride-hits-new-low-few-proud-political-system.aspx.

Buchanan, Patrick Joseph. "Cultural War Speech: Address to the Republican National Convention (August 17, 1992). *Voices of Democracy: University of Maryland*. Accessed July 8, 2019. https://voicesofdemocracy.umd.edu/buchanan-culture-war-speech-speech-text/.

Burke, Daniel. "The guilt-free gospel of Donald Trump" (October 24, 2016). *CNN.com*. Accessed February 13, 2020. https://www.cnn.com/2016/10/21/politics/trump-religion-gospel/index.html.

Broadcasting Board of Governors. Accessed December 3, 2019. https://www.usagm.gov.

Cise, Ed Van. "How Low Earth Orbit Astronauts Are the New Pioneers" (January 17, 2014). *Gizmodo*. Accessed May 29, 2018. https://gizmodo.com/how-low-earth-orbit-astronauts-are-the-new-pioneers-1503603924.

Condon, Stephanie. "Mount Vernon Statement Unveiled" (February 17, 2010). *CBS News*. Accessed March 30, 2020. https://www.cbsnews.com/news/mount-vernon-statement-unveiled/.

Dunkelman, Marc. "The Crisis of American Exceptionalism" (August 13, 2014). *Real Clear Politics*. Accessed January 25, 2020. https://www.realclearpolitics.com/articles/2014/08/13/the_crisis_of_american_exceptionalism_123644.html.

Freedom Eden. "Rick Santelli: Tea Party" (February 19, 2009). Accessed December 16, 2019. http://freedomeden.blogspot.com/2009/02/rick-santelli-tea-party.html.

Gamble, Richard. "Savior Nation: Woodrow Wilson and the Gospel of Service." Paper presented to *The Philadelphia Society*, April 21, 2001. Accessed February 27, 2017. https://phillysoc.org/gamble-savior-nation-woodrow-wilson-and-the-gospel-of-service/.

Gardiner, Nile & Morgan Lorraine Roach. "Barack Obama's Top 10 Apologies: How the President Has Humiliated a Superpower" (June 2,

2009). *Heritage Foundation*. Accessed January 15, 2020, https://www.heritage.org/node/14384/print-display.

Gist Junction. "GOP Buys Cuomo Ticket to Canada for Saying America Not Great" (August 16, 2018). Accessed August 21, 2018. https://gistjunction.com/2018/08/16/gop-buys-cuomo-ticket-to-canada-for-saying-america-not-great/.

Imdb. "Space Cowboys (2000)." Accessed May 29, 2019. https://www.imdb.com/title/tt0186566/.

Jackson, Jesse. "1984 Democratic National Convention Address" (18 July 1984). *American Rhetoric*. Accessed October 8, 2018. https://www.americanrhetoric.com/speeches/jessejackson1984dnc.htm.

Jefferson, Thomas. "To George Rogers Clark," (December 25, 1780). *National Archives*. Accessed June 11, 2018. https://founders.archives.gov/documents/Jefferson/01-04-02-0295.

– "Thomas Jefferson to Samuel Kercheval" (July 12, 1816). *Library of Congress*. Accessed May 15, 2018. https://www.loc.gov/resource/mtj1.049_0255_0262/.

Jones, Jeffrey M. "In U.S., Record-Low 47% Extremely Proud to Be Americans" (July 2, 2018). *Gallup.com*. Accessed January 25, 2020. https://news.gallup.com/poll/236420/record-low-extremely-proud-americans.aspx.

Kaplan, Richard. "Yellow Journalism of the 1890s." *Academia.com*. Accessed January 30, 2017, www.academia.edu/8114924/Yellow_Journalism_of_the_1890s_--_Encyclopedia_Entry.

Kennedy, Brian & Cary Funk. "Many Americans are skeptical about scientific research on climate and GM foods" (December 5, 2016). *Pew Research Center*. Accessed January 28, 2020. https://www.pewresearch.org/fact-tank/2016/12/05/many-americans-are-skeptical-about-scientific-research-on-climate-and-gm-foods/.

King Jr., Martin Luther. "The Montgomery Bus Boycott" (1955). *BlackPast.org*. Accessed February 19, 2018. http://www.blackpast.org/1955-martin-luther-king-jr-montgomery-bus-boycott.

– "Some Things We Must Do" (December 1957). *Stanford: The Martin Luther King, Jr. Research and Education Institute*. Accessed February 19, 2018. http://kingencyclopedia.stanford.edu/encyclopedia/documentsentry/some_things_we_must_do_address_delivered_at_the_second_annual_institute_on_/index.html.

Kipling, Rudyard. "The White Man's Burden, 1899." *Internet History Sourcebooks Project*. Accessed May 23, 2019. https://sourcebooks.fordham.edu/mod/kipling.asp.

Kraft, Emilie. "Ten Commandments Monument Controversy" (May 12, 2008). *Encyclopedia of Alabama*. Accessed March 27, 2019. http://www.encyclopediaofalabama.org/article/h-1525.

Kristol, Irving. "The Emerging American Imperium," (August 18, 1997). *AEI.com*. Accessed October 8, 2019. https://www.aei.org/articles/the-emerging-american-imperium/.

Lake, Anthony. "From Containment to Enlargement," (September 21, 1993). *Mount Holyoke*. Accessed July 11, 2019. https://www.mtholyoke.edu/acad/intrel/lakedoc.html.

Lerer, Lisa. "Obamamania verges on obsession" (February 20, 2008). *Politico*. Accessed October 21, 2019. http://www.politico.com/news/stories/0208/8605.html.

Lew, Jack. "Remarks of Secretary Lew at The Economic Club of New York" (June 11, 2014). *The U.S. Department of the Treasury*. Accessed January 25, 2020. https://www.treasury.gov/press-center/press-releases/Pages/jl2421.aspx.

Lizza, Ryan. "The Consequentialist: How the Arab Spring Remade Obama's foreign policy" (April 25, 2011). *New Yorker*. Accessed January 17, 2020. https://www.newyorker.com/magazine/2011/05/02/the-consequentalist.

Malik, Tariq. "Trump unveils new Space Force logo (yes, it looks like something from 'Star Trek')" (January 25, 2020). *Space.com*. Accessed March 31, 2020. https://www.space.com/space-force-logo-star-trek-insignia.html.

McCain, John. "Senator John McCain: Russians deserve better than Putin" (September 19, 2013). *Pravda.ru.* Accessed January 22, 2020. https://www.pravdareport.com/opinion/125705-McCain_for_pravda_ru/.

McClatchy Washington Bureau. "Republican Contract With America." Accessed July 8, 2019. http://media.mcclatchydc.com/static/pdf/1994-contract-with-america.pdf.

Mount Holyoke News. "Richard Olney: On American Jurisdiction in the Western Hemisphere Mount." U.S. Department of State, Papers Relating to Foreign Affairs, 1895, I: 545-562. Accessed January 23, 2017. http://www.mtholyoke.edu/acad/intrel/olney.htm.

   – "Grover Cleveland: American Interests in the Cuban Revolution." U.S., Department of State, Papers Relating to Foreign Affairs, 1896, xxvii-lxii." Accessed January 23, 2017. http://www.mtholyoke.edu/acad/intrel/gc26.htm.

Mr. Richman's Blog. "Four Minute Speech 1918." Accessed December 29, 2017. https://rickmanhchs.files.wordpress.com/2016/02/four-minute-speech-article.pdf.

National Endowment for Democracy. Accessed March 29, 2019. https://www.ned.org/about/history/.

Newport, Frank, Jeffrey M. Jones, & Lydia Saad, "Ronald Reagan From the People's Perspective: A Gallup Poll Review" (June 7, 2004). *Gallup.com.* Accessed February 13, 2019, https://news.gallup.com/poll/11887/Ronald-Reagan-From-Peoples-Perspective-Gallup-Poll-Review.aspx.

New World Encyclopedia. "Manifest Destiny." Accessed November 2, 2018. http://www.newworldencyclopedia.org/entry/Manifest_Destiny.

Nixon, Richard. "The Meaning Of Communism To Americans" (August 21, 1969). Watergate.info. Accessed June 26, 2018. http://watergate.info/1960/08/21/nixon-the-meaning-of-communism-to-americans.html.

O'Sullivan, John. "Annexation" (July-August 1845). *United States Magazine and Democratic Review* 17, no.1. Accessed March 30, 2020. https://pdcrodas.webs.ull.es/anglo/OSullivanAnnexation.pdf.

Page, William Tyler. "The American Creed." *US History.com*. Accessed May 20, 2019. http://www.ushistory.org/documents/creed.htm.

"Pragmatism" (March 14, 2019). *Stanford University of Philosophy*. Accessed January 10, 2020. https://plato.stanford.edu/entries/pragmatism/.

Pestritto, Ronald J. "Woodrow Wilson: Godfather of Liberalism" (July 31, 2012). *Heritage Foundation*. Accessed on March 8, 2017. http://www.heritage.org/political-process/report/woodrow-wilson-godfather-liberalism.

Pew Research Center. "Partisan Polarization Surges in Bush, Obama Years: Trends in American Values: 1987-2012" (June 4, 2012). Accessed February 24, 2020. https://www.people-press.org/2012/06/04/partisan-polarization-surges-in-bush-obama-years/.

- "2012 Republican Primary Voters: More Conservative Than GOP General Election Voters: A profile of the GOP primary electorate" (January 28, 2016). Accessed January 25, 2020. https://www.people-press.org/wp-content/uploads/sites/4/2016/01/1-28-16-Profile-of-2012-GOP-Primary-Voters-release.pdf.
- "The Partisan Divide on Political Values Grows Even Wider" (October 5, 2017). Accessed January 25, 2020. https://www.people-press.org/2017/10/05/3-foreign-policy/.
- "The Partisan Divide on Political Values Grows Even Wider" (October 5, 2017). Accessed January 25. 2020. https://www.people-press.org/2017/10/05/3-foreign-policy/.

Proctor, Redfield. "Cuban Reconcentration Policy and its Effects" (March 17, 1898). *Latin American Studies*. Accessed on February 1, 2017, www.latinamericanstudies.org/1895/reconcentration-camps.htm.

Province, Charles M. "The Famous Patton Speech" (June 5, 1944). *The Patton Society*. Accessed June 17, 2018, http://www.pattonhq.com/speech.html.

Reagan, Ronald. "Eureka College Commencement," (June 7, 1957) *The Reagan Speech Preservation Society.* Accessed November 19, 2018. http://www.poorrichardsprintshop.com/wiki/Default.aspx?Page=Eureka%20College%20Commencement&AspxAutoDetectCookieSupport=1.

Reinhart, R.J. "Protests Seen as Harming Civil Rights Movement in the '60s" (January 21, 2019). *Gallup.com.* Accessed January 23, 2019. https://news.gallup.com/vault/246167/protests-seen-harming-civil-rights-movement-60s.aspx?utm_source=alert&utm_medium=email&utm_content=morelink&utm_campaign=syndication.

    — "Gallup Vault: U.S. Opinion and the Start of World War II" (August 29, 2019). *Gallup.com.* Accessed September 4, 2019. https://news.gallup.com/vault/265865/gallup-vault-opinion-start-world-war.aspx?utm_source=alert&utm_medium=email&utm_content=morelink&utm_campaign=syndication.

Rice, Condoleezza. "Remarks at the American University in Cairo, Egypt" (June 20, 2005). *State.gov.* Accessed October 14, 2019. https://2001-2009.state.gov/secretary/rm/2005/48328.htm.

Roosevelt, Theodore. "In front of the Alamo" (April 7, 1905). *Theodore Roosevelt.* Accessed February 15, 2017. http://www.theodore-roosevelt.com/images/research/txtspeeches/132.txt.

    — "The New Nationalism" (August 31, 1910). *Theodore Roosevelt.* Accessed February 15, 2017. http://www.theo-dore-roosevelt.com/images/research/speeches/trnational-ismspeech.pdf.

Sad, Lydia. "Gallup Vault: Americans Favored Putting God in U.S. Pledge (October 5, 2017)." *Gallup.com.* Accessed October 13, 2017. http://news.gallup.com/vault/220232/gallup-vault-americans-favored-putting-god-pledge.aspx?utm_source=alert&utm_medium=email&utm_content=morelink&utm_campaign=syndication.

    — "Gallup Vault: Americans' Views of Socialism, 1949-1965" (August 10, 2018). *Gallup.com.* Accessed August

18, 2018. https://news.gallup.com/vault/240749/gallup-vault-americans-views-socialism-1949-1965.aspx?utm_source=alert&utm_medium=email&utm_content=morelink&utm_campaign=syndication.

Smith, Ben. "Obama on small-town Pa.: Clinging to religion, guns, xenophobia" (April 11, 2008). *Politico*. Accessed January 9, 2020. https://www.politico.com/blogs/ben-smith/2008/04/obama-on-small-town-pa-clinging-to-religion-guns-xenophobia-007737.

U.S. House of Representatives. "H.R.4655 - Iraq Liberation Act of 1998105th Congress (1997-1998)." Accessed October 7, 2019. https://www.congress.gov/bill/105th-congress/house-bill/4655.

Van Cise, Ed. "How Low Earth Orbit Astronauts Are the New Pioneers." *Gizmodo*, (January 17, 2014). https://gizmodo.com/how-low-earth-orbit-astronauts-are-the-new-pioneers-1503603924. Accessed May 29, 2018.

Winter, Yves. "Conquest." *Political Concepts: A Critical Lexicon*. www.politicalconcepts.org/issue1/conquest/. Accessed October 22, 2016.

Winthrop, John. "The City on a Hill" (1630). *Gilder Lehrman Institute of American History*. Accessed May 5, 2017. https://www.gilderlehrman.org/sites/default/files/inline-pdfs/Winthrop%27s%20City%20upon%20a%20Hill.pdf.

Wolfensberger, Don. "Congress and Woodrow Wilson's Military Forays Into Mexico: An Introductory Essay." *Wilson Center*. Accessed December 28, 2017. https://www.wilsoncenter.org/sites/default/files/ACF18F1.pdf.

World Factbook. *CIA*. Accessed October 29, 2018. https://www.cia.gov/library/publications/the-world-factbook/rankorder/2186rank.html.